THE INVESTOR'S GUI
WARRANTS

THE INVESTOR'S GUIDE TO

WARRANTS

Capitalize on the fastest growing sector of the Stock Exchange

Andrew McHattie

FINANCIAL TIMES

Prentice Hall

An imprint of Pearson Education

London · New York · San Francisco · Toronto · Sydney · Tokyo · Singapore
Hong Kong · Cape Town · Madrid · Paris · Milan · Munich · Amsterdam

PEARSON EDUCATION LIMITED

Head Office:
Edinburgh Gate
Harlow CM20 2JE
Tel: +44 (0)1279 623623
Fax: +44 (0)1279 431059

London Office:
128 Long Acre
London WC2E 9AN
Tel: +44 (0)20 7447 2000
Fax: +44 (0)20 7240 5771
Website www.business-minds.com

First published in Great Britain in 1992

British Library Cataloguing in Publication Data
A CIP catalogue record for this book can be obtained
from the British Library.

ISBN 0 273 65053 X

3 5 7 9 10 8 6 4

Typeset by Northern Phototypesetting Co. Ltd, Bolton
Printed and bound in Great Britain by
Biddles Ltd, Guildford and King's Lynn

*The Publishers' policy is to use paper manufactured
from sustainable forests.*

Andrew McHattie MA (Cantab) runs the investment publishing company, The McHattie Group. He has been Editor and Publisher of the *Warrants Alert* newsletter and the *Warrants Directory* since 1989. He also publishes *Covered Warrants Alert* and *Investment Trust Newsletter* and has written for a number of other investment magazines. In 1999 he founded  McHattie Investment Management, a fund management company which has launched a warrants unit trust. He previously worked for Phillips & Drew on international gilt trading and on their European equity desk.

The McHattie Group/McHattie Investment Management Ltd
Clifton Heights, Triangle West, Bristol BS8 1EJ, UK
Tel: (UK) 0117 925 8882
Fax: (UK) 0117 925 4441
e-mail: enquiries@mchattie.co.uk
http://www.mchattie.co.uk
http://www.tipsheets.co.uk

To my grandmother,
Margaret

ACKNOWLEDGEMENTS

I should like to thank numerous friends, colleagues and sources for their help and support in the preparation of this book. Sarah King, Rachel Lockyer, Wendy Sawyers, John McHattie, Harold Nass, Mark Mabin, Richard Kershaw, David Baker, Pascoe Gibbons, and Anthony Wah have all provided me with invaluable assistance. Benjamin Cooper deserves a special mention for his diligent work in updating data for tables and charts, as well as for his specialist knowledge of the covered warrants market.

Finally, I should like to thank Reuters for their permission to include examples of graphics from its Reuter Terminal Graphics Service.

CONTENTS

"Rich rewards await those who can select the best warrants, trade them shrewdly, and enjoy a little luck along the way."

INTRODUCTION

Warrants are possibly as close as international investors are likely to get to the ultimate speculative tool. As Japanese, European, Asian, and American investors have already discovered, warrants can provide fantastic profits during boom periods, as long as you can accept the associated risks. As one investor wrote recently*, warrants are 'as good as can be expected in bear markets, tremendous in bull markets.'

If shares are the normal vehicle for stockmarket investment, then warrants are the 'sports' model for the adventurous. They can certainly move rapidly enough. Warrants are a wonderful bull market instrument, and they can inject excitement into a pursuit which is too often as prim as it is profitable. If you intend to enjoy your dealing on the stockmarket, then warrants may be the instrument for you. Some of the more colourful market characters who have learnt about the market in depth and examined the finer points of warrants trading cannot understand why people want to buy shares at all when they can have warrants. Why settle for a 30 per cent gain when your profit might be 100 per cent? To put it another way, why invest in a share when an attached warrant will perform better at an annual growth rate of over 5 per cent? The premier attraction of warrants has always been their ability to produce huge profits from small market movements, yet few investors appreciate the wide range of applications for which warrants are suitable. Used as a hedging instrument, warrants can actually reduce risk, or they can be used in conjunction with capital shares or traditional options to offer enormous capital exposure from a small stake.

The very concept of a warrant is still a puzzle to the majority of investors in the UK, where warrants were very much a fledgeling market throughout the 1970s and 1980s, and still a minority instrument in the 1990s, never matching the overseas warrants markets in terms of size or public interest. As a result the market has not been widely exploited, although the sudden spurt in growth over the last 11 years has gained it a new prominence and a new confidence which has attracted a gathering of enthusiastic newcomers eager to learn about warrants. One reason why the market has not taken off before now is the widespread lack of understanding about warrants, how they work, and how they can be used for profit. Part of the difficulty has been that the small warrants fraternity has tended to shroud the market in a mist of esoteric terminology such as capital fulcrum point, premium, volatility ratio, parity ratio, time to maturity, and so on. In fact any reasonably intelligent investor can understand these concepts and use them

---

* A subscriber to the *Warrants Alert* newsletter, from Alresford in Hampshire

to considerable advantage in the same way as market professionals. There is no reason why a handful of mathematically minded stockbrokers should have a monopoly of warrant knowledge.

This problem has been compounded by the extraordinary lack of written material on the subject, which the first edition of this book attempted to address in 1992. This second edition attempts to continue this process of education by updating and extending the extant knowledge on the subject. Written for private investors, for professional advisers, for derivative traders, for institutional fund managers, for company directors, for stockbrokers, and for anyone else seeking a compelling new investment, this book is intended to be a comprehensive manual for everyone interested in the warrants market. In parts the text is necessarily complex and mathematical, but the intention has been to make the contents as accessible as possible for everyone.

Since the first edition of this book was published there has been much new material generated from the experience of the roaring bull market of 1993 and the moderately bearish one of 1994 and early 1995. In 1993 the average gain from UK-listed warrants was a staggering 221.95 per cent, and 70 per cent of warrants doubled or more in value over the year, but warrant investors came back down to earth in 1994 when the average change was a fall of 19.86 per cent. In both years the course of the market provided many extraordinary movements which taught all market participants a great deal and stimulated new analytical methods to identify future winners and avoid the worst falls.

The chapter on covered warrants is greatly expanded to reflect the rapid growth and increasing popularity of that sector, and a new chapter on American warrants has been inserted to demonstrate how warrant markets differ. Most of the examples in the book are still drawn from the UK, but these are used to illustrate general principles which are equally applicable across all warrant markets. Although the method of issue and the dealing procedures for UK warrants differ markedly from those overseas, the instrument is essentially standard, and the theoretical analysis may be applied equally to all forms of warrants.

Chapter 1 chronicles the remarkable recent growth in the UK market and looks at the reasons for issue by both commercial companies and investment trusts. Chapter 2 looks at the advantages and disadvantages of warrants *vis-à-vis* shares, and their general performance in relation to the stockmarket. Having established that their advantages make them worth looking at, Chapters 3, 4 and 5 concentrate on warrant assessment and selection. Chapter 3 outlines the basic elements of valuation which any investor could undertake, Chapter 4 looks at graphical approaches, and Chapter 5 delves deeper into the algebraic and computational methods which should be of interest to financial advisers. This chapter can easily be skipped by those who find it difficult. Now that the investor is able to select warrants, Chapter 6 addresses the question of risk and explains how to structure the warrant investment to suit your individual preferences.

Having chosen your warrants and your degree of risk, the next thing to discover is how to deal – this is the concern of Chapter 7. After dealing and holding warrants, the question of exercising subscription rights will arise, and Chapter 8 offers explanations and advice on this matter.

At this stage the book has taken investors right through the investment process, from simple definitions through to selection, dealing and exercising warrants before their expiry. The rest of the book is concerned with developing trading skills and taking full advantage of the opportunities which may become available at different times. Chapter 9 is a completely revised view of the covered warrants market which is of interest to more experienced investors and those dealing in larger size, Chapter 10 deals specifically with American warrants, Chapter 11 with other overseas warrants, and Chapter 12 with other risk instruments which may be complementary. Chapter 13 is the final chapter, which looks ahead to the second half of the 1990s and looks forward to the prospects for the development of international warrant markets. Appendix A provides a specific worked example of all calculations relating to warrants, which you may find useful for reference as you learn about the different methods of analysis, and Appendix B provides a comprehensive list of all UK equity warrants. The book is concluded with a glossary, sources of further information, and index.

This structure has been designed to provide a detailed and thorough view of extant knowledge and theory relating to warrants. Beginners should find most of the text comprehensible, and chapters 1–8 try to lead them by the hand through the investment process. These chapters should also be useful to the more experienced warrant investor, as they contain a lot of previously unpublished information, and certain sections which address complex theory and strategies. Furthermore, experienced investors and professionals should appreciate the overall scope of the book which contains both the introductory facts and the high-level analysis all together in one volume: this unique combination should make the book indispensable for anyone investing in warrants. A constantly recurring theme throughout the book is the need to learn about the market and to overcome the ignorance which is endemic at the present time. Armed with a sound knowledge of warrants and the way in which they work, it should be possible to combine substantial profits with the fascinating and enjoyable task of uncovering some astonishing bargains. Without this knowledge, investment in warrants is a lottery. There is nothing 'magical' about the way in which warrants perform. They are subject to market sentiment and fads as much as any other securities, of course, but there is an underlying logic to their issue, pricing and trading which any diligent and enthusiastic investor can study. Rich rewards await those who can select the best warrants, trade them shrewdly, and enjoy a little luck along the way.

"Poorly run companies will not find warrants to be the answer to their capital-raising problems, but well-run companies should be able to tap into the virtuous circle of warrant capital."

1

THE ISSUE OF WARRANTS

The first question asked by most investors is, understandably, 'what exactly is a warrant?' The answer is that warrants exist in many forms, each with their own characteristics and quirks, although many of the facets are common. This book is principally concerned with listed equity call warrants, and readers should assume that these are what are being referred to unless specifically stated otherwise. Later in the book covered warrants and put warrants are introduced and explained, but for the most part it should be assumed that the text is dealing with the standard form of issue which is what most private investors will understand by the word 'warrant'.

Equity warrants are transferable option certificates issued by companies and trusts which entitle the holder to buy a specific number of shares in that company at a specific price (exercise, subscription, or strike price) at a specific time in the future. To many investors they are basically long-term options. Like options, they present opportunities for capital gain which can make them an attractive medium for speculative investing. The two key differences from options are that, when exercised, the shares come from the company and not from another investor; and the maturity typically extends for a period of years rather than months.

This chapter explains in simple terms how the UK equity warrants market has developed, explains why warrants are issued, and describes the most important features of the issue documentation.

THE DEVELOPMENT OF THE UK WARRANTS MARKET

It is ironic that London should have provided the world trading centre for the huge Japanese warrants market, and yet have developed the domestic market at such a modest pace. Warrants first appeared in small numbers in the 1970s, but the market failed to achieve a significant presence until the mid-1980s when steady growth took hold. The initial flurry of interest was dissipated by the bear market of 1973–75 which virtually stopped the flow of new issues. A mere 13 warrants were issued from 1973 to 1980 inclusive, a total surpassed several times in a single month in the rapid expansion of the 1990s. With so few warrants being issued, the market inevitably shrank as earlier issues expired, and the total number of warrants in issue fell from 50 at the start of 1974 to just 23 by the start of 1981, as Figure 1.1 shows.

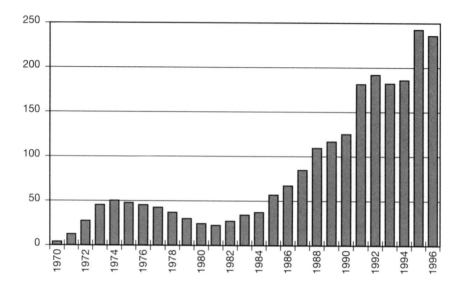

Figure 1.1 Number of warrants listed on the London Stock Exchange 1970–96

It was at this point that growth resumed, and the market began a steady if modest climb back over 50 warrants, and then over 100 warrants by the start of 1988. It seemed as though growth was accelerating and that the warrants market would finally begin to take off. As most investors will remember, however, the 'Crash' of 1987 caused widespread panic and nervousness which persisted well into 1988 in spite of the strong market recovery. A new note of caution was injected into the market, and this restrained the warrants market until confidence was restored and the market experienced its equal fastest year of growth in 1990, pushing the number of warrants from 129 at the start of 1990 to 183 a year later. The 200 barrier was finally broken in 1994 as expansion continued apace, pushing the number of warrants up to record highs. It is often a source of considerable surprise for private investors to learn that so many warrants are listed on the London Stock Exchange, partly because few receive any publicity, many even falling shy of a daily price listing in the *Financial Times*. Part of the reason for this is that many warrant issues are very small. Indeed the aggregate market capitalization of UK equity warrants at June 1995 was a modest £1,295 million, implying an average market capitalization per issue of marginally below £6 million.

Year	Number of warrants listed	Commercial	Finance/ Investment Trusts*
1970	2	2	0
1971	11	11	0
1972	28	23	5
1973	45	29	16
1974	50	31	19
1975	49	30	19
1976	47	28	19
1977	45	25	20
1978	38	21	17
1979	31	17	14
1980	24	13	11
1981	23	12	11
1982	30	13	17
1983	35	14	21
1984	39	12	27
1985	54	16	38
1986	70	22	48
1987	86	30	56
1988	110	39	71
1989	119	48	71
1990	129	51	78
1991	183	59	124
1992	193	59	134
1993	185	48	137
1994	190	51	139
1995	244	60	184
1996†	241	56	185

* Closed-end funds which may be registered overseas and denominated in US dollars are included within this definition as long as they are listed on the London Stock Exchange.
† Estimate.

Table 1.1 Number of UK equity warrants listed on the London Stock Exchange at start of each year, 1970–96

Just as 1981 proved to be the turning point for the warrants market as a whole, so it was also a pivotal moment for the composition of the market. Throughout the period up to 1981 the market comprised a majority of issues from commercial and industrial companies, with investment trusts playing a secondary role. The relative prominence of the two sectors in these early days is well illustrated with a list of the warrants in issue at the start of 1972. The five investment trust names are not likely to be familiar: Anglo-Welsh (Continental), Atlantic Assets Trust, Glendevon Investments, Jessel Securities, and the Thanet Investment Trust are not enduring fixtures. Yet in the list of 23 commercial warrants there is a string of famous companies, including Hill Samuel, National Westminster Bank, Burton Group, Grand Metropolitan Hotels, Lex Service, Trust Houses

Forte, Burmah, Trafalgar House, and Rio Tinto Zinc. The notorious name of Slater Walker also makes an appearance.

The leading position of commercial companies in the warrants market was overtaken during 1981, and investment trusts have subsequently come to dominate the market, gaining a three-quarters share by 1995. Figure 1.2 shows graphically the change in composition, and Table 1.1 gives the number of warrants listed, divided between commercial and investment trusts. There is no doubt that the warrants market has benefited substantially from the quite separate resurgence in the investment trust industry: whereas commercial warrants have exhibited a remarkably stable pattern of growth, the recent surge in numbers has come from the investment trust sector. This reflects the considerable promotional efforts of the Association of Investment Trust Companies (AITC), which has helped to spur the investment trust industry to stage a remarkable comeback in recent years, usurping the prominent role previously accorded to unit trusts. The movement from unit trusts to investment trusts has brought the leading managers across as well, with such prominent names as Morgan Grenfell, Fidelity, Kleinwort, Perpetual, Mercury and Schroder all moving into the investment trust market and issuing warrants for the first time in the 1990s. This augurs well for continued expansion.

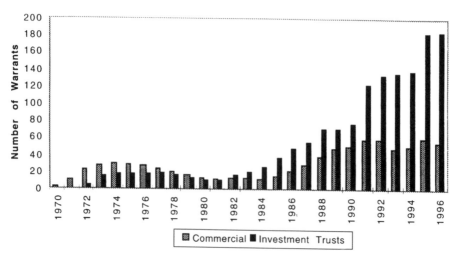

Figure 1.2 Commercial and investment trust warrants listed on the London Stock Exchange 1970–96

It is also revealing to look at the the two components governing net growth. New issues and expiries are analogous to births and deaths in determining population growth in the warrants market. Beginning with the new issues, Figure 1.3 shows how the first bubble of enthusiasm burst quickly, and how growth then resumed during 1981. The post-1987 'Crash' pause shows up clearly before the exceptional growth of 1990 and 1993/94 which has brought so many new investors into the warrants market. The pattern of expiries is also very much as expected: there is a lag of approximately 5–7 years following the issue of new warrants (although some warrants have much longer lives). The majority of the first set of issues expired between 1975 and 1979, contributing to the contraction of the market during this period. This was followed by a predictably low level of expiries in the early 1980s before the post-1981 issues began to expire from 1987. Figure 1.3 and Table 1.2 present this information. The number of expiries will rise sharply from 1995 when issues from 1990 onwards begin to reach final maturity in large numbers.

Year	New Issues	Expiries	Net Change
1969	2	0	+2
1970	9	0	+9
1971	17	0	+17
1972	18	1	+17
1973	6	1	+5
1974	0	1	−1
1975	0	2	−2
1976	3	5	−2
1977	3	10	−7
1978	0	7	−7
1979	0	7	−7
1980	1	2	−1
1981	9	2	+7
1982	9	4	+5
1983	8	4	+4
1984	23	8	+15
1985	20	4	+16
1986	20	4	+16
1987	32	8	+24
1988	21	12	+9
1989	28	18	+10
1990	65	11	+54
1991	33	23	+10
1992	27	35	−8
1993	39	34	+5
1994	62	8	+54
1995*	27	30	−3

* Estimate.

Table 1.2 New issues and expiries during each year 1969–95

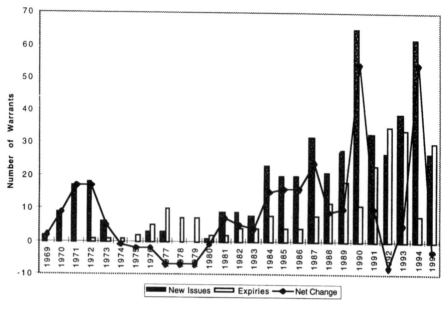

Figure 1.3 New issues, expiries and net change 1969–95

WHY COMPANIES ISSUE WARRANTS

The recent growth of the warrants market does not disguise the fact that it remains a very small sub-section of the market, and many more companies are now beginning to cast a favourable eye over what is still an underdeveloped field. The majority of companies launching new issues are using warrants for the first time, motivated by a broad range of attractions. Directors and corporate financiers fully aware of the range of benefits must see that a warrant issue can heap several advantages upon both the company and its shareholders – advantages which other forms of financing find hard to match.

The most tangible increment from a warrants issue is the capital-raising element. When the warrants are exercised, the holder must pay the exercise price in cash to the company in exchange for new shares. Assuming full exercise, this amount will be known at the outset, and may be used to plan for acquisition, investment or debt reduction. This method of raising additional capital is rather like a deferred rights issue, which can be of considerable advantage for corporate planning. Ordinary rights issues have the benefit of immediacy, but they cannot always be launched when desired. In poor market conditions, or where the market may already be overburdened with capital demands, companies may be unable to raise capital through a rights issue, which shareholders may simply decline to take up. This is not a problem with warrants, which can provide a specific amount of capital at a specific time or during a specific period in the future as long as the share price exceeds the warrant's exercise price. Warrant-holders who do not wish to participate in the eventual capital payments can sell in the market prior to final expiry. The final holder must pay the additional capital on the final subscription date or lose the value of the warrant entirely, thereby ensuring a near-100 per cent take-up rate as long as the warrant is 'in the money'.

The importance of this exercise money was emphasized in an announcement from the drug development company British Biotech in May 1995. 'We will need those warrants to be exercised,' said chief executive Keith McCullagh, who had in mind the £47.5m of funds the warrants would generate if exercised – cash which the company needed to finance further drug development. Should the warrants fail to be exercised, then the company would need to seek finance from a rights issue or from bank financing, both of which are far more costly in terms of both fees and effort. Warrants can be a simple method of raising large sums of money.

The best example of this is the industrial conglomerate BTR, which proved to be the most eager proponent of warrants at the start of the 1990s, making six annual issues from 1988 to 1993 and setting up a *de facto* rolling rights issue for each of the years 1992 to 1998 inclusive. Over this period full exercise of the outstanding warrants will result in the company receiving over £1.7 billion in exercise monies (compared with a market capitalization of around £12.3 billion) – a very useful contribution for a company which relies to some extent upon acquisitions for growth. It is no coincidence either that Eurotunnel, which has suffered such difficulties in obtaining the huge sums of finance necessary for the project, should have used the warrants market extensively as a way of raising cash.

Warrants can therefore provide a useful contribution to a company's capital requirements, while being less disruptive than a rights issue if the capital is not required straight away. Rights issues often carry negative side-effects, alienating some shareholders and casting a bearish shadow over the shares, but warrants avoid these difficulties entirely. Indeed the impact of a warrant issue can be quite the reverse. Warrants are often appreciated as a 'free gift' from the company to its shareholders, seemingly creating extra value at a stroke.

But surely a company cannot suddenly 'create' value in this way? The short-term benefit is real enough. A company issuing warrants on a 1-for-5 basis, on favourable terms, may be able to provide shareholders with an immediate one-off increase of up to around 10 per cent in the capital value of their holdings, as follows:

Widget plc shares 100p. Value of 10,000 shareholding = £10,000
Widget plc issues warrants free on a 1-for-5 basis.
Widget shares 100p; Widget warrants market value 35p.
Value of 10,000 shareholding + 2,000 warrants = £10,700 (+7.0%)

This gain accrues because the current share price fails to take full account of the equity dilution which will occur when the warrants are exercised. The issue of warrants has created a claim over new shares equivalent to 20 per cent of the existing capital, but since those new shares will not be issued for some years, the impact upon the current share price is minimal. Hence value is 'created'. This is in essence a subtle form of deception, as the warrant issue offers jam today instead of jam tomorrow, but few of the newly created warrant-holders have a full appreciation of this fact.

Anyone doubting the ability of warrants to make an immediate and positive contribution in this way should consider the example set by Lord Hanson, an acknowledged master of takeover bids. His creative use of warrants to help finance the takeovers of Consolidated Gold Fields in 1989 and Beazer in 1991 allowed the issue of new shares to be deferred until 1997. The first tranche of warrants appeared as part of the first offer which comprised £143 in cash and 11 new Hanson warrants for every 10 Gold Fields shares. At this point the warrants were not listed and so their value was uncertain. A brokers' forecast of 55p per warrant contained within the prospectus was sufficient to persuade doubtful Gold Fields' shareholders of the new warrants' value, and the offer was successful. In this instance the 160 million warrants formed only a small part of the offer package (around 4 per cent), but the precedent was set. In 1991 Hanson used warrants to play a far more prominent role in the acquisition of building group Beazer. As the market price of the warrants was well established by this time (albeit at the lower price of 33.5p) their value was readily identifiable, making it easier to use them as an alternative to new shares. Prior to the offer for Beazer shares, Hanson had taken a stake in ICI, bringing considerable political pressure and a short-term underperformance from the shares. Against this background it was preferable to avoid a rights issue to fund the new acquisition, so Hanson instead offered 90p cash and one new warrant for each Beazer share. This time the warrant element accounted for no less than 27 per cent of the value of the bid. This neatly avoided the need to issue new shares at a discount, Hanson shares rose, and the City naturally acclaimed the takeover as a positive move. Furthermore, in some respects Hanson was in a 'no-lose' situation with the new warrants. Should Hanson shares fail to perform well up to the final exercise date in 1997, then the warrants will not be exercised, Hanson will not have to issue any new shares, and this part of the bid will have been free. Conversely, if Hanson shares do perform well and the warrants are exercised, Hanson will benefit substantially from the payment of the exercise monies in 1997 or before.

Hanson's skilled use of warrants provides a wonderful example of the benefits they can offer to companies, but the use of warrants on this scale is unusual. More frequently, the ability of warrants to add value to an equity holding has been used in the role of 'sweetener' to aid difficult issues, often at the time of a takeover or an awkward corporate restructuring. The very fact that warrants should be used in this way speaks volumes for their utility as an instrument of corporate finance. The beauty of warrants, from the point of the issuer, is that they offer very low initial servicing costs. Warrants are cheap to issue, and they can actively reduce the cost of more expensive forms of finance. When attached to loan stock, for example, the addition of a warrants sweetener often allows the company to offer the stock at a lower coupon than might otherwise have been the case: this is the rationale behind the huge issues of Japanese warrants (see Chapter 11), the exercise monies from which provide the cash for the redemption of the bonds.

In the UK, most commercial warrants are not attached to other instruments now, but given 'free' to shareholders on a scrip basis. The warrants so issued provide shareholders with an added way of participating in the future growth of the company, and it has been argued that they draw attention to the forward value of a company's shares. It has not been proven that warrant issues benefit share prices in this way, but companies may argue that warrant purchasers are expressing confidence in the company by buying the right to subscribe for shares at a price higher (sometimes much higher) than the prevailing market price. This can stimulate some positive publicity, and in certain cases the issue of warrants has raised the media profile of companies considerably.

Another reason for the issue of scrip warrants by smaller companies is where liquidity is a problem for the underlying shares. In a minority of cases the shares are tightly held by institutions or company directors, who may be more willing to allow small warrant holdings to float freely in the market. These warrants can attract the sophisticated private investor, broadening the shareholder base once the warrants are exercised.

These are largely benefits external to the company, but one little-recognized benefit of warrants is in the provision of management intelligence. Warrants can act as a more sensitive barometer of confidence in the company than the share price. The vast majority of warrants command a conversion premium which means that the underlying equity must rise to justify the prevailing warrant price. Fluctuations in the premium are therefore indicative of confidence in the equity price, and in the company itself. The capital fulcrum point (CFP, explained in Chapter 3) measures this in a consistent way through time, and can be a powerful indicator of a company's standing in the market as long as it is placed in the proper context.

Last but not least, warrants can add some spice to what might otherwise be regarded as a dull investment proposition. Companies should not underestimate the power of this simple fact: the addition of warrants to the equity base can make a company stand out from the crowd, particularly if the warrants are given a high profile with newspaper price listings. There are over 3,000 ordinary shares listed on the London Stock Exchange, so a company must be able to present some specific attractions before it can expect to draw the attention of new investors. The issue of warrants achieves this at a stroke, and carries the benefit of appealing principally to private investors. Many companies seek a broad shareholder base with a substantial number of private investors, because individuals tend to be less aggressive than large institutional shareholders, and because a scattered shareholder base is more difficult for a predator to capture in the event of a bid. It is likely that an issue of warrants will result in a broadening of the shareholder base after exercise, and if the warrants were issued by way of a scrip issue then they may have increased the loyalty to the company felt by many private investors. This is a reason cited by some issuers, and it seems appropriate to close this section with a direct quote from the chairman and chief executive of one of the companies which has issued warrrants. When asked why his company had issued warrants, J David Abell said that industrial conglomerate Suter issued warrants in order to:

(a) 'Achieve more interest in the company. It was envisaged that the warrants would end up with high net worth individuals who would not necessarily buy the high-yielding ordinary shares.'
(b) 'To raise money without the cost and disruption associated with a rights issue.'

These benefits of issuing warrants are far from nebulous, yet they appear to be little understood or appreciated by the majority of finance directors of listed companies. There is still some degree of fear about warrants, a worry that they are somehow too complicated, too speculative, too flashy, that they make a future claim on equity at the expense of shareholders, and that they could expire worthless.

Addressing each of these points in turn, the fear that warrants are too complicated is borne out of ignorance. It is a fear of the unknown. Once people own warrants and see the way in which they work, much of the mystery is removed, and there is no need for the majority of holders to understand the finer points of algebraic valuation techniques. Warrants can simply be a welcome addition to a portfolio, particularly if there is no initial cost attached. The same applies to the company directors: while it is possible to use warrants to help finance takeovers and to achieve other sophisticated aims, they can equally be used to fulfil the simple aim of creating additional value for shareholders. The degree of complication may be tailored to suit the issue and the target investors, and a normal retail issue will carry simple conversion terms such as the following:

Incepta Group warrants each carry the right to subscribe for one share at 19.7p on 30 June in each of the years 1992 to 2000 inclusive.

Warrant terms need be no more complex than this, although the picture is clouded by the minority of warrant issues which are aimed directly at banks and financial institutions, such as the special 1991 issue from Eurotunnel. These warrants were issued directly to banks as part of a share warrant and credit agreement, and the subscription terms reflected this highly specific facility.

Eurotunnel 1991 warrants each carry the right to subscribe for 1.24 ELPC shares at £1.75 and 1.24 EPSA shares at FFr17.50 during the period of three months commencing on whichever first occurs of (i) the date when all indebtedness due to the banks under the financing agreements has been discharged; (ii) the date when the aggregate of all refinancing debt exceeds 10 per cent of the eligible prepayment amount; and (iii) 31 March 2000.

Terms such as these, where warrant-holders cannot even know the final maturity date with any certainty, are thankfully rare, and the large majority of warrants are relatively simple.

There is more substance to the point that warrants may be too speculative for some tastes. Where blue-chip companies are concerned, investors may buy ordinary shares as an alternative to safer, interest-bearing investments such as gilts, investment bonds, or building society accounts. Companies seeking these investors may feel that warrants fail to project the right image, being associated with Irish exploration stocks and more speculative concerns. It is true that the Irish exploration companies have consistently used warrants, as have 'hot stock' companies whose stars have fallen. But in a market which can boast issues from respected blue-chip companies such as Hanson, British Aerospace, BTR, and Pilkington, not to mention the array of conservatively managed investment trusts, this argument seems flawed.

Similarly, warrants are seen as attracting short-term speculators rather than solid long-term investors. This may be true to some extent, as warrants are an excellent instrument for investors concerned with short-term capital gains, but of course the majority of enfranchized warrant-holders never trade, and what better way of convincing investors of the long-term merits of your company than to provide them with excellent short- to medium-term gains? The true long-term investor will pocket his free warrants, thank you, ignore their price fluctuations, and then exercise the subscription rights for ordinary shares if the terms are favourable at exercise time.

The one major caveat, implied above, is that the company may experience a poor trading period and the shares may not reach the exercise price. In this event the warrant-holders have no incentive to exercise their subscription rights and the warrants will expire worthless. The company will not only fail to raise any capital, but also fall prey to the attendant negative publicity. When BTR's share price began to fall sharply in the autumn of 1994, it was extremely unfortunate that it did so immediately prior to the expiry of the 1993/94 series of warrants, which fell by 48 per cent in one trading session and had little time to recover. Whilst it would have been more helpful for the Press to have concentrated on the margin pressure which afflicted the shares, it was the precipitate decline in the warrants which was more newsworthy, and BTR was pilloried as a consequence. This Press coverage may have influenced the management decision to cease warrant issues, but the main problem which BTR encountered was that an annual call on shareholders did place some strain on both their pockets and their patience. So after six successive and successful issues, BTR decided to halt the practice. It seems that pressure was brought to bear by instutional shareholders who were concerned about the dilutive effect of the warrant issues when the proceeds were not being used for a specific purpose. This should not be a problem for companies issuing just one series, or even several series spaced a few years apart, but BTR has withdrawn for the moment, costing the UK warrants market its most prestigious example.

Problems such as these can and do happen in bear markets, but in normal market conditions the great majority of warrants are exercised with a minimum of fuss. Furthermore, from the standpoint of market efficiency there is an appealing logic to whichever outcome may transpire. Since warrants may be issued for a period of several years*, and with a subscription price chosen by the company, they will only expire worthless if the terms of subscription were misjudged initially, or the company has not performed as well as expected. In either event it may be argued that the company does not deserve to raise the additional capital and that the problem is directly related to their failure to plan or to perform adequately. Poorly run companies will not find warrants to be the answer to their capital-raising problems, but well-run companies should be able to tap into the virtuous circle of warrant capital. If the company performs well and the share price grows to exceed the exercise price, then the warrants will be exercised and the company will receive the proceeds, providing funds for further expansion.

THE TYPE OF COMPANIES WHICH ISSUE WARRANTS

Just as the reasons for issue can differ widely, so can type of issuer. As the market has grown, so has the range of issuing companies, and there is no standard set from which issuers are drawn: they vary from the smallest companies to very nearly the largest. Sectorally, there is again little pattern. Warrant issues have come from the fields of advertising, property, finance, engineering, conglomerates, and most others. What may be interpreted as a lack of consistency reflects the fact that warrants tend to provoke polarized opinions among the decision-makers who matter. Some consider warrants to be an excellent speculative tool with which they would like to be associated; others have a strong reaction against them, whatever the benefits. Seen in a more favourable light, the diversity of issuers may be considered a reflection of the equally diverse interests which warrants can serve.

One interesting question which has yet to attract empirical research is whether those companies issuing warrants might form a relatively successful sub-sector of

---

* The long terms of maturity available from warrants rule out short-term bear markets as a legitimate reason for worthless expiry.

the market. The reasoning behind this suggestion relates to the progressive attitudes of companies issuing warrants and to the provision of future capital, which implies growth. The issue of warrants is something which is more likely to be undertaken by dynamic, forward-looking management than by staid and conservative boards.

WHY INVESTMENT TRUSTS ISSUE WARRANTS

Whilst a relatively small proportion of commercial companies have issued warrants, they are far more widespread among investment trusts. It is not merely the number of investment trust warrant issues which outstrips the commercial sector, but also, far more dramatically, their concentration. Of the 373 companies listed under 'Investment Trusts' in the *Financial Times* in May 1995, some 176 (47 per cent) had warrants attached, and some of these boasted more than one series of warrants. Furthermore, the concentration is even greater amongst those investment trusts now coming to the market: with the exception of split-capital trusts, the large majority of new investment trusts (around 80 per cent) offer warrants as part of the initial package, usually 'free' on the basis of one warrant for every five or ten shares. The basic reason for this is simple. With most trusts starting to trade at an immediate discount to net assets, a 'sweetener' helps to persuade investors to pay a full price for those assets at the launch. The 'free' issue of warrants plugs the discount gap, and also provides the trust with additional funds when the warrants are exercised. A typical example runs as follows:

The Big Cheese Investment Trust plc – Offer for Sale at 100p per share, with warrants attached on a 1-for-5 basis. Estimated net asset value per share after deducting the costs of the offer: 96p.
Shares begin trading at 95p, warrants at 30p. Value of share bought as part of offer = 95p +(30p/5) = 101p. Investor has small paper profit.

For this reason the issue of warrants by investment trusts can be curiously perverse according to market conditions. During bullish periods when confidence is high, new trusts may feel sufficiently confident to issue shares without free warrants attached. One new issue in 1991, from the Moorgate Smaller Companies Income Trust, exemplified this point. This trust was very similar to the existing Moorgate Investment Trust which could point to an enviable investment record in its sector which allowed its shares to trade at a consistent (and unusual) premium to net assets. The managers judged, therefore, that as the market conditions appeared favourable, shares in the new trust might also trade at a premium, and that there was no necessity to provide a further incentive by way of free warrants. Even so, the numerous attractions of warrants were evident to the managers, so warrants were sold separately as part of the offer at 35p each. The result of the offer for sale vindicated this approach, as not only did the shares begin to trade at a premium, but the warrant issue was very popular. While the offer of 50 million shares was slightly undersubscribed, attracting applications for 48.53 million, the offer of 10 million warrants was nearly 5 per cent oversubscribed. The trust received the full £3.5 million from the initial price of the warrants, and will receive a further £10 million if the warrants are exercised in full.

In the Moorgate case the capital-raising benefit was prominent, but more generally the attraction of warrants in lending added spice to an offer for sale is a key facet for investment trusts. Although investment trusts now seem to have the battle won, they have fought for market share with competing forms of collective investment such as unit trusts. Warrants are one of the prime features which give investment trusts the edge, adding value to the investment trust package and offering a more exciting prospect. This can be important for many investors who are attracted by certain features of collective investment but wish for a less conservative holding than that offered by the shares alone. Consider, for example, an investor wishing to take a speculative stake in the stockmarkets of developing countries. It will be almost impossible for the investor to construct his own portfolio, and a battery of problems will be encountered if he tries to invest directly. Conducting research in such a variety of countries will be very difficult, there are still numerous restrictions on foreign investment, capital cannot always be repatriated, settlement may be difficult, the custody of certificates may be awkward and expensive to arrange, and many stocks are extremely illiquid. For all of these reasons it makes sense for the investor to enlist a professional manager to invest in a diversified portfolio on his behalf, and there are both unit trusts and investment trusts which invest in emerging markets. The drawback for the speculative investor is that the spread of investments will tend to moderate the return on capital, and this is where warrants play their part. The speculative investor will choose from the warrants attached to Abtrust Emerging Economies, Beta Global Emerging Markets, The Emerging Markets Country Fund, Fleming Emerging Markets, Foreign & Colonial Emerging Markets, Govett Emerging Markets, Kleinwort Emerging Markets, Murray Emerging Markets, and Templeton Emerging Markets investment trusts, probably exercising his warrants at the appropriate time if the trusts perform well.

In addition to these specific practical benefits, another reason why investment trusts issue warrants is simply that the precedent is very well-established. There is a strong element of inertia in the new issue market, which seems to have three components. First, there is competition. Just as there is competition between investment trusts and unit trusts, so there are competing investment trusts. Several fund management groups may have similar trusts with similar aims, investing into similar geographical regions or market sectors. When launching a new trust, the managers must be aware that they will very often be competing with existing trusts with warrants in issue, and they are unlikely to risk a narrower capital structure excluding warrants, which would rebuff those investors who prefer warrants or a warrant/share mix.

Second, and similarly, it may be difficult to raise capital from a new issue without warrants attached if similar trusts launched around the same time have made provision for their issue. Fashion seems to be a remarkable feature of the investment trust industry, and there are frequent spates of issues providing blanket coverage of certain regions or sectors. In early 1994, for example, Latin American investment trusts were in vogue, and three new trusts covering this sector were launched within three months. As the first two had both offered warrants, there was no way in which the third (the Scudder Latin America Investment Trust) was likely to proceed without free warrants attached, since the market had by this time built up a firm expectation that this was necessary and desirable.

Finally, there is quite simply the urge to comply with the prevailing standard. If the majority of new trusts are issuing warrants, then the default position is to follow the trend and to issue warrants. This 'copycat' approach is backed by the fact that many trusts have the same banks and stockbrokers advising on issues, so the same opinions are likely to be voiced repeatedly. More positively, the fear of warrants is diminished by familiarity. While many finance directors of commercial companies may be wary of warrants because they are uncommon, the merits of warrants are more freely appreciated in the investment trust market – both by the issuers and by investors.

THE PARTICULARS OF THE WARRANTS

When new warrants are issued, the documentation detailing the particulars of the warrants will include the conversion terms. This basic yet crucial information comprises the number of shares for subscription, price, and the subscription period – the primary factors which determine the value of the warrant.

Each warrant will usually confer the right to subscribe for one share, but this is not necessarily the case and it is always important to check before dealing. Some warrants do have special features – such as the Gartmore European Investment Trust plc, where one warrant confers the right to subscribe for four ordinary shares. The result is that the warrant price is higher than the price of a single share – something which repels most casual investors unfamiliar with the terms and often leaves the warrants undervalued. This is just one example of where the well-informed warrant investor can use his superior knowledge to take advantage of market pricing discrepancies, and in America, where the terms of subscription are extremely varied (see Chapter 10), there is no doubt that careful research is necessary.

The same applies to the subscription price. Commonly, this will be related to the price of the shares at the time of issue, and for this reason 100p is a price which frequently occurs, largely for the sake of simplicity. The price will usually be straightforward, although again the market can boast a few colourful mavericks. One of the most interesting is the London American Growth Trust plc, which offered the right to subscribe for one share at 110p in 1990, or at 125p in 1995, or at 140p in the year 2000. The price may also be denominated in a currency other than sterling. In recent years the London market has attracted listings from a range of closed-end funds incorporated in such exotic places as the Cayman Islands, Netherlands Antilles, Luxembourg, and Hong Kong. These funds are usually traded in US dollars, and the subscription price will usually be in the same currency as the shares.

The maturity, or life, of the warrant will tend to be several years. The average time to expiry of existing warrants in the UK equity warrants market is around four and three-quarter years, and this will tend to be approximately five to seven years for most new issues. There is a good deal of variation around this average, however, with the time preference determined largely by the individual motivations and capital requirements of each issuer. Thus, for example, the US Smaller Companies Investment Trust plc, launched in August 1991, issued warrants with the primary objectives of plugging the discount gap and creating additional value for shareholders. This meant that a high price was desirable for the warrants, and this was best achieved with a long time to expiry, in this case up to the year 2002. Conversely, the warrants issued on a scrip basis by the Alpine Group plc in September 1991 featured an unusually short maturity, lasting only until February 1992. This made them less of a warrant and more of a deferred rights issue dressed as a temporary traded option. Certainly the capital-raising motivation appeared prominent in this case.

Warrants will usually last until the end of their predetermined life, but there are four circumstances in which they may be terminated early. First, if the company itself ceases to exist in its current form before the warrants are due to expire. This may happen if the company is forced into liquidation or in the event of takeover. In the former case, the warrants will be worthless, but in the latter case there may be provisions to protect the value of the warrant (see Chapter 2). This can also be important in the second case – an early winding-up of the company or trust. Investment trusts do sometimes offer shareholders the right to vote for an early dissolution of the trust if it is not performing well. An example is provided by the Aberforth Smaller Companies Trust plc, which has warrants with a final expiry date in 2003. The shareholders can vote to have the trust wound up in 1995 and every three years thereafter, so some investors may fear that the warrants may not last into the next century. In this case the warrant-holders can rest assured that the time value of their warrants is fully protected (they would effectively be bought out at the prevailing market price), but this cannot be guaranteed in all cases.

Third, the company will usually retain the right to purchase warrants in the market or to make a tender offer at a price not exceeding 110 per cent of the middle market price. Any such warrants so purchased are cancelled and are not available for re-issue or re-sale. This rarely happens, as does the final reason for curtailment – a majority of early exercise. If immediately after a subscription date prior to the final exercise date, more than a certain percentage (usually 75 per cent, but sometimes up to 90 per cent) of the warrants have been exercised, then the company may be entitled to enforce exercise of the remaining warrants if the terms are favourable. As the large majority of warrants are normally exercised on the final exercise date this is unlikely to take place, but it is always wise to be aware of the detailed terms in the warrant particulars.

ADJUSTMENT OF SUBSCRIPTION RIGHTS

There are also circumstances in which the price and number of shares for subscription may be altered. Indeed, companies and trusts are obliged to adjust these terms for subsequent rights issues or capitalizations – a process which is undertaken in a standard manner. This is simple common sense: there is no legitimate reason for warrant-holders to be penalized because the company alters its equity structure. In the event of a rights issue, for example, with new shares offered at a price beneath the current market price, the ex-rights price will be lower, and the warrant-holder would lose out if the terms of subscription were not amended.

In the case of capitalizations the procedure is simple:

Adjusted subscription price

$$= \textit{subscription price} \times \frac{\textit{number of shares before capitalization}}{\textit{number of shares after capitalization}}$$

EXAMPLE

Scottish Investment Trust plc issued 16,944,000 warrants free to shareholders on a 1-for-5 basis. Subscription price 484p. February 1988, 2-for-1 capitalization issue (shares and warrants). Now 50,832,000 warrants in issue, subscription price adjusted:

$$\textit{Adjusted subscription price} = 484p \times \frac{84,720,000}{254,160,000}$$

$$= 484p \times 1/3$$
$$= 161.33p$$

The calculations for adjustment of both the subscription price and the number of warrants following a rights issue are more complex, and are outlined in the particulars of the warrants. These are generally written in vile legalistic prose along the lines of:

If and whenever the Company shall offer to holders of Ordinary Shares new ordinary shares for subscription by way of rights, or shall offer or grant to holders of Ordinary Shares any options, rights or warrants to subscribe for or purchase new Ordinary Shares, in each case at a price which is less than the market price per Ordinary Share on the dealing day next preceding the date of the announcement of the terms of the offer or grant, the Subscription Price shall be adjusted by multiplying the Subscription Price in force immediately before the date of the announcement of such offer or grant by a fraction of which the numerator is the number of Ordinary Shares in issue immediately before the date of such announcement plus the number of Ordinary Shares which is the aggregate of the amount (if any) payable for the rights, options or warrants and of the amount payable for the total number of new Ordinary Shares comprised therein would purchase at such market price and the denominator is the number of Ordinary Shares in issue immediately before the date of such announcement plus the aggregate number of Ordinary Shares offered for subscription or comprised in the total number of warrants. Such adjustment shall become effective on the date of issue of such Ordinary Shares or grant of such options, rights or warrants (as the case may be).

Newcomers to the warrants market will be thankful that it is not necessary to follow exactly how this adjustment is calculated. It is sufficient to understand that the provisions are written into the warrant particulars for your protection, and that the subscription price will be adjusted in a fair way. An example is provided below for those who do wish to look more closely:

EXAMPLE

New subscription price = old subscription price

$$\times \frac{shares\ in\ issue + (number\ of\ new\ shares \times (rights\ price\ /\ share\ price))}{shares\ in\ issue + number\ of\ new\ shares}$$

EXAMPLE

Ibstock plc, 198m shares in issue, market price 114p, warrants subscription price 170p. 4 April 1991, company announces 1-for-4 rights issue at 90p.

$$New\ subscription\ price = 170p \times \frac{198\ million + (49.45\ million \times (90p\ /\ 114p))}{198\ million + 49.45\ million}$$

$$New\ subscription\ price = 170p \times \frac{198\ million + 39\ million}{247.45\ million}$$

$$New\ subscription\ price = 170p \times 0.958 \qquad New\ subscription\ price = 162p$$

Furthermore, the company may issue additional warrants to existing warrant-holders at no extra charge, according to the formula:

New warrants = existing warrant holding

$$\times \frac{\textit{old subscription price} - \textit{new subscription price}}{\textit{new subscription price}}$$

And returning to the example of Ibstock:

$$\textit{New warrants} = \textit{existing warrant holding} \times \frac{170p - 162p}{162p}$$

New warrants = existing warrant holding $\times$ *0.0494*

This translates into 24 new warrants for every 500 warrants held.

Although the actual terms of warrants can vary widely, the adjustment terms are fairly standard, as is most of the wording. And the intention is clear: to provide a clearly defined investment with its value properly protected against external changes. The apparent complexity of some of the jargon need not prove a barrier to understanding, to issue, or to investment. Once the primary hurdle of ignorance is overcome, then many more companies are likely to be issuing new warrants, and thousands more investors becoming registered warrant-holders.

"You must not enter this high-risk area of investment with your eyes closed. There are arguments both for and against investment in warrants, and it is up to you, the individual, to decide whether they are a suitable place for your money."

2

SHOULD I INVEST IN WARRANTS?

Warrants have many attractions, and they can appeal to a broad range of investors with a broad range of different interests. It has even been suggested that warrants are suitable for children, who have a full capital gains tax allowance but a less favourable income position. Whether this is sensible or not, there is no doubt that warrants are an exciting and fascinating area of investment, at once both challenging and enticing.

That said, they are not a fitting investment for everybody, and there are certain disadvantages which it is as well to be aware of. Most importantly, it is possible to make heavy losses, due to bad luck, poor judgement, or more probably, simple ignorance. You must not enter this high-risk area of investment with your eyes closed. There are arguments both for and against investment in warrants, and it is up to you, the individual, to decide whether they are a suitable place for your money. Warrants attract strong opinions for and against, often depending upon the personal experience of the person voicing the opinion. Most warrants experts will tell you that warrants are the perfect vehicle for speculative investment, but that is little more than preaching by the converted. This chapter attempts to provide a balanced overview of the pros and cons of investing in warrants, listing ten points for and ten points against. Whatever your preconceived view of warrants, it makes sense to read both sections and to be aware of the other side of the coin.

THE SORT OF INVESTORS WHO BUY WARRANTS

The largest London stockbrokers deal in warrants, and so do retired colonels in Christchurch, shopkeepers in Sheffield, doctors in Dundee, and a broad spectrum of other people. You do not have to be a City professional or a wealthy landowner to buy warrants. Indeed the warrants market is increasingly attracting small investors who have dipped their toes into the waters of the stockmarket with the privatization shares, and now feel sufficiently confident to move into the rapids of speculative investing. Other newcomers to the warrants market are more experienced private investors who have become disenchanted with other forms of securities such as penny shares. In their heydays in the 1980s penny shares did produce some returns approaching those provided by warrants, but their performance has been very poor since the Crash of 1987. Similarly, other investors are turning to warrants instead of traded options, put off by the limited range, high commissions and short trading periods. Whatever their previous experiences, a large number of investors are now buying warrants for the first time.

Among those who already have some holdings, the first group is passive. Thousands of shareholders have become warrant-holders accidentally, as the companies in which they hold shares have issued them with 'free' warrants on a scrip basis. Many of these holders will simply ignore their new holdings until the time when they can be exercised at a profit, but others will follow the progress of the warrants, and if suitably impressed will then seek to invest in warrants directly. A practical illustration of warrant profits is the best salesman: if sceptical shareholders can see for themselves how well warrants can perform, then many will become convinced of their merits. It would hardly be a surprise if those fortunate holders of the first series of free BTR warrants who saw them rise from 55p after the issue in late 1988 to 253p a year later decided to take up investment in warrants.

Further along the spectrum of experience, there are of course some market professionals and specialists who use their knowledge of the market to trade on a regular basis. Some of these investors will use warrants as part of their overall investment strategy, using warrants to 'fine tune' the risk and return characteristics of portfolios or for hedging purposes. Others may invest the majority of their capital in warrants, a strategy which is only suitable for the most experienced and confident of investors. To pursue such a high-risk course you would need to have no doubts about the advantages of warrants over ordinary shares.

THE ADVANTAGES OF WARRANTS OVER SHARES

Gearing – where fortunes can be made

The principal advantage of warrants over ordinary shares is that they offer the potential for much larger gains in rising markets. Warrants concentrate exclusively on capital gain, leading to some spectacular profits on occasions. During bull markets or at other times of rising prices, shares cannot hope to match the sort of returns which are commonly available to warrant-holders. Even the most speculative forms of direct investment in equities such as penny shares are unable to keep pace.

Yorkshire Tyne Tees TV warrants have produced a heady schedule of gains for warrant investors who tuned in over the last couple of years (see Figure 2.1). From a low of just 6p at the start of March 1993 the warrants have been well worth watching. They doubled by 16 March 1993, and hit 60p for a ten-fold gain by early October. The warrants continued to rise as the stock was boosted by persistent takeover rumours, reached 100p in the first week of February 1994, then doubled again by the end of August, and added a further 100p by April 1995. The warrants have moved up to 393p at the time of writing in early July 1995. This 65-fold gain is an extraordinary achievement, not merely in its magnitude, but also in view of the fact that the shares rose by a far more modest 389 per cent over the same period. Anyone who invested £15,268 in the shares would have a holding worth a handsome £74,714 just over two and a quarter years later, but would have been made a millionaire from the same investment in the warrants.

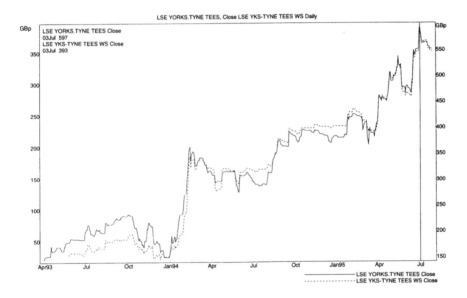

Figure 2.1 Yorkshire Tyne Tees TV shares and warrants 1993–95
(source: Reuters)

Another memorable example from a few years ago is provided by Airtours, the package holiday company, whose shares rose from 170p to 812p (up by a creditable 378 per cent) in the first ten months of 1991*, placing them among the best-performing shares during that period. The company was a major beneficiary of the cyclical upturn in holiday bookings, and had gained a large chunk of market share following the demise of a major competitor, ILG Intasun. Anyone investing £2,000 in Airtours shares at the start of the year would have an investment worth a shade over £9,550 by October, a more than satisfactory return. These investors had good reason to be happy – until they realized that they could have invested in the highly geared warrants. In January 1991 Airtours warrants

*From 1 January 1991 to 31 October 1991

were quoted at just 10p middle-price, and 12p to buy. During February they dipped to 7p before taking off and making a few shrewd investors very rich. By the end of October 1991 the warrants had risen to 590p, a rise in excess of 4,800 per cent from the buying price of 12p at the start of the year. Placing this in context, the investor preferring to place his £2,000 in Airtours warrants at a cost of 12p each in January would have an investment worth almost £98,300 by October. This is more than ten times the worth of the direct equity investment over the same period. It must be stressed that Airtours was the best-performing warrant for some time, and is by no means typical, but it does illustrate the enormous upside potential which draws speculators to the warrants market. Using warrants it is possible to make a small fortune, and occasionally a large one.

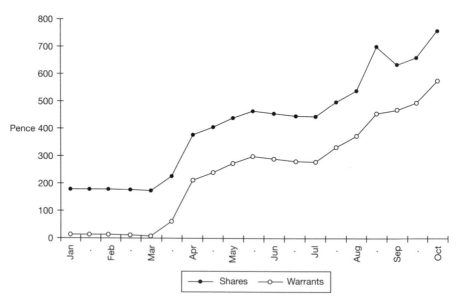

Figure 2.2 Airtours Shares and Warrants 1991 (prices)

As Figure 2.2 shows, Airtours shares and warrants moved very much in tandem throughout the period in question, so how did the warrants manage to magnify the return more than ten-fold? The answer lies in a concept known as 'gearing'. Essentially this reflects the lower price of warrants, which means that absolute changes are proportionately greater. If ABC shares are 100p and ABC warrants carry the right to subscribe for the shares at 70p, then each warrant may trade at 30p (assuming a zero premium for simplicity). A 15 per cent rise in the value of ABC shares to 115p means that the warrants must be worth at least 45p – a 50 per cent increase. Figure 2.3 shows the Airtours shares and warrants in terms of percentage gain.

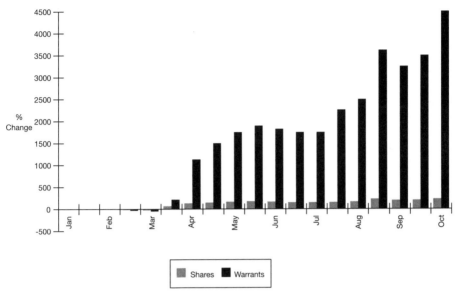

Figure 2.3 Airtours Shares and Warrants 1991 (percentage change)

Looking at this another way, the gearing benefit means that you can achieve a large equity exposure from a relatively small investment. In the case of Airtours above, for example, the £2,000 investment bought 1,176 shares if they were purchased directly at 170p, but that same investment would have bought 16,666 warrants at 12p each. As each warrant confers the right to subscribe for one share, this gives the warrant-holder rights over 16,666 shares, worth over £28,000 at the January price of 170p. This greater exposure carries with it the possibility of a commensurately larger gain.

More generally, the gearing element of warrants means that price changes in the warrants will exaggerate movements in the shares, as illustrated by three more examples taken from the start of 1995, and shown in Table 2.1.

This revealing table shows that warrants can provide heavily accentuated returns when shares are rising, whether or not this is established as a trend. For example, the steady growth of BTR shares throughout this period brought shareholders a creditable gain of 12.1 per cent, but one which was outstripped handsomely by the 40.95 per cent return to holders of the warrants. Investors in Five Arrows Chile had a more uneven ride, but the result was predictably the same – the warrant-holders fared markedly better over the period. This was also true for the Turkey Trust warrants, in spite of their relatively modest degree of gearing. This was still enough to produce a 41.98 per cent gain over the course of one bullish week and a 19.32 per cent gain overall from the period.

Warrants	Type of company	Gearing at start of 1991
BTR 1995/96	Blue-chip conglomerate	5.5 times (301.5p/54.5p)
Five Arrows Chile	Investment trust	5.5 times (US$2.46/US$0.45)
Turkey Trust	Investment trust	2.6 times (190p/37p)

Date wk end	BTR Shares	Wts	Five Arrows Chile Shares	Wts	Turkey Trust Shares	Wts
6 Jan	+2.73	+3.81	−2.38	−10.00	−8.65	-17.05
13 Jan	+1.33	+0.92	−1.63	−20.00	0.00	+1.37
20 Jan	+0.49	+1.82	−0.83	−8.33	−0.53	0.00
27 Jan	−0.81	−2.68	+1.25	−3.03	−2.12	−5.41
3 Feb	−0.16	−0.92	0.00	+6.25	−1.08	-4.29
10 Feb	+5.59	+20.37	+2.47	+23.53	0.00	−2.99
17 Feb	−3.12	−10.77	−1.61	−2.38	−2.19	−3.08
24 Feb	+1.45	+5.17	+3.27	+19.51	+3.35	+1.59
3 Mar	−0.32	0.00	−2.37	−4.08	0.00	0.00
10 Mar	+0.48	0.00	−11.34	−17.02	+1.08	0.00
17 Mar	+1.74	+3.28	+5.94	0.00	+2.14	+3.13
24 Mar	+1.40	+15.87	−0.86	0.00	+7.33	+12.12
31 Mar	+0.61	+2.74	+3.48	+2.56	+3.41	+9.46
7 Apr	+1.22	+5.33	+2.94	+7.50	+11.79	+41.98
14 Apr	+1.51	+3.80	+4.49	+11.63	−1.27	−4.35
21 Apr	−1.34	-3.66	+1.17	+6.25	+2.56	+4.55
28 Apr	−1.05	-6.33	+2.70	+9.80	−3.33	−8.70
Change over Period	**+12.10%**	**+40.95%**	**+5.56%**	**+12.00%**	**+11.54%**	**+19.32%**

Table 2.1 Weekly percentage price changes, first four months 1995

As the foregoing suggests, market timing is very important: if you can time your warrant investments to coincide with the beginning of a bull market then you will never look back. In rising markets the gearing benefit can be enormous, and the performance of warrants is certainly hard to rival.

Uses as a hedging instrument

We have already seen how investors can use their standard investment unit to 'gear up' using warrants, but the gearing benefit may also be used in another way. Instead of using the same amount of capital to gain greater exposure, a smaller amount of capital may be committed. Consider an investor with capital of £10,000 wishing to adopt a modest degree of risk while keeping his hand in the market. If XYZ shares are 100p each and XYZ warrants are 20p each, then an outlay of £2,000 in the warrants would confer rights over £10,000 worth of shares, and the remaining £8,000 may then be invested in other, lower-risk financial products. This feature makes warrants outstandingly appropriate for an investor seeking to make substantial capital gains from a small portion of his overall investment portfolio. Certainly the ability to use warrants in this way means that they can be consistent with an overall low-risk strategy, something which is explored further in Chapter 6.

Loss limitation

An attraction allied to the hedging approach is that your loss is limited to the amount you have invested, which may be much less that you might have invested in the shares. Returning to the case of Airtours, the investment of £2,000 in the warrants offered exposure to £28,000 worth of equity, made £96,000 profit, and yet the maximum loss was limited to £2,000. And in the hedging example, an investor switching out of £10,000 worth of XYZ shares and into £2,000 of warrants providing the same exposure is reducing his possible loss by the full £8,000 which may be removed from the market.

The excitement factor

Of course most investors focus upon profits rather than loss limitation, and investment in warrants can be exciting. For investors seeking to avoid risk there are a myriad of competing investment products from building society accounts to income bonds, but for the majority of investors who place their funds directly into the stockmarket the 'excitement factor' plays some part. Many people undertake stockmarket investment as a gripping and absorbing hobby, even if it is a serious one. Parallels with horse racing are overdone and should not be encouraged, but one common thrill is the ability to watch your selections perform.

On hearing of a large rise in the FT-SE Index on the news one evening, will your holdings of ordinary shares really compel you to rush towards your *Financial Times* the following morning to check the prices? Probably not. A 1 per cent rise in the value of your holdings is unlikely to set the heart pounding and to give you renewed faith in the stockmarket as a place where skilful analysis and selections can be liberally rewarded. A 5 per cent, 10 per cent or even a 20 per cent change in your warrants, by comparison, can animate even the most dour of personalities. Achieving a greater return in a single day than you might make in an entire year on deposit can be an exhilarating experience, and the gearing element of warrants means that they are far more likely to move by such a margin than the underlying shares.

No one would deny that an investment in Yorkshire Tyne Tees TV warrants from 1993 to 1995 would produce more of a stir of enthusiasm for stockmarket investment than a steady 10 per cent compound annual return from some convertible preference shares, yet this attraction of warrants is frequently denigrated. The excitement factor is often misconstrued as frivolity, resulting in various unflattering descriptions of warrants as 'go-go' securities or 'a gambler's market'. These views acknowledge this single aspect of warrants as a positive feature, but fail to take account of the serious role of skilful analysis in attempting to realise the potential of the market.

Short-term trading opportunities and price anomalies

In reality, it is a mixture of skill, experience and vigilance which enables investors to identify and exploit short-term opportunities. As implied above, such short-term opportunities occur because the percentage movements in the warrants market are so much larger, and a sizeable gain may be achieved in in a very short space of time. During volatile market conditions it can be possible to deal quickly and make substantial profits. Consider the failed Soviet *coup d'etat* in August 1991, which offered some excellent opportunities. At times like this it makes sense to stick with the common, easily tradeable warrants which can be dealt in good size and where the spread is reasonable, but where the gearing is high. In this case the outstanding candidate for trading was the BTR 1993/94 series, which were offered at 39p on the morning of Monday, 19 August when the shares were 405p. As the *coup* toppled and the market recovered, a good profit in excess of 10 per cent net was locked in within 24 hours. With this profit already in the bag, the investor could relax and sit on the investment until the end of that Stock Exchange account on 30 August, selling the warrants at 49p. This profit of 26 per cent before dealing charges compares with a profit of just 7 per cent before dealing charges for the shares.

This example was taking advantage of a market dislocation, but there are also price dislocations between the shares and the warrants. The warrants market is not like the market for blue-chip shares where new information is instantaneously incorporated into the price, and where the market works efficiently. Warrants are often much slower to react to news, and price anomalies frequently exist. At times of market flux, prices become misaligned, creating 'windows of opportunity' for those who can identify those discrepancies and take advantage of the bargains which are thrown up. It is reasonable to doubt whether this process can really occur in such simple fashion, but most experienced market traders will declare that it happens regularly. Part of the reason lies with the market-makers, who will not necessarily be the same for the shares and the warrants. Further, in cases where the warrants market is relatively illiquid, the market-maker may wait for signs of actual trading activity before moving the price, whereas the share price might simply be marked higher or lower along with the market.

The result is that price anomalies arise which can leave warrants looking far too cheap or far too expensive in relation to the underlying equity. Such discrepancies can last for days, weeks, or even months depending upon the dealing interest and activity in the warrants. Two fine example of temporary price misalignments are provided by the Martin Currie European Trust warrants and Pilot Investment Trust warrants, and it is interesting to note that the anomalies were corrected in both cases by sharply rising warrant prices. As Figure 2.4 shows, Martin Currie European warrants started to fall gently in the autumn of 1994 and kept falling until April 1995 whilst the equity actually fared quite well. From 31 October 1994 to 3 May 1995 the shares had fluctuated but were unchanged over-all at 113p, whilst the warrants had dropped from 36p to 25p over the same period. This clear anomaly was corrected by a leap in the warrant price to 34p on 8 May after the *Warrants Alert* newsletter had highlighted the position.

The second anomaly was created by Pilot Investment Trust warrants dropping too sharply in February 1994, but rising again at the end of April as the shares actually fell, re-establishing the close relationship with the shares again there-after (see Figure 2.5).

Warrant–share price anomalies are a major source of profit opportunities for sharp-eyed warrant investors, but even those who identify anomalies correctly are not always successful. The critical point to note is that it is not always the warrant price which will move to re-align the two securities. There are occasions when a buyer of the warrants may be disappointed, since the apparent divergence in performance may be corrected by a sharp fall in the share price while the warrants merely retain their value. This underlines the need to consider apparent anomalies in the light of the technical and fundamental position of the warrants.

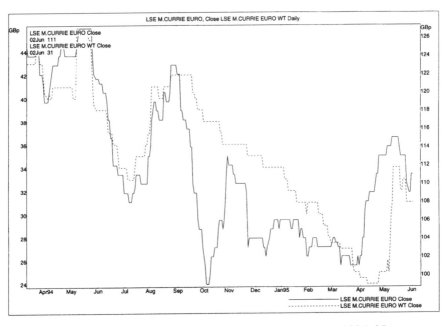

Figure 2.4 Martin Currie European Trust shares and warrants 1994–95
(*source: Reuters*)

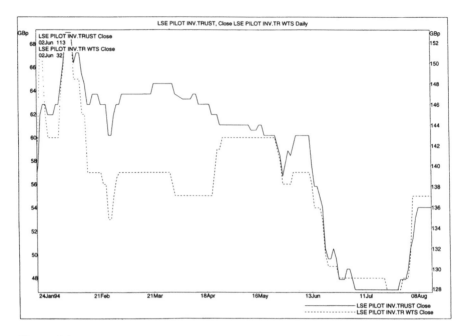

Figure 2.5 Pilot Investment Trust shares and warrants 1994
(*source: Reuters*)

Finally, pricing inefficiencies are often evident at the time of a new issue, where market-makers may struggle to find the right market level. Opportunities frequently arise for a quick profit on the first day of dealings, but only if you are suitably informed. The key here is to have a firm understanding of the terms of the warrants and to form an opinion on the likely opening price. Again there are some extraordinary examples here, generally provided by warrants which came to the market without the glare of publicity. Syndicate Capital Trust warrants, for example, crept on to the market in November 1993 with a very low profile and generating very little interest. The warrants began trading at 15p, then rose smartly to 29p before the morning was over.

Market is under-researched

In addition to the whims of market-makers, another reason why pricing ineffi-ciencies exist is simply because the market is under-researched. This is largely due to the modest market capitalization which means that many large stockbro-kers and other research organizations are not prepared to devote resources to an area which generates little in the way of commissions. Among the largest UK brokers and merchant banks it is doubtful whether there are more than one or two specialist warrant analysts – in the majority of cases warrants are tacked on to the responsibilities of analysts concerned with investment trusts or with wider derivatives. This does not help the quality of research.

While this may sound rather negative, it actually means that some excellent opportunities exist for the minority of investors who are armed with good information and advice. In a perfect market it is impossible for investors to leap ahead of the crowd, since all market participants have access to all current information and research, but in the warrants market this is manifestly not the case. Where investors have some knowledge of warrant histories, technical positions and fundamental prospects it is certainly possible to unearth some astounding bargains before they are discovered by other investors.

Private investors can exert real influence

The size of the market also influences the composition of investment funds. Among the majority of UK shares, institutions dominate trading, and the actions of private investors have little bearing on market prices. To many companies and market practitioners, private investors are at best a minor aid to liquidity, and at worst a downright nuisance. The result is that private investors are treated as second-class investors and are deprived of any real influence in the marketplace. In the shares of a large blue-chip corporation, private investors may come and go, but it is the large insurance and pension funds which determine the real value and direction of the shares.

In the warrants market there is no danger of small investors being considered incidental or insignificant. On the contrary, because many UK equity warrants are too small for institutions to bother with, the warrants market is a realm in which private investors really matter. From July 1995 this point became even more forceful as warrants were effectively banned from broker bond funds, which are used by financial advisers to manage clients' money. A revision to the Insurance Companies Act which came into force on 31 July redefined warrants as options instead of equities, implying that they may be used only for the purposes of efficient portfolio management, and not for direct investment. Private investors are not subject to such restrictions, and they have an important voice in the warrants market, exerting an influence which is rarely seen in the wider markets for equities and other instruments.

Taxation

For taxation purposes, warrants have the advantage of simplicity. Since warrants do not pay dividends, holders have no income tax liability and do not have to spend hours compiling dividend records for income tax returns. The capital gains tax (CGT) position is also clearly defined, allowing a certain amount of profit to be realised tax-free in each year (the personal allowance for individuals was £5,800 in the 1994/95 tax year). For CGT purposes warrants are treated in a similar way to ordinary shares, but one particular benefit is that the exercise of a warrant is not treated as a disposal. Instead the warrant is then aggregated with the share subscribed for, the original cost of the warrant is added to the subscription price payable on exercise of those subscription rights, and the gain or loss is established upon sale of those ordinary shares:

EXAMPLE

Year 1:   Investor buys 10,000 Widget warrants at 25p. Cost = £2,500.
Year 2:   Investor exercises subscription rights and converts 10,000 warrant into ordinary shares at a cost of 100p per share.
         Cost = £10,000.
Year 3:   Investor sells 10,000 Widget shares at 150p. Receipts = £15,000.

Capital gains liability occurs in year 3, on £15,000 – (£2,500 +£10,000) = £2,500.
Inflation indexing is ignored.

This removes the need for tax-conscious investors to seek warrants with specific maturities when planning a portfolio, although the timing of subsequent disposals to establish profits or losses may of course be influenced by the tax liability.

On this subject, the concise warrants factsheet published in 1991 by the Association of Investment Trust Companies advanced the interesting argument that warrants may be peculiarly suitable for children under 18. This argument relies upon the fact that children are entitled to a full CGT allowance, whereas their income must be added to that of their parents where they are the donors. This is no more than a side issue, but it is another factor in favour of warrants investment.

One loophole which has been closed though after some dispute relates to new issues. It is a source of regret that the 'free' warrants attached to new issue investment trusts cannot be apportioned a zero cost. This would have been attractive for investors who wished to sell the shares immediately, perhaps for slightly less than the 100p purchase price, but hold on to the 'free' warrants, deferring their capital gains tax liability for some time. Unfortunately the Inland Revenue has now decided that the cost of new investment trust issues with warrants attached should be apportioned on the basis of the opening prices:

EXAMPLE

Investment trust prices at 100p; warrants attached on a 1-for-5 basis.
Shares – price on first day 94p.
Warrants – price on first day 55p.

Total package value = 94p +11p (555/5) = 105p.

Purchase price for shares = *market price/package price*
                             = *94p/105p*
                             = *89.52p*

Purchase price for warrants = *market price/package price*
                             = *55p/105p*
                             = *52.38p*

This removes the market inefficiency which arose from pricing the warrants at zero. The 'base costs', as they are known, are usually available from the investment trust companies some time after launch.

Inflation

Inflation is widely regarded as an enemy of the markets, and shares tend to fall when investors believe governments may be structuring policies which favour growth at the expense of inflation. Warrants are in an unusual position in this circumstance though, since one element of their structure – the exercise price – is fixed. The fact that holders have the pre-determined right to buy at this fixed price in the future becomes more attractive at times of asset price inflation. Consider the example below where the warrant makes a handsome gain even though the underlying shares fail to produce any real post-inflation growth at all:

EXAMPLE

Warrant carries the right to subscribe for one share at 100p in six years' time.
Current share price 100p; current warrant price 30p.
Asset price inflation runs at 8 per cent per year; shares appreciate in line with this.
Share price at final expiry of warrants = 159p.
Warrant price at final expiry = 159p–100p = 59p.
Warrant almost doubles in value, and has gained 24 per cent in real terms over the period.

Whereas 'solid' assets such as gold, property, art and antiques are often thought of as good hedges against inflation, few investors would think of putting warrants in the same category. Yet the argument is far more convincing for warrants, being a simple mathematical case which carries more weight than nebulous notions about real assets maintaining a real value.

The early bird catches the worm

Last but not least, this is a developing market. Investors moving into warrants now may well find them in far greater demand later on as more funds flow into the market. It is possible that prices could be marked higher across the board if a few more unit trusts or other major investors catch on to the merits of warrants and start to build large portfolios. There is a lot to be said for buying good quality warrants now and waiting for the herd to follow. Furthermore, with the market growing all the time, investors who begin to acquire expertise and experience now will be well placed to benefit as the market matures and more opportunities become available.

THE DISADVANTAGES OF WARRANTS COMPARED TO SHARES

Complexity

Warrants are more complicated than ordinary shares, and this is for many investors their principal disadvantage. Whereas share prices are directly related to market movements and to the performance of companies, warrant prices can be very difficult to fathom, particularly if the investor has no previous experience of options. For some people the very concept of 'out of the money' warrants is a complete mystery, and when analytical devices such as the capital fulcrum point are mentioned then the mist becomes thicker still. An understanding can usually be gained, but only after some study and effort, which not everyone is prepared to make. Casual investors may not have much personal interest in their investments, preferring to rely upon stockbrokers' advice or newspaper share tips, in which case they are unlikely to be bothered with the complexities of warrants.

This is where problems start. Investors who have little grasp of the intricacies of warrants rarely make good profits, and it is when people with a scant understanding of warrants plough into the market that horrendous losses are made. The wrong warrants are bought (often long-shot warrants with little chance of reaching the exercise price) at inappropriate prices, with the inevitable result that some of the investments fall to zero. The ignorant investor has no idea why this has happened, blames the warrants, storms away from the market, and never returns, missing out on subsequent opportunities.

It is not difficult to avoid this scenario with the application of a little common sense. The key is to feel comfortable with your investments, which usually means knowing why you bought them, what the upside and the downside potential is, and at what point you might wish to sell. Some warrants will still fall, of course, but if you know why this has happened and understand the risk then it is much easier to accept your loss and to try and make up for it. To reach this point, it is not necessary to understand all of the analysis and all of the reasoning in this book. Some people probably will, but as long as you grasp the basic concepts and feel content with your level of understanding, then there is no reason why you should not become a successful warrants investor. The complexity of the warrants market is a disadvantage, but it is not an insuperable obstacle. Learning about the market can actually be enormously stimulating, and the more you know, the more enthusiastic you are likely to become. After all, if warrants were too simple they would also be boring.

Risk

A more concrete drawback, and one which no investor can avoid entirely, is the higher risk attached to warrants. This is of very considerable importance, and is attended to comprehensively in Chapter 6, which reminds readers that the value of warrants can fall to zero. If the share price falls below the exercise price for the whole of the remaining subscription period, then the warrant is effectively worthless. Warrants have no redemption value if not exercised, and their value can fall sharply. It would be naive to expect the promise of such fabulous rewards from the warrants market without a matching element of risk. Potential investors should be in no doubt: warrants are more risky than ordinary shares.

Gearing – where fortunes can be lost

The risk element is manifested most clearly in the concept of gearing. The tendency for warrant price changes to exaggerate changes in share prices and general market conditions is a prime attraction in rising markets, but a prime liability in a bear market. The gearing effect can work in reverse. A small fall in the price of the underlying shares can lead to a substantial decline in the value of your warrants, particularly if they are highly geared. A vivid illustration is provided by Eurotunnel '1993' warrants, from the first four months of 1995 (see Table 2.2). Over this period the shares, or units as they were called, fell sharply as the company suffered from cost overruns, delays in the service, financing problems, and a string of unfortunate PR disasters including a door falling off a train and VIP guests left waiting at a station. The warrants, which were highly geared, fell dramatically, including a fall of over 50 per cent in one week ending 14 April 1995.

If this decline were not warning enough, these warrants look, at the time of writing, as though they are likely to expire worthless in October 1995. More broadly, warrants do tend to amplify market movements and perform badly during bearish periods. The Gulf crisis, coupled with a recession and high interest rates, meant that 1990 was a poor year for the market, and the FT-SE Index fell by 11.5 per cent over the year. This decline was reflected right across the board in the warrants market, there were only a handful of rises, and of course most falls were amplified by the gearing element. The outcome was an average decline of 45 per cent in the value of UK equity warrants in 1990, and few were exempt from this depressing performance. Again, in 1994 the London market had a quietly disappointing year with the FT-SE 100 Index slipping by 10.3 per cent. This would not perturb many participants greatly, but for warrant investors the market felt much worse, with the average warrant posting a 19.86 per cent decline.

Date week ending	Eurotunnel Units (%)	Eurotunnel 1993 Warrants (%)
6 Jan	+10.92	+6.25
13 Jan	+1.27	+0.00
20 Jan	−6.90	−5.88
27 Jan	−1.01	−12.50
3 Feb	−2.38	+3.57
10 Feb	+3.83	−6.90
17 Feb	−1.34	−11.11
24 Feb	−2.04	−8.33
3 Mar	−7.64	−18.18
10 Mar	+1.13	−22.22
17 Mar	−2.60	−7.14
24 Mar	−10.31	−23.08
31 Mar	+3.40	+10.00
7 Apr	−0.41	0.00
14 Apr	−16.12	−54.55
21 Apr	0.00	+40.00
28 Apr	−6.40	0.00
Overall Period	**−33.1%**	**−78.13%**

Table 2.2 Weekly percentage changes, first four months 1995

At this point it bears repetition that market timing is very important: if you are unfortunate enough to time your warrant investments to coincide with the beginning of a bear market then your investments will be decimated. In falling markets the gearing detriment can be enormous, and the performance of warrants can make for unpleasant reading.

Dilution

Warrants usually cause dilution to ordinary shareholders when they are exercised. This occurs because new shares are issued at a price lower than the prevailing market price, and the value of the assets shared by existing shareholders is therefore diluted, as demonstrated below:

EXAMPLE

Company has 100 million shares in issue; net assets £200m; asset value per
*   share 200p*
Warrant-holders exercise 20 million warrants at 100p per share, raising £20m
Now 120 million shares in issue; net assets £200m +£20m = £220m; asset
*   value per share diluted to 183p (£220m ÷ 120m).*

This dilution can reduce the underlying share price into which warrant-hold-ers may be converting, thereby reducing the intrinsic value of the warrant. In practice this is less of a problem than it seems, as the factor of dilution is well known in advance and tends to be discounted over time so that the dilution is fully incorporated into the share price by the time warrant-holders come to exer-cise. Nevertheless, for this reason it is always important for investors to look at the fully diluted net asset value when analysing investment trusts with warrants, as it can differ substantially from the 'headline' net undiluted net asset value when there are warrants attached which are 'well in the money' (i.e., the exer-cise price is well below the share price).

EXAMPLE

Beta Global Emerging Markets Investment Trust plc
Unaudited and undiluted net asset value as at 31 May 1995 = 150.1p
Warrants exist which carry the right to subscribe at 100p, compared with a
*   share price of 149p. As a result the diluted NAV is lower.*
Unaudited diluted net asset value as at 31 May 1995 = 141.9p

It is always wise to be aware that dilution does occur, although this is not a rel-evant factor until the share price is above the exercise price of the warrants. There are even cases where ignorant warrant investors cause some reverse dilu-tion by exercising their subscription rights erroneously at a price higher than the prevailing share price.

No income

If you are investing for income, which is a preference for many retired investors in particular, then warrants should not form any more than a small proportion of your portfolio. Warrants do not rank for dividends, not even those attached to high income investment trusts. The aim is solely for capital gain.

Three exceptions to this rule are the 'subscription share' hybrids launched by the Touche Remnant management group and more recently by Jupiter Tyndall. These are warrants in disguise, offering the usual terms of subscription attached to warrants, but with the additional benefit of some income. The first of these innovative packages was the TR High Income Trust, launched in 1989, which pioneered subscription shares offering a fixed annual dividend of 1.5p each. These were followed in 1990 by the TR European Growth Trust 'participating subscription shares' (PSSs) which carry the additional benefit of the full dividend entitlement. This offer was not entirely altruistic, as the extra value of the dividend entitlement allowed the trust to sell the PSSs separately to raise an extra £1.45 million as part of the issue, but it was nevertheless an interesting and worthwhile differentiation of the normal warrant structure. The Investment Trust of Investment Trusts, launched by Jupiter Tyndall in February 1995, offered warrants with a fixed dividend entitlement of 4.4p, showing that the concept is still alive, if rarely considered. In this case the trust decided to trade off the extra attraction of the income element for a higher exercise price, thereby reducing the potential dilution. The cost in terms of the income stream which the trust would have to generate was of course known, whilst the future dilution could not be known at that stage. It could be argued that this trade-off gave shareholders more certainty about the future value of their investments, thereby making the issue more attractive, and it would not be surprising to see more trusts testing this concept.

Other rights also limited

In adddition to the lack of income, warrant-holders' rights are severely limited in other ways. Warrants do not confer any rights upon the holder other than the right to buy shares on the terms stipulated. Since warrants do not form part of the issued share capital of a company until they are exercised, warrants do not carry voting rights or the right to attend ordinary shareholders' meetings. This may not disturb many investors in the normal course of events, but there are occasional situations where the right to vote and to voice an opinion can become important.

Takeovers – a thorn in the side?

One such situation is a takeover bid for the company in which you hold warrants. For shareholders other than the company directors and employees, a takeover bid is usually welcomed as a way of increasing the value of your investment. As the value of warrants is linked to the value of the underlying shares, it might appear at first glance as though warrant-holders will also benefit. Unfortunately this is not necessarily the case, and it is possible in certain circumstances for warrants to lose their entire value in the event of takeover. This is because the value of the warrants may be composed entirely of premium which may disappear at a stroke. For years investors have faced the absurd possibility of losing their entire investment in the event of takeover as the 'time value' could disappear without recompense.

As you can see from Case A below, where time value is not protected and where the warrant has no intrinsic value (i.e., it is 'out of the money'), warrant-holders can lose their investment in the event of a takeover bid pitched below the subscription price. This is an additional risk which you must take into account when buying such warrants.

CASE A

WIDGET INDUSTRIES PLC (no protection of time value)

Warrants in issue to subscribe for one share at 100p on 31 March 1993 to 1996 inclusive. October 1990 share price 70p; warrant price 15p.

Takeover bid received at 90p per share

Warrant-holders offered the right to exercise their subscription rights early, but as the warrant has no intrinsic value, its value falls to zero. Clearly there is no incentive for the warrant-holder to subscribe 100p per share now when the value of the offer is only 90p per share. The 15p time value of the warrant has disappeared, and it becomes worthless.

Result: Warrant-holders lose their investment.

In practice, it is far from certain that this situation would be allowed to happen, and the bidding company might in fact make some offer to the warrant-holders. The bidder will be aware that the majority of warrant-holders will also be share-holders, so he will not wish to anger them or to foster any negative publicity which might ensue from a loss of warrant value. There are, therefore, some reasons why this threat may not be quite as stark as it appears, although investors should certainly be aware of the risk which exists.

The risk of non-compensation is taken seriously in the market, and it can consign some warrants to a persistently low rating. A good example provided, ironically, by the top-performing Yorkshire Tyne Tees TV warrants which appear to have lost their premium prematurely because a takeover is widely expected to occur. This fear is less common in the investment trust sector, and although it was heightened following the takeover of the Globe Investment Trust in 1990, it has receded somewhat since this time.

Until a few years ago this considerable drawback of warrants investment was something which warrant-holders had to accept as part of the risk. Very few warrants offered any formal protection, and there was no standard formula for doing so. Fortunately this has changed as the warrants market has grown, and now the large majority of new investment trust issues use a standard formula for reducing the subscription price of the warrants to compensate holders for the loss of time value.

This formula is shown in Case B below:

CASE B

THE WIDGET INVESTMENT TRUST PLC (time value protected)

Warrants in issue to subscribe for one share at 100p on 31 March 1993 to 1996 inclusive. October 1990 share price 70p; warrant price 15p.

Takeover bid received at 90p per share

The standard formula which would be applied in this case is as follows:

$A = (B+C) - D$

where A = the reduction in the subscription price
B = the subscription price ruling immediately before the adjustment (100p)
C = the average of the mean of the quotations as derived from the Daily Official List of The Stock Exchange in London for one warrant for the ten consecutive Stock Exchange dealing days ending on the Stock Exchange dealing day immediately preceding the date of the adjustment (assume the price was stable at 15p)
D = the value (as determined by the auditors) of the consideration per ordinary share offered to ordinary shareholders of the company by the offeror (90p)

So:

Reduction in subscription price = (100p + 15p) - 90p

Subscription price reduced by 25p to 75p. With the bid at 90p this gives the warrants an intrinsic value of 15p.

Result: Warrant-holders are protected and the value of the warrant is maintained.

This formula was also adopted by a commercial company for the first time in early 1991, with the issue of warrants by MMI plc (now called Incepta Group). Their exemplary terms of conversion were fashioned by the chairman, the late Patrick Morris, an enthusiast for the warrants market who was equally concerned that his warrant-holders should have their rights properly protected. His lead has been followed by some other commercial issues, and the precedent is now established for new issues of all kinds.

There are two main reasons for the development of this time value protection, both reflecting the growth of the warrants market. The first is simply the higher status now accorded to warrants as they have become a more common and favoured security. And second, it used to be the case that nearly all warrant-holders were also shareholders who would gain on balance from a takeover even if their warrants lost value. With the increase in independent interest and investment in warrants this assumption is no longer valid – hence the need for added protection. Not all issues comply with this new standard though, and it is always sensible to check the terms of the warrants if the underlying security is subject to a takeover threat. Where the formula is used, it is incorporated in the particulars of the warrants which are published at the time of issue. This document will usually be made available upon request from the company, or you can consult a specialist publication such as *The Warrants Directory*.

It is pleasing to report that this specious risk is largely being removed as a barrier to warrant investment, representing an improvement in the quality of the warrants now being issued. This recognition of the separate rights of warrant-holders is a major step forward, and is symbolic of the increasing acceptance of warrants as an integral part of the UK stockmarket.

Limited range

At present, the range of UK equity warrants is still extremely limited. Although it is growing quickly, the warrants market is very small in relation to the equity market, and there is a danger that you could miss out on the best opportunities elsewhere if you restrict your scope to the warrants universe. This argument has some merit, but the difficulty may easily be overcome if warrants are used in conjunction with other, more wide-ranging instruments. This is not a case against using warrants where they are available. Furthermore, few investors will be able to achieve an informed coverage of the entire equity market anyway – your knowledge and interest is probably limited to a small number of stocks. A good analogy is that of vocabulary. Most people are aware of a large number of words, but actually have a working vocabulary which is very much smaller. The same tends to be true of stockmarket coverage, and all but the most demanding of investors will find that the spread of warrants is now sufficiently broad to offer exposure to most sectors.

Indeed there is a counter-argument based upon the fact that the 250 or so warrants provide such a broad coverage. This means that investors who follow them may achieve a comprehensive understanding across all market sectors from conglomerates and water companies through to oil exploration, investment in the Philippines, and even Brazilian smaller companies. A balanced view based upon the whole of the warrants market is surely preferable to a patchy knowledge of a few corners of the overall equity market.

Lack of media coverage

Investors seeking this balanced view will run into some problems though. It is a constant source of irritation that warrant prices are not to be found in any newspaper apart from the *Financial Times*, and even there not all warrants are listed. To be fair to the newspapers, this is because the companies and trusts involved do not wish to pay for an extra listing. The media is perhaps more culpable in its failure to say very much about new warrant issues or to produce informative articles on the subject. Those few articles which are written tend to be very introductory, and it is left to the intermediate or experienced investor to plunder primary sources themselves in the quest for information. It is without doubt much more difficult for investors to obtain information and opinions about warrants and the warrants market than it is for ordinary shares.

Once again, this is not a black and white issue. The lack of media coverage can be a serious disincentive for the casual investor, but for the well-informed investor with a well-established source of specialist information it can mean the preservation of certain benefits. As long as the market remains at least partially hidden from public view, price anomalies will persist and canny market players will be able to take advantage of some well-kept secrets.

Dealing difficulties

One problem which has virtually no redeeming features is the difficulty in dealing in warrants (explained more fully in Chapter 7). Too often you might find a warrant you like, conduct all of your analysis on the basis of the middle price, and decide to buy, only to discover that the spread is very wide and that the market-maker is only prepared to deal in small size. This can prove to be a real bane for larger investors, who may need to be both patient and cautious in order to buy the right warrants at the right prices.

Indeed this is a particular problem for warrant funds, which can often find it difficult to place new cash into the market quickly, and it is impossible for managers to make meaningful short-term investments with a view to a quick gain. Instead they are first in the queue for the large lines of warrants which occasionally become available at good prices, buying sound warrants for the medium- and longer term, forced to place a strong emphasis on long-term quality because they cannot move in and out of the market quickly at reasonable prices, and they cannot unload holdings at short notice if something goes wrong. This places certain limits on the investment strategies which funds can pursue, but it does not prevent successful investment.

The important thing is to be aware that dealing may be awkward and to take care accordingly. The dealing difficulties which exist can restrict your room for manoeuvre, and they are certainly frustrating on occasions, but with a good stockbroker and a flexible investment policy the majority of problems can be overcome.

CONCLUSION

The balance of the discussion must be that warrants are worth looking at – if you can find the right ones, buy them at the right time, and deal at the right price. There will always be pros and cons to warrants investment, but many of the disadvantages listed above are being ameliorated as the market develops, or may be lessened by the individual investor. You can learn about warrants to overcome the problem of ignorance, you can control your level of risk, there is increasing use of the formula for time value protection, the range of warrants is growing all of the time, the media is starting to pick up on warrants, and a good stockbroker can bypass many of the dealing problems. A recurring theme is that the well-informed investor can make the most of the advantages of warrants while keeping the disadvantages to a practical minimum. The ignorant or careless investor, by contrast, may on occasions find the disadvantages overwhelming. For this reason it is hardly surprising that most investors who are knowledgeable about the warrants market feel that it has considerable merits – they are, after all, able to use their expertise to make the most of the opportunities as they occur.

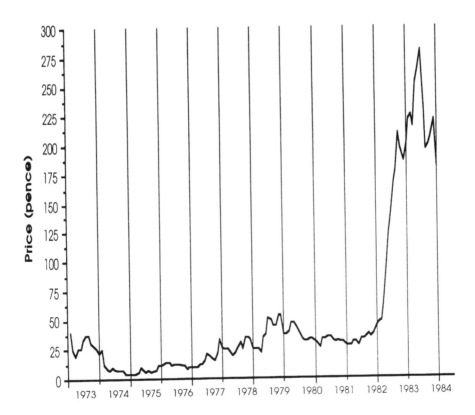

Figure 2.6 Lex Service 2nd series warrants 1973–84

In addition to knowledge and information, the other key factor which emerges is market timing. Warrants undoubtedly have an exceptional role to play in taking full advantage of bullish market conditions while they last. Your shares may do well at times of rising prices, but using warrants you could be doing much better. Take, for example, the case of Lex Service plc 2nd series warrants from 1973 to 1984, a period which illustrates both the downside and the upside features of gearing. The warrants began 1973 at 40p, collapsed to 3.5p in late 1974, and then made the most extraordinary profits in the decade thereafter. The warrants reached a peak of 280p in 1984 – an 80-fold increase over ten years.

The sort of graph shown in Figure 2.6 can inspire both awe and incredulity. Whatever the reaction, it is perhaps the most eloquent case which can be made for investment in warrants. Regrettably, private investors tend to see graphs such as this after periods when the markets have been strong, and it is a source of continual sadness and bemusement that investors come into warrant markets only after they have proved their worth with a string of highly profitable examples. Usually that means that investors come in near to the top of the market and suffer falls thereafter. Many then walk away, but more intelligent investors can learn from the experience and stay with the market until bullish conditions predominate once again.

"The warrants market is under-researched in comparison with most securities markets, so an investor armed with good information and analysis can often move ahead of the crowd."

3

ASSESSING WARRANTS PART 1 – BASIC CALCULATIONS

It is not easy to assess the value of a warrant. If it were, everyone would have a perfect knowledge of the value of every warrant, and the opportunities for profit would be strictly limited. Instead, investors tend to have very hazy ideas regarding warrant valuation, and some are simply naive. There is no excuse for this. True, private investors will not have access to the complex computer simulations which govern the investment decisions of the most sophisticated investors and institutions, but there are some elementary 'back of the envelope' calculations which may be used to provide a firm base for simple comparisons. Armed with these, it should be possible to avoid expensive mistakes and to steer towards those warrants with better prospects for capital growth.

With warrants moving very sharply on occasions, the need for some form of analysis is quite clear. Much of the basic 'value' approach is a matter of common sense, which can fly out of the window when inexperienced investors sense the whiff of speculation in their nostrils. Elementary analysis has a precautionary role to play, but it can also have considerable predictive value. The fact that ordinary warrants are ineligible for any income simplifies the analytical process considerably: it is solely the prospects for capital gain which are important.

Conversely, because warrants are not generally standardized – the conversion terms for different warrants differ substantially – it does require some effort to compare alternatives. For this reason the basic techniques for warrant selection are structured to provide a framework for standardized statistical information which may be applied to all warrants. While the examples in the chapter are drawn from the London Stock Exchange, the analytical techniques are applicable to all forms of warrants, and will reveal their various characteristics irrespective of the nature of the underlying security.

LOOK BEFORE YOU LEAP

The first rule is that just as warrants have a separate price and a separate listing from the shares, so they are valued in a separate way. The underlying security may appear cheap, but the warrant may not be. This is axiomatic, but it is astonishing to see the approach of some credulous investors who like the look of a security, see warrants attached at a lower price, and rush in to buy them on the assumption that they are better value. This happened with the warrants attached to the small exploration companies listed on the London Stock Exchange in 1990/91. A group of these warrants looked perilously overvalued in mid-1990, with the shares a long, long way from the exercise price and a short time to expiry. The companies would have to strike oil or gold to give the warrants any real value. Yet because these companies were favourites of the penny share newsletters, a lot of private investors were lured by the lower price of the warrants, and bought barrowfuls for a few pence each. Predictably, most of them expired worthless a few months later – something which was considered very likely by those who had troubled to undertake even the most basic of calculations.

It is not surprising that this example involved low-priced warrants. Just as penny shares attract casual investors because they look like bargains, the same applies to the very low-priced warrants which may look a steal at 1p or 2p, especially if they have fallen from considerably higher levels. Yet on balance the penny warrants are a bad proposition – certainly much worse than average. They are low-priced for a reason, after all. The reasons for a low price may be categorized as follows:

1. attached to low-priced share
2. share price a long way beneath the exercise price
3. no intrinsic value and a short time to expiry

In the second and third cases, the likelihood is that the value will fall to zero as the time value diminishes. Such warrants with little realistic chance of gaining any worth by the final exercise date will often be quoted at a nominal price because this is a mid-price. Where a warrant is listed at a penny the quoted spread may be 0p–2p. In other words, the warrant has no saleable value. This fact is rarely appreciated by those investors who find the glister of a low price irresistible.

The lesson from this is that it is essential to undertake at least some simple analysis yourself, or take advice from a specialist who undertakes research on your behalf. Sometimes of course a low-priced warrant will represent genuine good value, and in full-blown bull markets, some low-priced warrants offering high gearing may be the best performers. In such cases the attractions will become apparent from the basic analytical approach outlined below, and not from the mere fact of the low price itself. This chapter explains the basic procedures for warrant analysis, with further elaboration in the following two chapters.

HOW WARRANTS ARE EVALUATED

Warrant evaluation has two essential strands, which may be termed fundamental analysis and technical analysis. To begin with, all warrants carry the right to subscribe for some form of security, whether that right is truly exerciseable or not. As such, their price is related to some extent to the price of that security. As a general rule, the warrant price is likely to move in the same direction as the underlying security price (opposite for put warrants), although this will not always be the case. For this reason it is important to form an opinion on this likely direction, using fundamental analysis. Second, once you have established that the prospects for the underlying security are positive, technical analysis can help to suggest whether the warrants will move favourably, and to what extent.

Fundamental analysis and technical analysis work together. Neither will suffice alone, and using them in conjunction is largely a matter of common sense. There is no point in buying a warrant with an excellent technical position if the shares are on a downward spiral, and there is no point in purchasing warrants in anticipation of 25 per cent per annum growth if they require an annual growth rate of 30 per cent to outperform the shares.

FUNDAMENTAL ANALYSIS

The form of the fundamental analysis and the sources of information for this will vary according to the sort of underlying security. This is the sort of analysis you would undertake before dealing in the underlying security, so in the case of UK equity warrants this is the sort of analysis which one would undertake before investing in shares. This is largely beyond the scope of this book, but a brief overview of the factors involved in fundamental evaluation is incorporated below.

The aim of fundamental analysis is to gauge the prospects for capital growth in the underlying share. This can involve a broad range of factors which influence share prices, including current rating, sectoral prospects, large shareholdings, net asset value, management ability, new products, competition, directors' dealings, brokers' forecasts, dividend payments, plus a host of additional factors specific to the companies concerned. There are a large number of books which cover this subject, and there is also a great deal of comment from stockbrokers, newspapers and magazines. Most investors will find information and advice plentiful for this purpose, unlike the more formal analysis applied to the warrants themselves.

For investment trust warrants the analysis usually considers the prospects for increasing the assets of the trust, coupled with any change in the relationship between the share price and those assets. As far as the assets of the trust are concerned, analysts need to gauge the prospects for the underlying market, together with the skill of the manager in maximizing the returns from that market. When analysing a Japanese smaller companies trust, for example, the most important determinant of future growth will be the outlook for Japanese smaller companies. No matter how good the manager may be, if his remit is to invest in a sector of the market which is falling heavily, then the assets will fall. Managers can make a substantial difference to the performance of a trust within its peer group, however, and it is worth consulting tables of historic performance to gain some impression of the quality of the manager. Third, if the sector goes up, and the manager has bought the right stocks, will the shares of the trust necessarily follow the assets? No, not necessarily, because the discount to net assets may widen. Conversely, if you can identify a trust trading on an unusually large discount to the net asset value, then the shares may appreciate without any change in the assets. The ideal investment trust combines a capital growth objective in a promising market sector together with a top quality manager boasting a strong long-term track record, and a wide discount to net asset value.

TECHNICAL ANALYSIS

So, once you have found a company or trust which you like, should you buy the warrants? Not necessarily. Sometimes the underlying equity can appear very attractive, but the valuation of the warrants can be extremely high, perhaps including a built-in expectation of considerable gain. This is where technical analysis becomes indispensable.

Technical analysis means the analysis of price, and price alone. It does not concern itself with the value of the underlying security, but provides some revealing perspectives on the actual market valuation of the warrant. This has several aspects which are covered below, including intrinsic value, premium, time to expiry, the capital fulcrum point, gearing, leverage, volatility, and income forgone. These are known collectively as the technical factors, and these are the basic tools which any investor can use to reveal the nature of specific warrants and to provide an insight into their likely prospects.

WHERE TO FIND WARRANT PRICES

Before undertaking any form of technical analysis it is necessary to have two forms of basic data, the first of which is the prices of the shares and warrants. Although warrants frequently give the impression of being part of a 'hidden' market, price information is far more accessible than many investors realize. There are quite a number of sources for prices, and this should certainly not prove a meaningful obstacle.

The first and most public source is the newspapers. The *Financial Times* carries many warrant prices every day, listed immediately beneath their respective share prices in the 'London Share Service' section towards the rear of the paper. At the time of writing approximately 75 per cent of the UK equity warrants in issue are listed every day. This compares with around 60 per cent when the first edition of this book was written, so it is pleasing to note that the market is becoming more transparent. Many of the other warrants are listed just once a week on the Saturday 'Dealings' page which gives prices for many of the lesser-traded securities. Other newspapers are sadly less comprehensive, and prices will only be found for a handful of the largest or most popular warrants. A recent alternative is provided by the television teletext facility on Channel 4, which lists a large number of Stock Exchange prices updated every night. Most warrant prices are listed, although it can take some patience to wait for the relevant prices to be displayed.

Periodicals can be a useful source for those longer-term investors who do not feel the need to check prices frequently. The quarterly *Investment Trusts* magazine carries a list of most investment trust warrant prices (it excludes those trusts registered offshore), and the monthly factsheet from the Association of Investment Trust Companies (AITC) contains prices for those affiliated trusts with warrants in issue. This is helpful, but not comprehensive. Much the same can be said of the *Warrants Alert* monthly newsletter which provides updates on a minority of recommended warrants.

For those seeking a complete and authoritative list of prices, the Stock Exchange *Daily Official List* is still the publication to consult. Published daily by the London Stock Exchange, the list may be available (possibly on microfiche) in some local business libraries, and it is also available on subscription. The terms for the protection of time value found in company warrant particulars use the *Daily Official List* as the source for prices.

Of course all of these written sources have the disadvantage of being out of date by the time they are published. This is not the ideal position to be in when dealing in high-risk securities. Possibly the best source for those prepared to absorb the expense are the 'real-time' premium telephone services which offer updated prices direct from the Stock Exchange. Comprehensive services such as *Teleshare* cover nearly all warrants, enabling you to check prices before you deal, probe for short-term price anomalies, and generally stay in touch with all of the latest movements. The drawback is that these premium telephone services are charged at the 'M' rate (currently 39p per minute cheap rate, 49p other times), which can work out expensive if you check prices regularly.

For investors who spend a great deal of time checking prices, and who are trading actively, it may be worth considering a screen-based service. Several exist which list all warrant prices in real-time, but most will be beyond the pocket of the private investor. One which seems reasonably priced for what it offers is the *Market-Eye* system run by ICV. Available on home PCs as well as on dedicated terminals, this service provides bid and offer prices for the vast majority of listed warrants together with a limited news service, an excellent 'ticker' showing price changes as they happen, and tables of biggest risers and fallers, new issues etc. The screen is an excellent way of staying in touch, and is very cheap to run once the subscription is paid, but many investors will still find it difficult to justify the cost unless they are making frequent deals of a short-term nature. Equally, many investors who invest in warrants as a part-time hobby will not be able to consult their screen during working hours and will not be able to spare the time which a screen-based system usually demands. *Market-Eye* makes for compelling viewing.

Finally there is the option of getting prices straight from the horse's mouth. Assuming that you have found a sympathetic stockbroker, you may be able to ask for a limited number of prices from him. This is particularly helpful if you are thinking of dealing, and if you explain this, then your broker will usually be happy to give you the latest price. This amenity will not always be available from the 'no-frills' execution-only services, although some are happy to provide limited information.

WHERE TO FIND THE CONVERSION TERMS

Just as it is essential that you have the latest price, so it is essential that you understand the conversion terms of the warrants. It is impossible to undertake any technical analysis of warrants without knowledge of the full conversion terms. Again, these details are available from a variety of sources.

First and foremost is *The Warrants Directory*, published by the *Warrants Alert* newsletter service. This publication gives the full terms for every warrant in issue, together with other vital information such as the number in issue and company address.

Investors not wishing to go to the expense of buying this publication can usually discover the terms with a little detective work of their own. The first stop must be the company annual report and accounts which will often (but not always) give the conversion terms of the warrants together with the number in issue. This has the virtue of being reliable, but the drawback of brevity. Fuller details, including information about the protection of time value in the event of takeover, will be found in the original placing, offer, bonus or scrip issue documents published when the warrants were first issued. These provide comprehensive details, but they may not be available if the issue was made several years ago. Further, conversion terms change when companies make rights issues and scrip issues, so the subscription terms may have changed since the document was issued. Finally, investors can always write to the appropriate company secretary with a request for the specific information required.

Further afield, warrant conversion terms are usually to be found on the Extel Company Information cards which may be available in local business libraries. For domestic investment trusts only, the quarterly *Investment Trusts* magazine carries a list, and the AITC carries a similar list in its monthly information service, although this only carries data on warrants attached to affiliated investment trust companies. As such it is far from complete.

Last but not least there is your broker, who might know, although equally this is unlikely unless he has some specialization in warrants. The level of ignorance among practitioners remains alarmingly high, and in this circumstance where it is essential to have entirely reliable and accurate information it is probably best to check the terms for yourself.

INTRINSIC VALUE

Intrinsic value is often the first stop for the 'value' investor with relatively little understanding of warrants. Even the least informed investor can see that a warrant carrying the right to subscribe for one share at 100p will have a value of 50p if that share is trading at 150p. This is the intrinsic value: the value which a warrant would have if it were to be exercised immediately, i.e.:

Intrinsic value = share price – exercise price

A warrant which has a positive intrinsic value is said to be 'in the money', and a warrant without intrinsic value is said to be 'out of the money'. Where the share price is exactly equal to the exercise price the warrant is said to have achieved parity. The extent of intrinsic value is often measured in terms of the parity ratio, which is simply the share price divided by the exercise price:

Parity ratio = share price/exercise price

Warrants with intrinsic value have a parity ratio above 1.0, while out of the money warrants have a parity ratio below 1.0. It may surprise some investors to discover that the average parity ratio for UK equity warrants is around 0.9, meaning that the average warrant is slightly 'out of the money'. This is largely due to the high proportion of new issues, since most warrants are either 'at the money' or 'out of the money' when they are first issued.

In market conditions when share prices are rising, the intrinsic value and the parity ratio of warrants will increase as they near maturity. This does not mean, however, that intrinsic value is necessarily related to the time to expiry across the spectrum of available warrants. This depends upon the individual conversion terms and performance of each security, which can differ substantially.

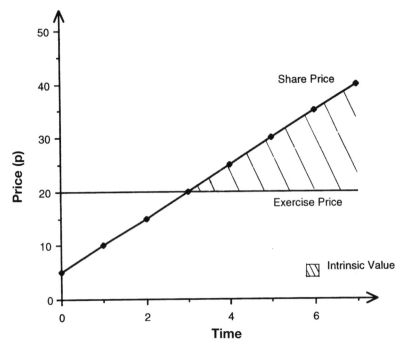

Figure 3.1 An illustration of intrinsic value

The fact that intrinsic value is a function purely of the share price and the exercise price (as illustrated in Figure 3.1), ignoring the actual warrant price, provides a clue that it is a superficial and incomplete measure of value. The warrant price is tautologically composed of two elements – intrinsic value and the premium. In most cases the latter is more important for analytical purposes, and intrinsic value is unlikely to be a primary consideration unless you are a very cautious investor, market conditions are poor, or the warrant is close to final expiry. Intrinsic value relates to the exercise value of the warrant, so it is most relevant when a warrant is bought with a view to exercise rather than trading.

THE PREMIUM

In practice, warrants will not trade simply at their intrinsic value, because investors will be willing to pay an extra amount for the benefits which warrants confer. A share price just 1 per cent beneath the exercise price will offer no intrinsic value, but it is absurd to expect a warrant with several years of life remaining to have no value in these circumstances. A speculator expecting the share price to rise would pay for the right to purchase those shares at a fixed price in the future, even if that price is higher than the current share price.

The introduction of future expectations explains the most elementary quandary which can confront new investors. Why on earth would anyone want to pay for the right to buy shares at 150p five years from now, when they can be bought today for 100p? The answer is of course that the shares may be well above 150p in five years' time, but the warrant-holder will still have the right to purchase them at that fixed price.

This second element of a warrant price, the premium, is often seen as the key to value. It is not used in the same sense as for traded options, where it is simply the price of the option, but as the extra amount which warrant investors must pay for the benefits which warrants confer. The premium, which is normally expressed as a percentage of the share price, may be defined as the percentage by which the warrant price plus the exercise price exceeds the current share price:

$$Premium\ (\%) = \frac{warrant + exercise\ price - share\ price}{share\ price} \times 100$$

EXAMPLE

Widget plc share price 120p, exercise price 100p, warrant price 50p.

$$Premium = \frac{(50p + 100p - 120p)}{120p} \times 100$$

Premium = 25%

Alternatively, the premium may be calculated using intrinsic value, which is simply a restatement of the equation above:

$$Premium\ (\%) = \frac{warrant\ price - intrinsic\ value}{share\ price} \times 100$$

Obviously the intrinsic value can only change when the share price changes, and it cannot change independently. The premium value of a warrant behaves differently, and will change according to investors' expectations of the future.

EXAMPLE

Big Cheese plc share price 100p; warrants carry the right to subscribe for one share each at 60p in five years' time. If investors believe that Big Cheese shares will rise to 150p over the next five years then they may be prepared to pay up to 90p for the warrants – a premium of 50 per cent. Should investors take a less positive view, and expect the Big Cheese share price to appreciate to only 120p over the next five years, then they may only pay up to 60p for the warrants – a premium of 20 per cent.

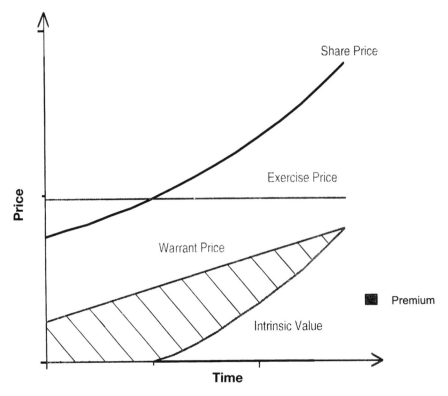

Figure 3.2 An illustration of the diminishing premium

For any given warrant, the higher the premium rises, the greater the rise being discounted, and the more expensive that warrant becomes. This is because the underlying shares must rise by a percentage equal to the premium by the time of final expiry if the investor is to recover his investment in the warrants – a premise which may be derived intuitively from the example above.

The reason why the shares must rise by the amount of the premium is simply that the premium disappears as the time of final expiry approaches, and will fall to zero by the end of the warrant's life. At the time of exercise, the warrant price is composed entirely of intrinsic value. This may be illustrated with an elaboration of Figure 3.1 from the section above (see Figure 3.2).

This characteristic of the premium is important, and indeed the premium is sometimes referred to as the 'time value' of a warrant for this reason.

This can be formalized with the 'break-even' formula, which provides the annual percentage rise in the equity required for a warrant-holder to recover the current warrant price:

$$Break\text{-}Even = \left[\left(\frac{exercise\ price + warrant\ price}{share\ price}\right)^{1/y} - 1\right] \times 100$$

Where y = years remaining to expiry.

EXAMPLE

Universe plc warrants with five years' life remaining, exercise price 100p; share price 85p; warrant price 15p.

$$Break\text{-}Even = \left[\left(\frac{100 + 15}{85}\right)^{1/5} - 1\right] \times 100$$

Break-even = 6.23 per cent

Check:
Year 0: shares 85p
Year 1: shares gain 6.23 per cent: 90.3p
Year 2: shares gain 6.23 per cent: 95.9p
Year 3: shares gain 6.23 per cent: 101.9p
Year 4: shares gain 6.23 per cent: 108.2p
Year 5: shares gain 6.23 per cent: 115.0p

Warrant exercised at 100p; intrinsic worth 15p. Warrant-holder breaks even.

It can be seen that the premium is a key indicator of the expectations built into the warrant price, which must be compared with the expectation of the would-be purchaser. The principal drawback with the premium is that it is critically dependent upon the time to expiry, yet it takes no explicit account of this factor. As such it is limited in its utility as a comparative indicator when used in isolation, and it must always be considered in the individual context of each warrant. Even when the time to expiry is incorporated into the break-even formula, the result tells only of the annual growth required for the investor to avoid a loss from the present position, and adds nothing of more predictive value.

TIME TO EXPIRY

UK equity warrants have an average time to final expiry, or maturity, of approximately four and three-quarter years, but there is considerable variation around this average. At any one time there will be several with only weeks or months to run, and others lasting well beyond the year 2000. This time to expiry has a critical role to play in assessing the premium, as explained above, and it has a further importance in relation to the time-preference of investors.

Time to expiry, if lengthy, is one of the significant advantages of warrants over many other derivative instruments which have very short maturities. Warrants can be used for short-term speculation, but with the confidence of a longer time perspective if necessary. This has been an important factor in the growth of the warrants market. Speculators lost some of their taste for the very short-term bets after the market crash of 1987 and looked for instruments with a longer time to expiry. They discovered warrants.

There are four major benefits of a longer time to expiry. First, the longer maturity allows room for error. No one invests in warrants expecting to make a short-term loss, but if market conditions are unfavourable, or the underlying security runs into unexpected difficulties, then the price of warrants can fall sharply. Should this happen with a short-dated option then the holder has little choice but to shrug his shoulders and take a loss. With longer-dated warrants, however, the holder does have a choice. It may be prudent to accept a large loss and sell in order to recover at least part of the investment, or the investor may choose to hold on to the warrants in anticipation of a recovery. At least this choice exists. Many warrant investors have seen initial losses turn into profits once they have held the warrants for some time.

Some forms of speculation are simply ruled out by short-dated securities. In a scenario, for example, where an investor expects a sharp one-off rise in a share price (due to a product breakthrough, drilling success, victory in litigation, analysts' re-rating, etc.), but is not sure when this will happen, a long-dated warrant is ideal, particularly if it offers high gearing. The investor can place his money into the warrants and wait for the event to happen. Such an approach may not be feasible using an instrument such as a traditional option where the maximum term is three months. The investor could not commit his entire stake at once, since a small misjudgement in timing could result in a total loss, and of course if he commits only a part of his stake then the potential profit is commensurately smaller.

Second, warrants offer a particular convenience for the longer-term risk speculator. It is usually assumed that the high-risk speculator is seeking, and will take, a short-term profit, but this need not necessarily be the case. For a host of reasons a speculator may not wish to trade frequently: warrants with a longer time to expiry avoid the need to keep buying and selling short-term contracts and paying out commissions each time.

Third, the longer time to expiry is useful to investors buying warrants with the ultimate intention of exercising them, because they can defer the outlay of capital needed for exercise. This benefit may be evaluated using the technique of present value discounting, as follows:

EXAMPLE

Grommet plc series 1 warrants, exercise price 100p in two years. Interest rate 9 per cent.

$$\text{Present value of exercise price} = \frac{\text{exercise price}}{(1+r)^{y}}$$

$$= \frac{100}{(1.09)^{2}}$$

$$= 84.2p$$

This means that at an interest rate of 9 per cent the investor must set aside 84.2p now to meet the 100p payment in two years time.

The investor buying Grommet series 2 warrants which are exerciseable at 100p in five years, does not have to set aside as much money:

$$= \frac{100}{(1.09)^{5}}$$

$$= 65.0p$$

Fourth, and possibly most interestingly, the longer time frame of warrants encourages a broader range of investors to use the market. Warrants are not only suitable for the short-term speculator, but for a wide range of investors with varying objectives. This is beneficial because it implies that participants will not always be making the same decisions. This aids liquidity, reduces unnecessarily large price fluctuations, and makes the market a more interesting place. It also means that small investors can win. In a market where the majority of players have the same objective, it is those with the best information who are first in, first out, and emerge with the largest profits. In a market with differing objectives these are less likely to be mutually exclusive. The idea that 'for every winner there is a loser' has always been false, but this fallacy is even more evident where objectives differ widely. A good deal for one client selling, perhaps to take a short-term profit, can also be a good deal for the buyer who sees longer-term fundamental value in the warrants.

In general, a longer time to expiry is preferable, and not just for the cautious investor wishing to leave plenty of time for the investment to perform.

THE CAPITAL FULCRUM POINT

The capital fulcrum point (CFP) may also be considered as the fulcrum of basic understanding. It can appear as a rather daunting algebraic concept, but its importance should not be underestimated, and all serious investors should endeavour to achieve an understanding of this key indicator. Although there is no single computation which will suffice, this is by far the most important single technical indicator for valuing warrants. The beauty of the CFP is that it combines the premium and the time to expiry to provide a compound indicator which is of more use than either component. It has been argued for some time that the CFP has made the premium largely redundant as a separate indicator, since the latter is of little comparative relevance. Even so, the CFP is under-utilized as a valuation tool, principally due to a lack of understanding. It is unfortunate that one leading firm of financial advisers which advertised a free warrant guide throughout 1994 confirmed the axiom that 'you get what you pay for' by defining the break-even formula incorrectly as the CFP, thereby causing much confusion among UK private investors.

The CFP is essentially a more sophisticated version of the 'break-even' formula, and measures the annual percentage growth of the equity required for you to do equally well in terms of capital appreciation with either the equity or the warrant. In other words, if the CFP = 7 per cent and the share price actually rises by 8 per cent per annum to the final conversion date, then the warrants will outperform the shares over this period, and vice versa.

The formula for calculating the CFP is as follows:

$$CFP = \left[\left(\frac{e}{s-w}\right)^{1/y} - 1\right] \times 100 \text{ per cent}$$

where e = exercise price
s = share price
w = warrant price
and y = years to expiry.

EXAMPLE

Universe plc warrants with five years' life remaining, exercise price 100p; share price 85p; warrant price 15p.

$$CFP = \left[\left(\frac{100}{85-15}\right)^{1/5} - 1\right] \times 100\%$$

$$CFP = \left[\left(\frac{100}{70}\right)^{1/5} - 1\right] \times 100\%$$

$$CFP = \left[1.4286^{1/5} - 1\right] \times 100\%$$

It is this next stage which sometimes causes confusion, especially for those unfamiliar with the notation. What must be calculated next is 1.4286 to the power of ⅕. Most scientific calculators can do this easily, usually with an 'inverse power' button marked X $^{1/y}$. In this case, 1.4286 is entered first, followed by the 'inverse power' button, then 5 and =. The answer is 1.0739.

$$CFP = \left[1.0739 - 1\right] \times 100\%$$

$$CFP = 7.39\%$$

In putting the CFP to use, it is important to understand that it has great power as a comparative yardstick, in three distinct ways. First the CFP standardizes the time factor to an annual rate of growth, enabling comparison between different warrants. If one warrant has a CFP of 7 per cent and another a CFP of 10 per cent then the former is discounting less future growth and is cheaper, other things being equal. When using the CFP in this way is is helpful to have some idea of the average CFP for the market – around 9 per cent for UK equity warrants at the time of writing. This figure can be volatile, and reacts most strongly to general market movements. In bullish periods when warrants are gaining in intrinsic value, the average CFP will tend to fall; during bearish periods the average CFP will tend to rise. For this reason it is not possible to say that a certain CFP is always good value: as with so many aspects of warrant valuation, it depends upon the context. Figure 3.3 shows the average CFP from October 1989 to April 1995.

Second, the CFP is perhaps most widely applied to comparisons between warrants and their underlying shares. An investor who has identified a company with favourable prospects can make use of the CFP in deciding whether to invest in the shares or the warrants. If the CFP is low then the warrants may be better value, and vice versa.

Third, and related to the above, the CFP provides a figure which may be compared with the investor's expectations. In deciding what constitutes a 'low' CFP, expectations are clearly important. As a general rule, if the CFP is below the expected growth rate for the equity, then the warrants should be bought. Using the example above, an expectation of 10 per cent equity growth suggests that the warrants should be bought, since the CFP is only 7.39 per cent:

EXAMPLE

Equity growth of 10 per cent per annum from base of 85p implies a share price at the end of five years of 136.9p – an overall rise of 61.05 per cent. The warrant carrying the right to exercise into one share at 100p will have intrinsic value of 36.9p after five years – an increase of 146 per cent over the current 15p.

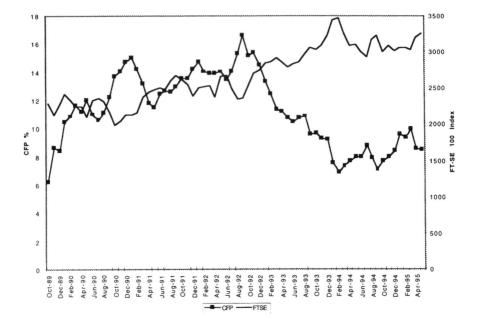

Figure 3.3 Average CFP and market movements, October 1989 to April 1995

This information may be demonstrated graphically, showing the percentage changes in the equity and warrant for a range of expected growth rates (see Figure 3.4). This graph also illustrates one principal difficulty in using the CFP. An investor expecting a growth rate below 6.23 per cent will anticipate a loss on the warrant and will not invest, yet another investor expecting a growth rate above 7.39 per cent will not only expect to make a gain on the warrants, but will prefer the warrants to the shares. Given that most investors have a blurred idea of their expectations, the CFP is not best used as a spuriously precise technical measure of value, but as a general comparative guide. In general, it makes little practical difference whether the CFP is 7.39 per cent, or 7.5 per cent, although the figures can provide an excellent screen for selecting a shortlist of warrants and for pinpointing extreme valuations.

In extreme cases the CFP can highlight short-term opportunities, but it is generally used as a guide to medium-term and long-term investment decisions where value is more important than speculative movements. As inexperienced investors often shy away from high premiums, it can be a good strategy to buy high premium warrants with a long time to expiry, where the CFP is actually quite low. There is evidence to suggest that warrants with more than seven or eight years to run are often comparatively undervalued, something which the long-term investor can discover by calculating the CFP.

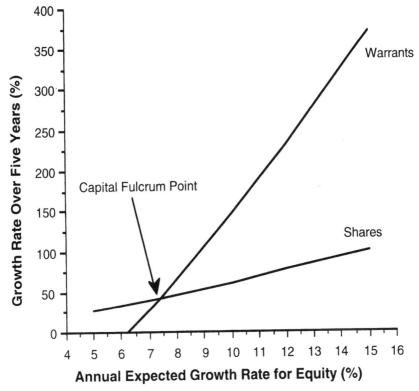

Note: negative growth rates are ignored, since neither the shares nor the warrants would be attractive under this expectation.

Figure 3.4 A graphic representation of the CFP

Finally, the CFP provides a nice illustration of the way in which the technical approach works in tandem with fundamental considerations. Although the CFP is an algebraic, technical factor, it is fundamental in origin since it relates the warrant position to the underlying expectation of share price performance. In this role it provides an excellent capital computation, incorporating a number of other technical factors.

INCOME

As the majority of warrant investors are seeking capital gain, the CFP has a good deal of power in spite of the fact that it ignores any income accruing to share-holders. Warrants do not rank for the dividends paid on the underlying shares, so when considering the relative merits of the warrants and shares, an accurate assessment will take note of the income forgone on the shares. There are two reasons for this. First, if the share carries a high yield this is a plus point in comparison with the warrants which carry zero yield. At least, the very large majority of warrants carry zero yield. The fact that some investors prefer to have some level of income on their investments, however modest, was recognized by the two TR subscription shares and the Investment Trust of Investment Trusts (see Chapter 2), which are essentially warrants with some income attached. These have a welcome place in the warrants market, but they have not proved popular enough to start a trend – the majority of warrant-holders would probably see income as a bonus and not as a prerequisite.

The second impact of a high income is that it may hold some implications for the scope for capital appreciation. This is particularly true of high income investment trust shares, which concentrate on the yield with some sacrifice to the capital gain. Income trust shares are likely to appreciate more slowly than shares with the principal objective of capital growth. When considering these shares, therefore, is it wise to check the historical capital performance which may not have kept pace with the market. In such cases the fundamental rating of the shares may be downgraded for the purposes of warrant evaluation.

The nature of the underlying share can be important when valuing investment trust warrants, and those attached to split-level investment trusts in particular. A large proportion of these trusts feature warrants attached to capital shares which carry no income and which are themselves geared. The CFP on these warrants can be extremely high, yet the double dose of gearing available can mean big profits in bullish market conditions (see Chapter 12).

ADJUSTING THE CFP FOR INCOME

Ideally, the CFP should be adjusted to take full account of the income available to shareholders in the underlying stock, thereby allowing a proper comparison not merely across time, but across different types of share. One particular problem with this is that in order to make an accurate adjustment it is necessary to forecast the level of dividend payments each year until the expiry of the warrant. This can be a difficult task, and one which is prone to introducing considerable estimating errors into what was before an admirably accurate equation.

This problem may be tackled in three ways. The first is to group the underlying shares into distinct income bands, say with yields of 0 per cent–3 per cent, 3 per cent–6 per cent, and 6 per cent and above, and to compare warrants within those bands. Whilst this measure is clearly an *ad hoc* approach which still allows considerable variations in the levels of income, there is more chance that warrants will be compared on a like-for-like basis. High income trust warrants will be compared with other high income trust warrants. A more useful, but equally simple approach is to add the current dividend yield, expressed as a percentage, to the basic CFP. This seems intuitively to be a sound approach, as a proportion of the assets equivalent to the yield effectively 'disappears' each year to shareholders, and should be added back in to the equation when determining the rate of growth required from the total asset base. An immediate benefit from this approach is that investors can see that the low CFPs boasted by high income trust warrants are often illusory, as in the example below where the growth trust warrant is marginally cheaper after the dividend yield is added in.

High income trust warrant
8 years of life remaining, exercisable at 100p
share price 100p, warrant price 18.5p
CFP = 2.59% Yield = 6.30% Adjusted CFP = 8.89%

Growth trust warrant
5.5 years of life remaining, exercisable at 100p
share price 100p, warrant price 32p
CFP = 7.26% Yield = 1.20% Adjusted CFP = 8.46%

Again, though, this is a rough measure which suffers from a series of shortcomings. First, the yield is a historic measure, based upon the last dividend payment which may have been unrepresentative. Second, it is well known that companies are reluctant to reduce dividend payments during what are perceived as temporary downturns. At these times the dividend yield will rise and the adjusted CFP will rise, implying that the capital growth prospects from the warrants seem less attractive. In practice, however, the growth prospects from these troughs are generally superior than at times when the yield is lower, and the shares may have the added attraction of having their downside risk protected by this high yield.

Among the more sophisticated adjustments which may be made, one suggested by a private investor, Mr DV Connell from Portugal, seems to have some validity. His derivation assumes the dividend payment amount (as distinct from the yield) will remain constant until the expiry date – an assumption which is valid in many cases where the maturity is relatively short. The formula for this adjusted CFP is then as follows:

$$Adjusted\ CFP = \left[\left(\frac{(e + ryw)}{s - w} \right)^{1/y} - 1 \right] \times 100\%$$

where r = the rate of dividend yield.

Thus, using the example of the high income trust above:

High income trust warrant
8 years of life remaining, exercisable at 100p
share price 100p, warrant price 18.5p
CFP = 2.59%   Yield = 6.30%

$$Adjusted\ CFP\ =\ \left[\frac{100 +(0.063 \times 8 \times 18.5)}{100-18.5}^{1/8} - 1\right] \times\ 100\%$$

$$=\ \left[\frac{109.32}{81.5}^{1/8} - 1\right] \times\ 100\%$$

$$=\ 3.74\%$$

Check: share gain 100p × (1.0374)^8 + 6.3p dividends × 8 = 184.54p = gain of 84.54%
warrant value at expiry = 134.14p – 100p = 34.14p = gain of 84.54%

Here the assumption of a fixed and constant dividend payment may be flawed, since a high income trust with a share price of 134p at the end of the period and a dividend payment of 6.3p would be yielding a more modest 4.7 per cent. Nevertheless this is an interesting algebraic approach which is worthy of consideration, if imperfect.

GEARING

Whereas the premium, CFP and loss of income provide measures of the additional costs of warrants investment which the investor seeks to minimize, gearing is one of the principal benefits of investing in warrants. As any good mechanic will tell you, gears enable one cog wheel to control the movement of another cog wheel of a different size, and the extent of gearing measures the relationship between the two. With regard to warrants, the simple gearing factor is calculated as follows:

Gearing factor = Share price / Warrant price

EXAMPLE

Warrants share price 400p; warrant price 40p.

Gearing = 400/40
Gearing = 10.0 times

Using this example, £1 invested in warrants confers rights over £10 worth of shares – a benefit which may be exploited in two distinct ways. On the one hand, the speculative investor using warrants can gain much more equity exposure from a given investment, and on the other hand a more cautious investor can achieve his ordinary equity exposure at a much reduced outlay. Which approach is adopted depends upon the investment aims, and also the market conditions. During difficult markets it can be a major advantage to use warrants to keep your hand in the market while committing much less capital. Conversely, during a bull market, warrants can be used to maximize the potential capital gains from a given amount of capital. These approaches are covered more fully in Chapter 6, which explains how this gearing benefit can be used to manipulate the level of risk.

However the investor chooses to interpret this gearing advantage, it clearly is a major attraction, and high gearing is considered an important factor in the technical analysis of any warrant.

LEVERAGE: IMPLIED GEARING

As far as gearing is concerned, this level of sophistication is sufficient for most investors, providing a clear picture of how much equity exposure a warrant provides. What few investors realize, though, is that this simple measure of gearing is only half the picture. The point of the combination of wheels is usually to effect a change in the speed of revolution. The smaller cog wheel turns faster. Similarly, with warrants, gearing enables larger percentage gains (or losses) on warrants because of their lower price relative to the equity. The measure of this price relationship is known as leverage. The higher the leverage, the higher the percentage change in the warrant price for any given change in the share price.

Where there is no premium the calculation is very simple, and gearing is synonymous with leverage:

EXAMPLE

Widget plc share price 100p; warrant price 25p; exercise price 75p; gearing 4.0 times; no premium.
Widget shares move up by 10 per cent to 110p – shareholder makes 10 per cent gain.
Warrants also move up 10p in response – warrant-holder makes 40 per cent gain.

In most cases, however, a premium exists, and simple gearing will overstate the extent of leverage. This is because the premium tends to fall as the warrant gains in intrinsic value:

EXAMPLE

*Widget plc share price 100p; warrant price 40p; exercise price 75p; gearing
2.5 times; premium 15 per cent*

*Widget shares move up by 10 per cent to 110p – shareholder makes 10 per cent
gain.*

*Warrants may move up 8p in response – warrant-holder makes 20 per cent
gain.*

To measure leverage, it is necessary to have prior knowledge of how the
warrants will react to changes in the share price – knowledge which no one can
claim.

$$Leverage = \frac{\% \text{ change in warrant price}}{\% \text{ change in share price}}$$

One way around this is to estimate leverage using what is known as implied
gearing. This is often based on the special assumption that the premium will fall
to zero if the share price doubles. This is not entirely satisfactory, since warrants
with a low parity ratio (a long way out of the money) or a long time to expiry
may still trade with a premium even if the shares double. Indeed, this must be the
case if the parity ratio is less than 0.5. On this basis the formula is as follows:

$$Implied \text{ } gearing = \frac{(2pr-1)}{wr} - 1$$

where *pr* = parity ratio (share price/exercise price) and *wr* = warrant ratio (warrant price/exercise price)

EXAMPLE

*BTR 1993/94 warrants share price 400p; warrants 40p; exercise price 480p;
parity ratio 0.833.*

$$\begin{aligned}
Implied \text{ } gearing &= \frac{((2 \times 0.833) - 1)}{(40/480)} - 1 \\
&= \frac{0.666}{0.083} - 1 \\
&= 7.0
\end{aligned}$$

*In other words, implied gearing suggests that a 1 per cent variation in the BTR
share price would create a 7 per cent variation in the BTR 1993/94 warrant
price.*

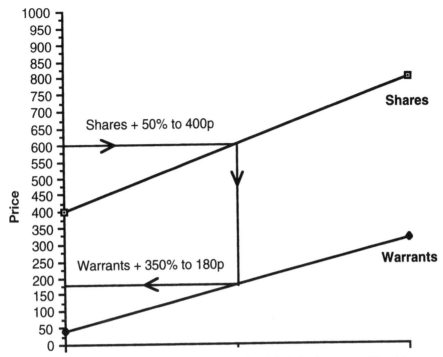

Note: this graph is constructed using the BTR example, and on the basis that the warrants will lose their premium if the shares double to 800p. This implies a price for the warrants of 800p−480p exercise = 320p. For any given share price the warrant price can be read off as shown, illustrating the leverage of 7.0 times.

Time

Figure 3.5 An
illustration of implied gearing

To be more certain, and to eliminate many of the unsatisfactory results, the equation may alternatively be based upon the similar assumption that the premium will fall to zero if the share price *triples*. This will provide a reasonable approximation for any warrants with a parity ratio greater than 0.33.

The formula in this case is:

$$\textit{Implied gearing} = \frac{(3pr-1)}{2wr} - 0.5$$

where pr = parity ratio and wr = warrant ratio

EXAMPLE

BTR 1993/94 warrants share price 400p; warrants 40p; exercise price 480p; parity ratio 0.833.

$$Implied\ gearing\quad =\quad \frac{((3\ \times\ 0.833)-1)}{2\times (40/480)}-0.5$$

$$=\quad \frac{1.499}{0.166}-0.5$$

$$=\quad 8.53$$

As illustrated, the result varies considerably depending upon which scenario is chosen, so this choice is of some importance. It seems most sensible to relate this to the average warrant, which currently has approximately four and three-quarter years of life remaining and a parity ratio of 0.9. In this case the additional safety of the 'triple' formula is somewhat superfluous, and the compound growth rate of 15 per cent required for a share to double over a five year period is more reasonable than the 25 per cent required for it to triple.

The greater sophistication of the implied gearing approach will usually provide a more accurate approximation of leverage than simple gearing, but it does remain an approximation. It cannot offer foresight. For this reason the private investor may well feel that simple gearing is satisfactory, particularly in cases where the premium is expected to remain fairly constant in the short term.

VOLATILITY

Although warrants are known as a risk instrument, this does not mean that they will all give holders an exciting ride. It is wrong to assume that the prices of all warrants fluctuate wildly. In practice some are rather docile, reflecting either the quiet position of the underlying security or the lack of trading. Whether the investor desires a highly volatile warrant or not depends once again upon the risk preference, but in general the higher the volatility the more attractive a warrant is considered to be. This is because it is more likely to reach the exercise price if it is volatile, and it will of course throw up more trading opportunities.

This argument may be understood by considering the extreme cases. A warrant which rarely moves (low volatility) will be unattractive to most investors seeking capital gains, and it is likely to suffer from low liquidity. Conversely, a volatile warrant should present plenty of opportunities for both trading and investment. In addition to these sober factors, there is the thrill and enjoyment of investing in a fast-moving security – an ingredient which can carry a great deal of weight. Investors do not generally buy warrants, any more than they buy penny shares or traded options, for a quiet and modest trading pattern where the warrants can move by a penny if there is an 'r' in the month. Warrants can be exciting – if you choose the volatile ones.

This is not to say, however, that everyone will wish to invest in the most volatile warrants. They can be exciting, but of course they can swing downwards just as quickly and violently as they can lurch upwards. In some cases you need the stomach for a roller-coaster ride. It is important also to bear in mind the market conditions. During difficult periods it may not be sensible to choose a highly geared, volatile warrant, but during a bullish or recovery phase these may be the best performers.

Volatility can provide a useful indicator of both risk and the ability of a warrant to play a full part in any market-led gains, and it is important for investors to have some appreciation of the likely range of movement. This need not involve a lot of calculation. Sometimes a basic visual approach can be helpful if you have a good graph of the warrant price over time. This is a simple approach, of course, but a glance over a graph can often indicate the approximate extent of a warrant's volatility. A graph can also illustrate whether a warrant stays within a narrow trading range, or whether it displays price 'stickiness' at certain levels. Figures 3.6 and 3.7 are examples of such graphs.

The main drawback with graphs is that they are obviously limited in their precision, and they can be misleading if scales are applied casually. Volatility is of most use as a statistical indicator, and to actually measure volatility it is necessary to have historical price data. Effective measurement requires prices input daily or weekly over a reasonable period of time, although private investors can gain a very simple *ad hoc* measure by observing the gap between the high and low prices for the year. This is not a very satisfactory measure, since a warrant may have jumped from the low price to the high price in one discrete step and remained unchanged thereafter. It has the considerable attraction of simplicity though, and a measure may be obtained simply by dividing the high price by the low price:

EXAMPLE

Warrant A: *High 120p*   *Low 76p*   *Volatility = 120/76*   *= 1.6*
Warrant B: *High 16p*   *Low 5p*   *Volatility = 16/5*   *= 3.2*

A better measure is to calculate the standard deviation of a range of past monthly prices, and then adjust this to a standard warrant price as follows:

$$Volatility = \times \; \frac{standard\ deviation\ (monthly\ prices\ of\ z\ warrants)}{average\ monthly\ price\ of\ z\ warrants} \times \frac{average\ market\ warrant\ price}{}$$

This is a relatively simple method of calculating historical volatility, one of numerous methods of varying sophistication. A more standard, and more complex technique involves computations which are best dealt with by a spreadsheet,

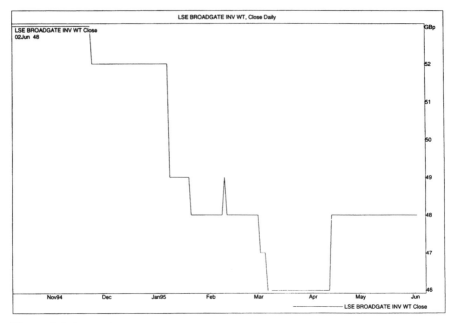

Figure 3.6 Low volatility: Broadgate investment warrants, November 1994 to June 1995
(source: Reuters)

although a keen investor could invest some time in manual calculations. This standard approach calculates annual volatility based upon prices collected daily, weekly or monthly. The first step is to divide the most recent price by the previous entry, and then to find the natural logarithm for this number. Next, the standard deviation is calculated for this range of natural logarithms, and the answer is multiplied by the square root of the number of entries per year (260 daily, 52 weekly, 12 monthly). This figure may then be written as a percentage.

EXAMPLE

Month	Price	$Price_t/Price_{t-1}$	Natural Log
1	100p	–	–
2	110p	1.100	0.095
3	95p	0.864	−0.147
4	90p	0.947	−0.054
5	80p	0.889	−0.118
6	85p	1.063	0.061
7	100p	1.176	0.163
8	120p	1.200	0.182
9	135p	1.125	0.118
10	130p	0.963	−0.038
11	130p	1.000	0.000
		Standard Deviation:	*0.1152*

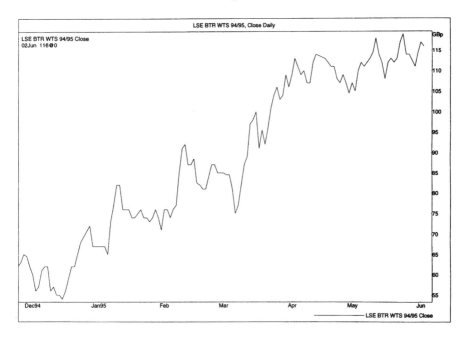

Figure 3.7 High volatility: BTR warrants, December 1994 to June 1995 (source: Reuters)

$$Volatility = 0.1152 \times \sqrt{12}$$
$$= 0.3991$$
$$= 39.91 \ per \ cent$$

Note: just 11 months' prices are used to show that the full year's data is not necessary.

It is revealing to look at at an empirical example such as the volatility table for BTR shares and four sets of warrants attached (see Table 3.1). This illustrates and upholds the theoretical proposition that gearing should make the warrants more volatile than the shares.

Yet even this approach fails to close the debate. There is some question over whether the volatility of the underlying share is actually more relevant, since the price of the warrant is ultimately dependent upon the price of the share. This argument has some force for the shorter-dated warrants, but for the longer-dated variants their ability to move independently of the shares makes the volatility of the warrants themselves more interesting.

Not surprisingly, volatility bears a strong relationship to gearing. Highly geared warrants tend to be more sensitive to changes in the underlying equity and to move through a broader price range. Most warrants with low gearing have a low volatility, and vice versa. However, volatility is also dependent upon a range

BTR Shares	P/P₋₁	Natural Log	BTR Wts 1994/95	P/P₋₁	Natural Log	BTR Wts 1995/96	P/P₋₁	Natural Log	BTR Wts 1997	P/P₋₁	Natural Log	BTR Wts 1998	P/P₋₁	Natural Log
293.5p			67p			53p			63.5p			32.25p		
301.5p	1.02726	0.02689238	73p	1.0896	0.08576682	55p	1.03774	0.3704127	63p	0.9921	-0.00790518	32p	0.99224806	-0.0077821
305.5p	1.01327	0.01317976	76p	1.0411	0.0402739	55p	1	0	66p	1.0476	0.04652002	32p	1	0
307p	1.00491	0.00489797	76p	1	0	56p	1.01818	0.01801851	66p	1	0	32p	1	0
304.5p	0.99186	-0.0081767	76p	1	0	55p	0.98214	-0.01801851	63.5	0.9621	-0.03861484	31p	0.96875	-0.0317487
304p	0.99836	-0.00016434	74p	0.9737	-0.0266682	54p	0.98182	-0.01834914	63.5p	1	0	28p	0.90322581	-0.1017827
321p	1.05592	0.05441342	92p	1.2432	0.21772348	65p	1.2037	0.18540322	74p	1.1654	0.15302519	32.5	1.16071429	0.14903558
311p	0.96885	-0.0316482	82p	0.8913	-0.1150693	58p	0.89231	-0.11394426	67.5p	0.9122	-0.0919375	31p	0.95384615	-0.0472529
315.5p	1.01447	0.01436577	87p	1.061	0.05918887	61p	1.05172	0.05043085	70p	1.037	0.03636764	32.5p	1.0483871	0.04725288
314.4p	0.99683	-0.0031746	84.5p	0.9713	-0.0291566	61p	1	0	70.5p	1.0071	0.00711747	31p	0.95384615	-0.0472529
316p	1.00477	0.00475814	87p	1.0296	0.02915658	61p	1	0	70.5p	1	0	32p	1.03225806	0.0317487
321.5p	1.01741	0.01725533	91p	1.046	0.04495139	63p	1.03279	0.03226086	72p	1.0213	0.02105341	32.5p	1.015625	0.01550419
326p	1.014	0.01389984	104p	1.1429	0.13353199	73p	1.15873	0.1473247	79.5p	1.1042	0.0990909	34p	1.04615385	0.04512044
328p	1.00613	0.00611623	106p	1.0192	0.01904819	75p	1.0274	0.02702867	79p	0.9937	-0.00630917	35.5p	1.04411765	0.04317217
332p	1.0122	0.01212136	110p	1.0377	0.03704127	79p	1.05333	0.05195974	81.5p	1.0316	0.03115517	37.5p	1.05633803	0.05480824
337p	1.01506	0.01494796	114p	1.0364	0.03571808	82p	1.03797	0.03727139	85p	1.0429	0.04204824	38p	1.01333333	0.01324523
332.5p	0.98665	-0.0134431	111p	0.9737	-0.0266682	79p	0.96341	-0.03727139	82p	0.9647	-0.03593201	37.5p	0.98684211	-0.0132452
329p	0.98947	-0.0105821	104.5p	0.9414	-0.0603431	74p	0.93671	-0.06538276	77p	0.939	-0.06291383	35p	0.93333333	-0.0689929
332.5p	1.01064	0.01058211	111p	1.0622	0.06034313	78p	1.05405	0.05264373	78.5p	1.0195	0.0192932	34.5p	0.98571429	-0.0143887
337.5p	1.01504	0.01492565	114p	1.027	0.02666825	80p	1.02564	0.02531781	82p	1.0446	0.04362062	35p	1.01449275	0.01438874
339p	1.00444	0.0044346	112p	0.9825	-0.0176996	78p	0.975	-0.02531781	80p	0.9756	-0.02469261	34p	0.97142857	-0.0289875
338.5	0.99853	-0.001476	114p	1.0179	0.01769958	80p	1.02564	0.02531781	81p	1.0125	0.01242252	32.5p	0.95588235	-0.0451204
341.5p	1.0086	0.00882359	116p	1.0175	0.01739174	82p	1.025	0.02469261	83p	1.0247	0.02439145	32.75p	1.00769231	0.00766287
Standard Deviation:		0.01658311	Standard Deviation:		0.06702456	Standard Deviation:		0.06253925	Standard Deviation:		0.05146626	Standard Deviation:		0.05207111
x√52		0.11958249	x√52		0.48332099	x√52		0.45097692	x√52		0.3711285	x√52		0.37549012
		11.96%			48.33%			45.10%			37.11%			37.55%

Table 3.1: Volatility table for BTR shares and warrants

of other factors. In particular, the type of underlying security is important. High income trusts often have a very stable capital value, hence a low volatility share price, and the warrants reflect this in their volatility. Conversely, where the underlying security is itself of a volatile nature, this will tend again to be reflected in the warrant. Similarly, the amount of trading is important. Popular and accessible warrants such as BTR will tend to have a greater volatility than more obscure and thinly traded warrants, simply because the market is more active. And finally, the time to expiry can have an influence in some circumstances, and warrants nearing their final expiry date are likely to be more volatile than their long-dated counterparts. If a warrant has ten years to run, and it is a long way out of the money, then a small move in the shares will not necessarily trigger any move in the value of the warrants. Should the warrant be close to its final expiry, however, it is more likely to track the share price closely, and far more likely to respond to changes.

AMALGAMATING THE RESULTS: INEXTRICABLE LINKAGES

This chapter has outlined the basic tenets of analysis, and it can be seen that investors should look for certain traits before investing in a specific series of warrants. The desirable elements are a positive fundamental position, some intrinsic value, a low premium, a long time to expiry, a low CFP, high gearing and leverage, high volatility, and low income on the shares.

In practice, these elements are unlikely to be combined in a perfect blend, and there is no such thing as a perfect warrant. This may disappoint some investors, but the search for the ideal warrant is a search for a chimera. Rather, warrant selection involves a realization that certain merits assume a great importance at certain times, while other merits assume paramount importance at other times. There are horses for courses, and there are warrants for markets. During bull markets the greatest gains will probably come from the highly geared, volatile warrants, probably well out of the money. During more uncertain times, it is usually better to moderate the risk and settle for a good value CFP with reasonable gearing. Furthermore, what is suitable for one investor is not necessarily suitable for another. Some investors may adopt an aggressive, high-risk approach, while others may prefer to look for sound medium-term value. Each will choose different warrants according to these preferences. For this reason it is not entirely satisfactory to assign standard weighting factors to each element and then to buy the warrants with the highest rating. Rather, the results need to be interpreted according to need, and warrant selections can be tailored according to individual preferences. Markets cannot claim to offer warrants bespoke, but as the range improves, so most investors will find warrants which provide a snug fit to their requirements.

Another reason why the separate weighting of factors seems too simplistic is that the factors are inextricably linked. Some are almost amalgams in their own right. The intrinsic value and the premium together make up the warrant price, the premium and time to expiry combine to make up the CFP, the erosion of the premium differentiates gearing from leverage, and both gearing and the time to expiry affect volatility. For this reason it is most important to get the overall picture rather than looking for perfection in one or two indicators.

HOW IMPORTANT ARE TECHNICAL FACTORS?

This is rather like asking 'how long is a piece of string?' It is difficult to assess the extent to which technical factors can be reliable, as technical analysis should always be used in conjunction with fundamental analysis, and vice versa. Each one is of little use without the other to back it up. With this in mind, it is important not to have unrealistic expectations of what technical analysis can achieve alone. It will not provide a magic answer. Technical analysis determines the value of the warrants in relation to the shares, and it can be put to good use as a method of weeding out the overvalued warrants. Investors may wish to concentrate on warrants with gearing over four times, for example, or those with more than eight years to run, or those with a CFP below 10 per cent, or those with volatility over 50 per cent. Used in this way, technical analysis cannot guarantee success, but it can stack the odds in your favour – a good technical position may be seen as a necessary but not a sufficient condition for success.

For short-term investors, technical factors may be helpful for identifying temporary misalignments. Warrants can and do move independently of shares, and occasionally in the opposite direction. This can lead to some surprising anomalies which technical analysis can uncover, revealing some excellent short-term opportunities. The warrants market is under-researched in comparison with most securities markets, so an investor armed with good information and analysis can often move ahead of the crowd.

Sometimes a technical imbalance is so strikingly obvious that the fundamental position is nearly (but not quite) irrelevant. This realization usually arises when an investor has been tracking the shares and warrants of a company closely, observing the 'normal' levels for the premium, gearing, CFP and volatility. For some reason this normal relationship, if one exists, may be disturbed and the warrants may become very cheap (or very expensive) for a short period of time.

Other factors such as fashion and sentiment govern and determine short-term market movements, but technical analysis can provide a more consistent approach for medium to long-term investment. An investor picking warrants with sound fundamental prospects, a long life, low CFP, and high gearing should find them to be a rewarding investment over the long-term.

Returning to the example of the junior oil exploration warrants cited at the beginning of the chapter, these provide a remarkable illustration of the power of technical analysis. In August 1990 the Iraqi invasion of Kuwait breathed new life into an oil sector which was looking drowsy, and into the more speculative stocks in particular. Speculators were looking for a substantial leap in the oil price, and in their search for a low-priced, geared investment they rushed into the oil exploration warrants. In the two weeks to mid-August 1990 these warrants exhibited some strong gains in a falling market:

Cluff Resources   +63.5 per cent
Oliver Resources   +50.0 per cent
Tullow Oil   +14.3 per cent
Gaelic Resources   +11.8 per cent

These low-priced warrants continued to be popular with small investors in particular, who pushed the warrants to unrealistically high levels when technical analysis showed them to be critically overvalued.

Stock and Terms	Shares Aug 1990	Warrants Aug 1990	Premium	Gearing	CFP	Warrants Oct 1991	Change
Atlantic Resources							
One share at 15p at any time to 3 October 1990	8.0p	0.5p	93.75%	16.0	>1000%	0p*	–100.0%
Cluff Resources							
Exerciseable during four-week period to 31 August 1989 to 1991 at 140p per share	81p	18p	95.06%	4.5	114.71%	0p*	–100.0%
The Exploration Company of Louisiana Inc.							
One share at 240p at any time to 30 July 1993	183p	43p	54.64%	4.3	20.01%	5p	–88.4%
Gaelic Resources							
One Ordinary share at IR15p at any time from 21 May 1990 to 31 January 1991	11p	4.75p	66.98%	2.3	166.34%	0p*	–100.0%
Oliver Resources							
One share at 20p at any time to 30 April 1991	16p	6p	62.50%	2.7	167.30%	0p*	–100.0%
Tullow Oil							
One share at IR18.5p at any time to 30 April 1991	15.5p	4p	33.82%	3.9	70.36%	0p*	–100.0%
United Energy							
One share at 2p in subscription periods up to 31 December 1995	1.75p	0.5p	42.86%	3.5	9.14%	1.25p	+150.0%

* expired worthless

Table 3.2 Oil exploration warrants 1990–91

As Table 3.2 shows, with one notable exception the resulting falls from grace were quite dramatic. This was partly because the equity prices fell back, but the unfeasibly high CFPs made steep declines appear very likely in any case. Only United Energy warrants boasted a single-digit CFP, and they subsequently managed to buck the trend. For all of the other warrants it was a real case of *caveat emptor*, as technical analysis made quite plain.

For an assessment of whether technical analysis can be of equal help in selecting winners as well as avoiding losers, it is instructive to consider the 'Technical Merit' section published in the *Warrants Alert* newsletter. This section is devoted to a brief overview of some of the warrants which have been highlighted by its computer model as undervalued or overvalued. The valuation is not based upon a full analysis, but solely upon technical merit – i.e., premium, time to expiry, CFP and gearing factor. In the 70 months for which this table has been published at the time of writing, the undervalued selections have outperformed the overvalued selections in 59 months – a success rate of 84 per cent.

Another thing to remember is that the analysis above provides only a static indicator of the technical merit of a warrant. For a diversity of reasons some warrants always look cheap, and some knowledge of price history can be invaluable. Technical analysis in all forms of securities markets can gain a bad name when it is used dogmatically: it is essential that algebraic niceties do not overcome simple common sense and experience. Warrant evaluation remains an inexact science, indeed some people consider it more of an art, so private investors should not feel intimidated if the foregoing seems difficult. These tools of basic analysis are available to be used, explored and enjoyed, at whatever level.

"If graphs are used sensibly, and you are aware of their limitations, then they must be a useful addition to your analytical armoury."

4

ASSESSING WARRANTS PART 2
– GRAPHS

If a picture can paint a thousand words, then a few warrant graphs must be worth a lot of textual comment. The liberal use of graphs throughout this book suggests that they must have some application, even if the purpose is merely illustrative. Most observers would also agree that they have a function beyond this level: used in conjunction with other forms of technical and fundamental knowledge, graphs can be an invaluable aid to understanding the way in which warrants work. They can be particularly useful in considering the relationship between the share price and the warrant price, and they can also provide some insight into trading bands and volatility. Graphs are not, however, a magic canvas for producing easy answers, nor are they an alternative to other forms of analysis. A graph is of limited use on its own, and is of little practical value without the twin engines of fundamental and technical analysis.

GENERAL USE OF GRAPHS

Some analysts and investors give graphs a prominent place in their analytical armoury. The 'technical chartists' who look at moving averages, momentum indicators, flag patterns, head and shoulders and numerous other signals known only to themselves, have never besieged warrants as they have traded options, yet there are those who would transfer their standard techniques directly to the warrants market. The prime difficulty which they encounter is that the volatility of warrants tends to present many false signals, and that basic chart analysis ignores the strong relationship between warrants and the underlying equity price. Chart analysis on the underlying equities makes more sense, although this can at best paint just half a picture, being unable to predict how the warrants might react to changes in the shares.

The inappropriateness of traditional chartist techniques has led to some specific forms of graphic analysis being developed for warrants, although the great weight of attention remains with the fundamental and technical aspects of warrant valuation. The graphs which are used are unlikely to provide much in the way of unique information, but they still have a number of uses.

First, graphs can provide an effective medium for comparison. When considering the relative position of several warrants it is often difficult to assimilate and digest numerical information which might usually be presented in tabular form. Frequently it will be possible to present this information conveniently in graphic form. The result is often an appealing visual overview which allows the simultaneous presentation of a considerable amount of data which may be absorbed in its proper relative context. Once the data is presented in this way, it may cast new light upon the figures, backing up or casting doubt upon the results from other forms of analysis. Last, and perhaps of most practical use, graphs can be useful for highlighting possible cases for investigation. It is possible to scan a number of graphs and to find certain oddities or apparent anomalies in valuation which seem to merit further attention. For detailed analytical work there is no substitute for raw numerical data or information, but for the purposes of preview and overview graphs have the attraction of simplicity – something which can be of considerable benefit in areas where complexity is the chief enemy of understanding.

DOUBLE-AXIS GRAPHS

These are the most widely used and almost certainly the most helpful form of graphs for analysing the relationship between warrants and their underlying shares. Quite simply, the double-axis graph plots both the share price and the warrant price over time, on the same graph, but with separate axes so that the performance may be compared directly. It is normal for the share price to be plotted using the right-hand axis, and the warrant price using the left-hand axis as Figure 4.1 exemplifies.

One immediate attraction of this graph is that it requires no pre-calculation to format the data. Daily, weekly, or monthly prices may be plotted directly, with no need to perform any normalization, indexation or other statistical functions. For this reason this approach is useful for the private investor who is prepared to accept a strictly limited degree of sophistication.

In spite of the apparently primitive nature of the graph, it can be of service in a variety of ways. Investors may find that double-axis graphs are an aid to understanding each of the following aspects:

1 The history of the share and the warrant
2 Trading ranges and bands
3 The relationship between the share and warrant prices
4 Volatility
5 Short-term price anomalies

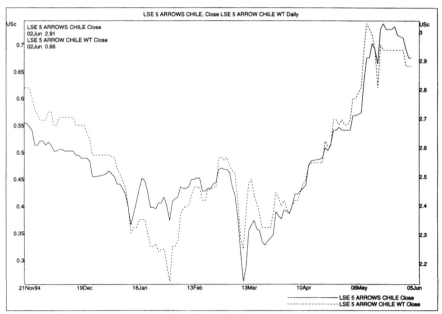

Figure 4.1 Five Arrows Chile Fund share and warrants, November 1994 to June 1995
(source: Reuters)

Considering each point in turn, the ability to recall the past history of share and warrant trading is one which is often underestimated. Lessons may be learnt from past performance, although this is not necessarily a guide to the future. A general understanding of the way in which shares and warrants have performed in the past enables a greater appreciation of the potential risks and rewards, and in individual cases it may provide some indication of the scope for growth. Should you be looking for warrants attached to recovery stocks, for example, then it may be useful to see which shares and warrants have fallen furthest, and over what period. Conversely, should your search be for warrants in your port-folio which might be ripe for selling, then it can be useful to see whether the shares and warrants had previously established any resistance levels at which the price was likely to stall (see Figure 4.2).

In this case the Pilkington shares appeared to run into definite resistance around 200–205p, failing on at least seven occasions to break through this ceil-ing with any conviction. The implication was that the warrants might find it dif-ficult to achieve short-term gains, a hypothesis which was proved correct over the following six months (see Figure 4.3).

Exactly the same reasoning applies to 'floor' prices, which can be of particu-lar significance for low-priced warrants. Should a warrant perform badly and fall to a nominal level, then it may reach the ranks of the penny warrants and reach

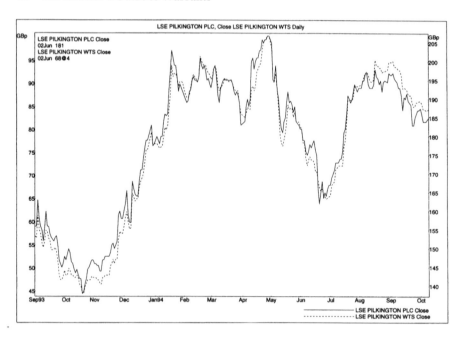

Figure 4.2 Pilkington shares and warrants, September 1993 to October 1994
(source: Reuters)

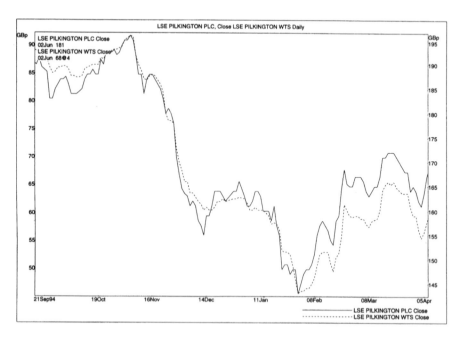

Figure 4.3 Pilkington shares and warrants, September 1994 to April 1995
(source: Reuters)

a level from which it is unlikely to fall further. The penny warrants are a risky proposition for all but the most skilful investors, but a 'floor' price might occasionally make a high-risk strategy worthwhile, particularly if the warrant has a long time still to run and some prospect therefore of retaining or increasing its time value.

In a similar vein to the high-low ranges, trading bands can be interesting to observe. If you can identify a trading band within which a warrant has been trading for some time, then dealing within this band might prove profitable. This is appealing in principle, but three problems need to be taken into account. First, the current Stock Exchange trading system does not allow short selling, so trading can only take place in one direction. You can buy at the bottom of the band and then sell at the top if you are lucky, but not vice versa. The second and more fundamental problem is that dealing spreads and liquidity problems may make it difficult to trade in and out of the market in all but the largest and most active warrant issues. Even in these warrants, trading within the band may not be successful. All trading ranges are broken sooner or later, often with a substantial move in one direction. Restriction of price movements within a narrow trading band for any period of time inevitably reflects a battle between buyers and sellers which one side will eventually win. When this happens the release of buying or selling pressure will often stimulate a large 'breakout'. Should the warrants break downwards then the consequences will be unpleasant for the trader caught with stock. A legitimate application of trading-band observation is indeed to predict when they have been broken and to trade accordingly, especially if certain chart patterns exist. The predictive value of chart patterns such, as double-tops, double-bottoms, and head and shoulders, attract polarized opinions, but some investors consider them to be of value. From experience it is noticeable that certain chart patterns work for certain warrants, and if you find something which appears to work, then of course it is right to apply that analysis.

That said, technical chartism does not seem not wholly reliable when applied to warrants. Warrant trading is affected by too many factors to offer such spurious precision. Further, chart patterns tend to make the assumption that trading occurs in a vacuum and that external influences are unimportant. This condition does not hold for warrants, which are heavily influenced by the underlying equity and by the prevailing market conditions.

The relationship between warrants and their underlying equities is clearly important, and the double-axis graph can provide a visual estimate of the correlation. Warrants which are well 'in the money' and without a premium can be expected to follow the shares almost penny for penny, with the implication that few anomalies are likely to occur (and those which do arise will be corrected swiftly). Where the warrants have virtually no independent trading pattern it is clearly the fundamental prospects for the underlying shares which are the prime determinant of warrant performance (see Figure 4.4).

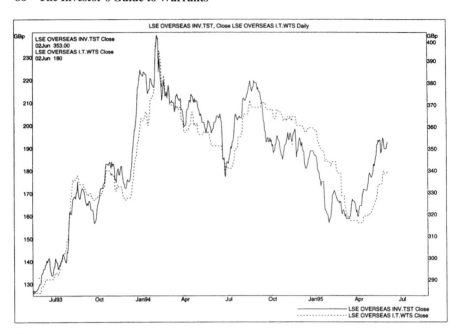

Figure 4.4 Overseas investment trust shares and warrants, July 1993 to June 1995
(source: Reuters)

More usually, most warrants will be influenced by the share price, but not rigidly so. At certain times some warrants may be subject to revaluations which are quite separate from the performance of the shares. In the case of Abtrust New Dawn, below, there was a de-coupling at the start of 1994 which placed the 'B' series warrants on a separate track from the shares (see Figure 4.5). In cases such as this, the technical valuation is of obvious importance in determining whether or not the upward lurch of the warrants was justified (in this case probably not).

The importance of volatility is documented in Chapter 3, but the difficulty of calculating the sophisticated statistical measures means that many private investors may prefer to rely upon a graphical representation. In this instance graphs are an alternative to numerical analysis, but for the majority of purposes graphs should be used in conjunction with other forms of analysis. Nowhere is this more true than when using graphs to identify price anomalies. Figure 4.6 shows that at November 1994 there was a clear divergence between the INVESCO Korea share price and the warrant price which had previously exhibited a fairly close relationship. Your immediate reaction might be that the warrants had failed to react to the shares' upward movement and should be bought. But consider the technical position. Even after the decline in the warrant price, the gearing was a moderate 1.8 times, yet the capital fulcrum point was well above average at 14.53 per cent. This suggested that the weak performance

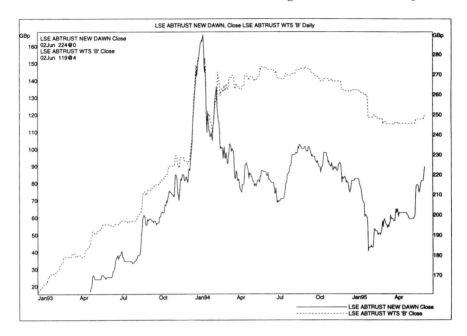

Figure 4.5 Abtrust New Dawn investment trust shares and 'B' warrants, January 1993 to June 1995
(source: Reuters)

may be an overdue correction and that the devaluation may persist. Fundamental considerations back up this reasoning, especially as high expectations encouraged by the strong performance of the Asian region in 1993 had been disappointed by the subsequent performance. The longer this poor performance continued, the less likely it was that the warrants would be able to sustain their high valuation, which was at a clear premium to the market. Technical and fundamental considerations did not support the chart hypothesis.

The outcome was, not surprisingly, that the technical analysis was correct. As Figure 4.7 shows, shares in the INVESCO Korea Trust fell by 25p over the following six months, but the warrants slumped by even more in absolute terms. The 29p fall in the warrants cost holders a painful 35 per cent of their investment.

As the double-axis graph goes some way to meeting several different needs, it must be considered both a useful and versatile instrument of analysis – if used with care. Double-axis graphs can easily mislead, and particular attention needs to be paid to the choice of axis limits. Inappropriate scales will produce graphs which are at best confusing and at worst subject to complete misinterpretation.

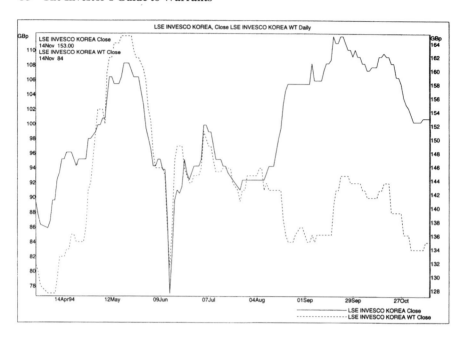

Figure 4.6 INVESCO Korea Trust shares and warrants, March to November 1994 (source: Reuters)

SHARE-WARRANT SCATTER GRAPHS

Using the same data which was used to construct the double-axis graphs, the share price may be plotted against the warrant price for each day, week or month to produce a simple scatter graph. Each point which is plotted represents the relative position of the shares and warrants at a given point in time, and the overall effect is to illustrate the strength or weakness of that relationship. Should the points be scattered in a random fashion then the relationship is weak; should the points be clusterered along an identifiable line then the relationship is strong.

A 'line of best fit' may be drawn on each scatter diagram to help with this observation. Points beneath the line represent below-average valuations for that warrant, and vice versa, again enabling the observer to highlight possible cases for investigation. More specifically, the line can be used for quantifying the apparent undervaluation or overvaluation. An equation for this purpose may be derived from the line of best fit using regression analysis (see Appendix A). The resulting equation for calculating the warrant price (y) for any given share price (x) can provide a useful back-of-the-envelope method for valuing warrants, although it must be stressed that this is a very basic measure. It is not based upon

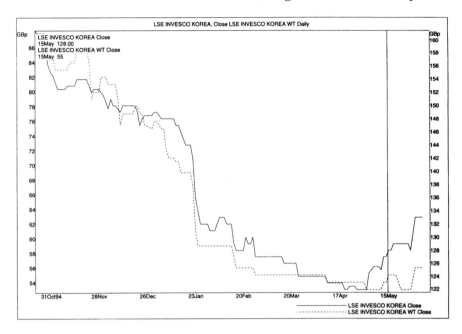

Figure 4.7 INVESCO Korea Trust shares and warrants, September 1994 to May 1995
(source: Reuters)

any fundamental or technical valuation factors, but merely on the past performance of the share and warrant prices. Further, the result of this equation is likely
to overstate the warrant price slightly since the relationship between the share
price and the warrant price will change as time value diminishes.

With these caveats in mind, the equations can still yield some useful information, particularly when the share price and warrant price are closely related
(where the correlation coefficient 'R' is close to 1). Where R is lower than 0.85
the equation is of limited use. In the case of the Fleming Emerging Markets
Investment Trust, where R = 0.99, a share price of 180p yields a theoretical warrant price of 102p from the equation regression analysis (see Figure 4.8). The
equation can be helpful when asking 'what if' questions. For example, what if
Fleming Emerging Markets shares suddenly rose by 25 per cent? How far might
the warrants fall if the shares slid by 20 per cent? It can be sensible to estimate
gains or using regression analysis, although these must be taken as a rough guide
only, and it can be useful to compare answers calculated in this way with those
derived from implied gearing.

The principal limitation of this approach is that the share-warrant relationship
is not linear over time. Warrants will have a greater value relative to the shares
early in their lives, when there is plenty of 'time value' remaining, but as the

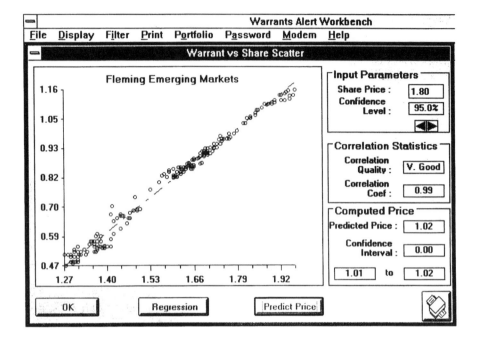

Figure 4.8 Fleming Emerging Markets investment trust – scatter graph
(source: Warrants Alert Workbench)

premium disappears, so the line of best fit will tend to overestimate the warrant value.

SCHEMATIC WARRANT CURVE

The next refinement from the basic scatter graph is to adopt a schematic adaptation which takes account of the fact that warrant premiums tend to fall to zero when the warrants are a long way 'in the money'. The graph makes use of 'normalized' warrant and share prices, both of which are divided by the exercise price to enable direct comparison. A warrant achieves intrinsic value when the normalized share price reaches 100 (i.e., it reaches the exercise price), and this intrinsic value is thereafter represented by the straight 'parity line' (DE) along which the warrant has zero premium. The schematic warrant curve (AB) shows that warrants tend to approach this parity line as they reach high levels of intrinsic value (see Figure 4.9).

Interesting though this is, a single curve will rarely provide a good fit for individual warrant data. The 'premium track' will shift downwards as time value

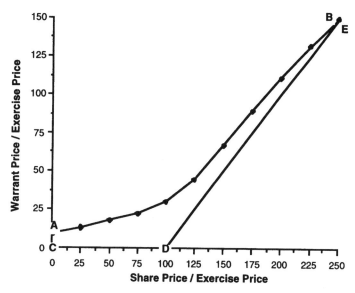

Figure 4.9 Schematic warrant curve

diminishes* and the value of the warrant at final expiry will lie along the line CDE – that is, along the line CD if it expires worthless, and along line DE if it is 'in the money'. For this reason the basic curve is of little predictive value if used with data points from a long period of time, since the data may actually represent a series of curves. Equally, it is of little use with a small number of clustered data points, so prices should ideally be entered daily as part of a 12-month moving data series. The work involved may deter all but the most serious of investors from using these graphs.

THE 30 PER CENT CURVE

A similar theoretical approach lies behind the 30 per cent curve, which was developed to illustrate an 'observed behavioural relationship' between share prices and warrant prices at various levels. Keenly promoted by Donald Cornelius, a well-known stockbroker who specialized in warrants from 1970 to

---

* The premium track may also shift in response to a number of other influences, most notably changing market sentiment. Bullish conditions will encourage higher premiums and vice versa. Other factors include the status of the underlying shares, the income forgone on the shares, and the interest rate obtainable on uninvested funds.

1990, when he retired from James Capel, the 30 per cent curve differs in two key aspects from the schematic curve above. First, the curve is derived from actual market data, and second, it is applied to the market as a whole rather than to individual warrants. The result is a visual overview which provides some ready differentiation between highly valued and modestly valued warrants.

As with the schematic curve, both the warrant price and share price are normalized by dividing them by the exercise price, which allows for direct comparisons. The results are plotted on a scatter graph, and a curve fitted to the data. Warrants with less than two years of life remaining are excluded, since the premium tends to fall steadily to zero at expiry.

The resulting curve is known as the 30 per cent curve because when the underlying share is at parity, a warrant with several years of life will normally stand at a price equal to approximately 30 per cent of the exercise price*. If the share price rises above the exercise price then the warrant will acquire *pro rata* intrinsic value, but the premium payable above this, the 'time value', will decline. From 30 per cent it will come down to around 15 per cent when the share price has risen to 150 per cent of the exercise price (warrant price comprises 50 per cent intrinsic value plus 15 per cent premium = 65 per cent of exercise price). Even further along the curve, when the share is more than twice the exercise price the warrant will probably not be far from its intrinsic value with little if any time value. This is because gearing is likely to be minimal at this stage, and investors will not be prepared to pay a significant premium.

Figure 4.10 shows how the 30 per cent curve applies to the market as a whole during May 1995. The points beneath the curve represent relatively cheap warrants (which may be numbered for identification), while those above the curve appear relatively expensive against the rest of the market. Of the other warrants identified as undervalued by this method, most accord with the findings of traditional technical analysis, suggesting that the curve has some use, either as a preliminary screen for eliminating overvalued warrants, or as a check for the results of technical analysis.

As ever though, there are some weaknesses in this approach. The main caveat is the failure to take full account of the time remaining to maturity, which means that the curve is biased against long-dated warrants. These are far more likely to appear relatively expensive, even though the additional 'time value' may be entirely justified. The fact that warrants expiring in the years 1995 and 2005 are treated equally in the graph means that some care is needed in interpreting the results. The graph is, after all, there to be used, not to dictate.

---

* This level is historically around 30 per cent, although it may vary. In bullish conditions it may reach 35 per cent, but in weaker market conditions only 25 per cent. It is an empirical measure, and therefore reflects the state of investor confidence.

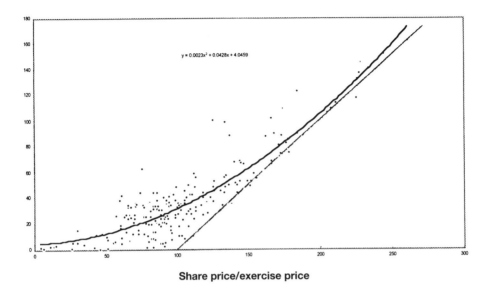

$$y = 0.0023x^2 + 0.0428x + 4.0459$$

Share price/exercise price

Figure 4.10 The 30 per cent curve (for data May 1995)

THE GEARING RATIO CURVE

A similar graph which is found in some warrants literature is the gearing ratio curve (see Figure 4.11). This uses the same data as the 30 per cent curve for the horizontal axis. On the vertical axis, however, it is the gearing which is plotted (share price divided by warrant price) instead of the normalized warrant price (warrant price divided by exercise price). This is subtly different. Less subtle is the fact that points above the line now represent cheap warrants and vice versa, because the warrant price is now the numerator instead of the denominator. This also explains the opposite slope of the curve.

The rationale behind this graph is relatively straightforward, and rests with the need for high gearing to compensate investors for the risk of holding warrants which are a long way out of the money. The greater the gearing for any given parity ratio, the better the value. As with the 30 per cent curve, the main problem is that the basic graph fails to take account of the varying time to expiry. Whereas it is quite reasonable, for example, to expect a warrant with ten years of life remaining to be well 'out of the money' with modest gearing, a much higher level of gearing will be required to entice investors to hold a similar warrant with only three years of life remaining. For this reason it is sensible to plot different

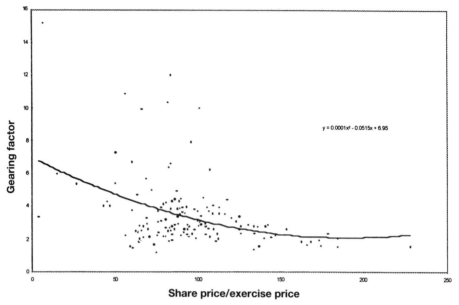

Figure 4.11 Gearing ratio curve (for data May 1995; maturities beyond 1998)

curves for different maturities, which may be divided into less than three years, three to six years, and six years and over.

The outcome is again that the results match the technical data reasonably well, although there are a few exceptions.

THE CFP/GEARING SCATTER GRAPH

Finally, the CFP/gearing scatter graph provides what is probably the closest graphic approximation of the technical approach to analysis, plotting the two most important factors against each other (see Figure 4.12). In basic terms, the chart plots the major benefit of warrants (gearing) against the major cost measured in a consistent way (the capital fulcrum point). Clearly the graph should then show which warrants offer a relatively positive combination and which do not. It is the points beneath the line of best fit which represent undervalued warrants, as investors will seek high gearing and a low CFP. One outstanding warrant on this basis is Jersey Phoenix Trust, also selected as an undervalued warrant by technical analysis.

In addition to differentiating between warrants, this graph is also helpful for the visual understanding of the two variables. It is clear to see the cluster of warrants around the average gearing level of 3 times, but while the average CFP is 8.52 per cent, this is influenced by a few high examples and there are a considerable number of warrants below this level. Again, the discerning investor

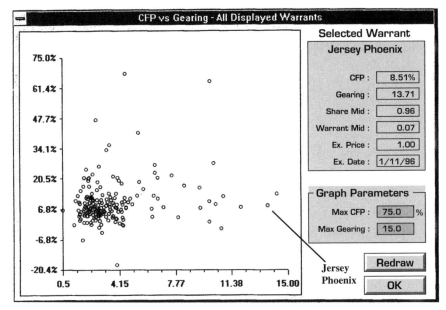

Figure 4.12 Gearing/CFP graph (for data May 1995; extreme valuations removed)
(*source: Warrants Alert Workbench*

looking for good value will see that warrants with a CFP below 7 per cent or 8 per cent are relatively numerous, while the highly-geared warrants with gearing over eight times are a rarer sight.

CONCLUSION

If graphs are used sensibly, and you are aware of their limitations, then they must be a useful addition to your analytical armoury. They can assist other forms of evaluation, and very occasionally serve as alternatives. Useful results cannot be acquired without effort though, and the compilation, manipulation and input of data can be very time-consuming. Furthermore, a considerable amount of re-drawing will be necessary if charts are kept by hand: for many practical purposes a computer is almost essential and of considerable benefit if you have access to 'smart' graphics software which can select axes automatically and calculate the lines of best fit accurately.

It is for the individual to decide whether the time and expense can be justified by the results. The only published sources are the *Warrants Alert Chart Books*, which plot double-axis graphs for 145 warrants, using around 65,000 share and warrant prices as the source data. Software such as *Warrants Alert Workbench* may also be used for generating graphs.

A few final words about the use of graphs. If you find that they help, or that one particular type of graph provides you with some insight, then use them as you see fit. This chapter sought to present an overview of the types of graphic approaches which have been developed for warrant trading, but you should not feel confined to using them in the precise formats explained. Create your own, experiment, throw the received wisdom out of the window if it fails to be of assistance. Graphs are your servants, not your masters.

"Technical analysis and fundamental analysis should always work hand-in-hand, as indeed should complex analysis and common sense."

5

ASSESSING WARRANTS PART 3 – COMPLEX ANALYSIS

For the majority of private investors and for many stockbrokers the level of analysis contained within the previous two chapters will be sufficient. Since most activity within the UK warrants market is based upon a relatively simplistic approach to selection, it is not necessary to undertake highly sophisticated calculations in order to identify the anomalies and opportunities which commonly arise. The existence of such pricing inefficiencies reflects the embryonic status of the UK market which has yet to mature and to attract the more skilful and experienced professional investors who will undertake arbitrage activities to remove discrepancies. Until then, the result is that even moderately well-informed investors can find themselves in a very strong position.

As the market develops, however, pricing will undoubtedly become more efficient, and the basic analytical techniques may well be surpassed. In order to take full advantage of the continuing opportunities offered by the developing market it may become necessary to explore more complex forms of analysis which incorporate the primary factors such as gearing and premium into an overall scheme. This chapters considers the development of more sophisticated and integrated models which should be of interest to larger investors and to professional advisers. Some of the text is unavoidably complicated, but this chapter may be skipped by those who find it difficult.

THEORETICAL BEGINNINGS: GIGUERE

There is no simple, magic formula which can be applied to evaluate warrants. This must be the prime conclusion from any study of early warrant pricing theory, which centred around the warrant price as a simple function of the parity ratio between the share price and the exercise price. This was the approach of Giguere (1958), who postulated a simple relationship between the warrant price and share price. His model yields an appealingly simple equation, which may be written as follows:

$$warrant\ price = \frac{parity\ ratio^2}{4} \times exercise\ price$$

where   parity ratio is ≤ 2

or

warrant price = (parity ratio -1) $\times$ exercise price

where   parity ratio is ≥ 2

This looks almost too simple to be of any practical use, but the result is a warrant curve (see Figure 5.1) which bears remarkable similarity to the 30 per cent curve outlined in Chapter 4, except that the Giguere curve is a 25 per cent curve. As such it is of some value, and has identified the property of warrants a long way 'in the money' losing their premium, but it is prey to some key criticisms. In particular, no account is taken of the time to maturity, yet it is clear that a warrant with ten years of life remaining should be valued differently from one with a week to run, particularly if the warrant has no intrinsic value. For this reason it needs to be applied with care.

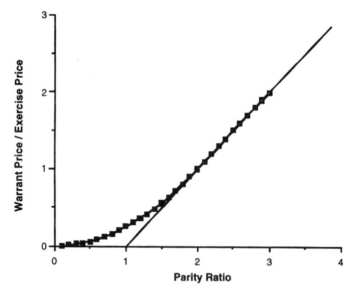

Fig 5.1: The Giguere warrant curve

In short, investors should not be lured by the ease of computation. Whilst Giguere made a valuable contribution by identifying the warrant curve, it would be impractical to apply the formulae directly to individual warrants. Kassouf (1967) went one step further by acknowledging that the position of the warrant curve will be determined by a number of variables including the time to expiry, but again the early theory is more instructive than it is practical.

REGRESSION ANALYSIS

Just as Giguere concentrated on the single feature of parity, so there are other analytical approaches which concentrate on a single feature of warrants. One of these is regression analysis, which concentrates solely upon the past performance of the equity as a guide to the future. Regression analysis works very simply by extrapolating from past growth to predict the warrant price at final expiry. This may be shown graphically with a line of best fit, or by simple calculation:

EXAMPLE

Widget plc share price 100p; warrants 30p; exercise price 95p; 5 years remaining; interest rate 11 per cent.

Performance of Widget plc shares in each of last five years = +30.7 per cent; –16.8 per cent; +12.2 per cent; +4.4 per cent; +20.0 per cent. Average growth = 8.86 per cent per annum. Extrapolate this for next five years and share price rises to 153p. Predicted warrant price at final expiry = share price of 153p – exercise price of 95p = 58p. This is a return of 93 per cent compared with 53 per cent for the shares.

The main objection to this approach will be familiar to any investor who has read literature relating to stockmarket investments. *Past performance is not necessarily a guide to the future.* This may be a hackneyed phrase, but it is true. Neither shares nor warrants grow in a predictable manner, whether linear or exponential, and future growth may differ markedly from that exhibited in the past. Furthermore, while regression analysis may have some application in determining and extrapolating from long-term growth rates, the very nature of warrants means that this is unlikely to be possible. The majority of UK warrants come to the market attached to new issues without any historical price record at all, and of those already in existence the average time to expiry at around three and a three-quarter years is less than one short-term economic cycle. As such the remaining time may be spread over an upturn or a downturn in economic activity, and it is extremely doubtful whether long-term price performance has any meaningful predictive value in all but a handful of cases. Basic regression analysis is too simple for practical use, although it may be used as a starting point for a predictive facility based upon macroeconomic, cyclical or sectoral reasoning. Even these more complex approaches may still be flawed for individual company issues, but for generic warrants such as those on market indices, currencies and interest rates the approach may have some validity.

PRESENT VALUE DISCOUNTING

In the event of a more developed approach providing some reasonable outcomes, the regression analysis will provide a predicted value for the warrants at final expiry. It will not predict a fair price for the current time: for this a further refinement is needed. One possible answer lies with present value discounting (PVD) which introduces the interest rate as a method of calculating a fair current warrant price from a predicted future price.

The concept underlying this theory is a simple one, namely that money available to the investor now will be worth more in five years' time, since it can be invested in a risk-free instrument providing a positive rate of interest. Working backwards, in order to derive the present value of a future sum of money it must be discounted by that rate of interest, as follows:

$$Present\ discounted\ value = \frac{predicted\ value\ at\ expiry}{(1+r)^y}$$

where r = annual percentage rate of interest; and y = years of life remaining

and using the example above:

$$Present\ discounted\ value = \frac{58p}{(1 + 0.11)^5}$$

*Present discounted value = **34.42p***

In this case, as the current value of the warrant is beneath the present discounted value, then an investment in the warrants would outperform the risk-free return available from an interest-bearing account. Of course, given the high levels of risk which can be involved in warrant investment (see Chapter 6), you may decide that the extra return predicted from the warrants needs to exceed the risk-free return by some margin before it can be justified. With this proviso, the compound result from the regression analysis and the PVD for the example provided is that the warrants are likely to provide the best return ahead of cash in second place and the equity in third place. Once again, the benefit of gearing is paramount.

BLACK-SCHOLES FORMULA

The interest rate is incorporated in a more sophisticated way in the Black-Scholes formula, the most widely used mathematical model for evaluating all forms of options. Formulated in 1973 by Fischer Black and Myron Scholes, this formula has become the benchmark against which all other pricing models are judged. There has been some argument over whether this and other option pricing models may be applied to longer-term instruments such as warrants, but it must be recognized that some market practitioners will be using Black-Scholes as the basis for modified calculations. Even for sceptics, therefore, the formula is of some importance.

The Black-Scholes formula is as follows:

$$Valuation = S\,N(d_1) - \frac{e}{2.71828^{ry}} \times N(d_2)$$

where

$$d_1 = \frac{ln\,(S/e) + (r + 0.5v^2)y}{v\,\sqrt{y}}$$

$$d_2 = \frac{ln\,(S/e) + (r - 0.5v^2)y}{v\,\sqrt{y}}$$

where S = share price; e = exercise price; $N(d)$ = normal distribution function of d; r = rate of interest; y = time to expiry in years; v = volatility; $ln(S/e)$ = natural logarithm of (S/e).

EXAMPLE

Widget plc share price 100p; exercise price 110p; warrant price 40p; 5 years remaining to expiry; volatility 50 per cent; rate of interest 10 per cent.

$$Valuation = 100 \times N(d_1) - \frac{110}{2.71828^{(0.1 \times 5)}} \times N(d_2)$$

$$d_1 = \frac{ln\,(100/110) + (0.1 + (0.5 \times 0.5^2)) \times 5}{0.5 \times \sqrt{5}} = \frac{-0.0953 + 1.125}{1.118} = 0.921 \; N = 0.82$$

$$d_2 = \frac{ln\,(100/110) + (0.1 - (0.5 \times 0.5^2)) \times 5}{0.5 \times \sqrt{5}} = \frac{-0.0953 + -0.125}{1.118} = -0.197 \; N = 0.42$$

$$Valuation = 100 \times 0.82 - \frac{110}{1.6487} \times 0.42 \;\; = 82 - 28 = \mathbf{54p}$$

For the purposes of this formula it is assumed that volatility is known and constant, that the interest rate is constant, that options will not be exercised early, and that the underlying shares pay no dividends. In practice the longer time to maturity offered by warrants will infringe upon these assumptions and casts doubt upon the validity of the results achieved. Further, the results from the formula, when presented in unmodified form, tend to show that almost all UK equity warrants are undervalued – a conclusion which is of little practical value. It is clear that if the Black-Scholes formula is to be used at all, then it should at least be adapted in some way to fit the requirements of the warrants market. It may then provide a useful check against other methods of analysis, and may be used to confirm or deny valuations derived in other ways.

IMPLIED VOLATILITY

An alternative approach favoured by many analysts is to use the formula to derive what is known as 'implied volatility'. Instead of attempting to derive a fair value for the options or warrants from the standard set of inputs including historical volatility, the current warrant price is substituted into the formula and volatility is omitted. It is then possible to work backwards through the equation to calculate a figure for volatility implied by the current warrant price. The reason for this is that many observers consider the assumption of constant historical volatility to be a prime weakness in the model, especially as the formula is highly sensitive to small changes in volatility. By re-organizing the formula to make volatility the unknown variable, the result provides a better measure of relative value. If the implied volatility is lower than the historical volatility and/or your expectations of volatility then the warrant is relatively cheap, and vice versa. Using the example above, the implied volatility of the warrant at the market price of 40p is just 26 per cent. As this is below the historical volatility of 50 per cent, the warrant is undervalued according to the model – a result confirmed by the 'straight' use of the formula which produced a theoretical price of 54p against 40p in the market.

Implied volatility is a useful and valid measure for comparing different warrants – those with the lowest implied volatilities will be the best value – and it has the added advantage that it can be calculated from any model which incorporates volatility as a variable. The Black-Scholes formula is more widely applied than any other, but there are other pricing models such as Cox-Rubenstein which may also be used.

THE EXTENDED BLACK-SCHOLES MODEL

With many of these models it is difficult to know when to stop adding variables which are of less importance, but it is certainly possible to extend models for greater levels of sophistication and accuracy. The Black-Scholes model outlined below has been extended to handle dilution, which can be a particularly relevant factor where a warrant may have had a long life and may expire a long way 'in the money'.

$$Valuation = \frac{ns}{ns + nw} \times \left[\frac{(ns \times s) + (nw \times w)}{ns} \times N(d_1) - \frac{e}{2.71828^{ry}} \times N(d_2) \right]$$

$$where \ d_1 = \frac{ln \ [(ns \times s) + (nw \times w)/(ns \times e)] + (r + 0.5v^2)y}{v \sqrt{y}}$$

$$and \ d_2 = \frac{ln \ [(ns \times s) + (nw \times w)/(ns \times e)] + (r - 0.5^2)y}{v \sqrt{y}}$$

where ns = number of shares in issue; nw = number of warrants in issue; s = share price; w = warrant price; e = exercise price; r = rate of interest; y = time remaining in years; v = volatility; N = normal distribution function.

Using the example used for the basic Black-Scholes formula above, one would intuitively expect the forecast warrant price to be lower once dilution was incorporated into the model, as is shown by reworking the example above.

EXAMPLE

Widget plc share price 100p; exercise price 110p; warrant price 40p; five years remaining to expiry; volatility 50 per cent; rate of interest 10 per cent; 10m shares in issue; 2m warrants in issue.

$$Valuation = \frac{10m}{10m + 2m} \times \left[\frac{(10m \times 100) + (2m \times 40)}{10m} \times N(d_1) - \frac{110}{2.71828^{(0.1 \times 5)}} \times N(d_2) \right]$$

$$= 0.833 \times \left[\frac{1080m}{10m} \times N(d_1) - \frac{110}{1.6487} \times N(d_2) \right]$$

$$= 0.833 \times [\ 108 \times N(d_1) - 66.72 \times N(d_2)]$$

$$d_1 = \frac{ln \ [10.8m/(11m)] + [0.1 + (0.5 \times 0.5^2) \times 5]}{0.5 \times \sqrt{5}}$$

$$d_1 = \frac{ln \ [.981818] + 1.125}{1.118}$$

$$d_1 = \frac{-0.018349 + 1.125}{1.118}$$

$$d_1 = 0.989849 \quad N = 0.84$$

$$d_2 = \frac{-0.018349 - 0.125}{1.118}$$

$$d_2 = -0.12822 \quad N = 0.45$$

$$Valuation = \ = 0.833 \times [(108 \times 0.84) - (66.72 \times 0.45)]$$
$$= 0.833 \times [90.72 - 30.024]$$
$$= \textbf{50.56p}$$

It is important to realize, however, that no matter how powerful a predictive mass of equations may appear, no algebraic model will be perfect, and caution should be exercised when considering the results. Whereas algebra can have a useful role to play in defining the relationships between variables, it is no panacea and cannot always provide the answers. Too often algebra is used as a way of edifying the analyst, of proving his own erudition without actually achieving very much. It is easy to fall into the trap of explaining something in detailed algebraic terminology, only to end up with a solution which is no more than common sense.

DELTA

The wealth of literature on futures and options yields a number of useful measures which may be applied with equal validity to warrants. One key indicator which warrant investors have only recently started to use is the 'delta' which can be used in two distinct ways to aid understanding.

As any mathematician will tell you, delta usually refers to a rate of change, and in this context it refers to the change in a warrant price expected from a given change in the underlying stock price. In essence the delta provides an estimate of the true gearing or leverage which has actually been observed in the market. Fortunately investors need not enter into more tortuous calculations to find the delta – it is simply $N(d1)$ in the Black-Scholes formula above, or 0.82 in the example. This means that for every 1p change in the share price we would expect a 0.82p change (in the same direction) in the warrant price. The delta will always fall between 0 and 1 for 'call' warrants in normal circumstances, and between 0 and –1 for 'put' warrants. To have such a precise measure of the true leverage is clearly very helpful for investors seeking to hedge investments accurately or just to ensure that they are securing the greatest potential for their cash outlay.

Perhaps more interestingly, the delta may also be used as a measure of the likelihood of a particular warrant finishing in the money. This is of enormous importance when considering a warrant with a short time to expiry where the share price may be hovering around the exercise price, or where investors may be struggling to decide whether to exercise a warrant or sell in the market. To be able to quantify the risk of such a warrant expiring 'out of the money', effectively worthless, is of considerable value, as Table 5.1 demonstrates (Thornton Asian warrants, for example, were given a 66 per cent chance of finishing in the money).

There are two interesting points to note from this table. The first is that volatility is clearly important and that the parity ratio fails to tell the whole story. Hence Lucas Industries warrants have a lower delta than Paribas French 'A' warrants in spite of

Name	Share price	Exercise price	Parity ratio	Expiry	Delta
Greenfriar Investment Co	387p	334p	1.16	1 April	1.00
Sphere Investment Trust	33.5p	50p	0.67	5 May	0.03
Thornton Asian Emerging	101p	100p	1.01	17 May	0.66
Pacific Assets Trust	442p	100p	4.42	31 May	1.00
Ibstock	80p	162p	0.49	30 June	0.00
Lucas Industries	190p	172p	1.10	30 June	0.79
Paribas French 'A'	115p	110p	1.05	30 June	0.88
Throgmorton 1000 Smallest	127p	100p	1.27	1 July	1.00
Anglo-Eastern Plantations	107p	86p	1.24	31 July	0.89
German Smaller Companies	180p	100p	1.80	31 August	1.00
BTR 1994/95	311p	222p	1.40	15 October	1.00
Navan Resources	135p	30p	4.50	23 October	1.00
North American Gas Inv Trust	70p	100p	0.70	31 October	0.01
Pacific Horizon Trust	38.5p	50p	0.77	3 Nov	0.03
Baillie Gifford Japan	599p	655p	0.91	30 Nov	0.34
Mediterranean Fund	259p	318.79p	0.81	31 December	0.01
Raglan Property	32p	30p	1.07	31 December	0.75
United Energy	14p	40p	0.35	31 December	0.00

Table 5.1 Deltas for Expiring UK warrants, February 1995

a higher parity ratio, because Lucas is more volatile and therefore more likely to fall below the exercise price. Second, it is notable that the results are polarized, with many deltas either at 1.0 or approaching zero. This is because the expiry dates are near. The delta will tend to move towards these figures as warrants mature, and at the very end of a warrant's life the delta will of course equal 1.0 or zero, as it will be known with certainty whether the warrant will expire 'in the money' or 'out of the money'. A table of warrants with several years of maturity remaining will tend to show a far more scattered range of deltas, although it will depend upon the subset chosen. As a warrant moves further 'into the money', its delta will approach 1.0, and as it moves further out of the money, the delta will approach zero.

Whilst the delta will not itself generate a buying or selling signal, it will provide a fair appraisal of the position which enables a sensible decision to be made. Later in this book we explain how the delta provides an extra indication of risk, with particular reference to the American warrants market.

COMPUTING A FIGURE FOR LEVERAGE

Using the delta it is possible to define the rate of change, and when this is coupled with gearing – the amount of additional exposure – it is possible to compute a figure for the actual amount of leverage. Leverage is what many investors mistakenly believe gearing measures, namely the degree of extra gain or loss likely from a given investment. Leverage is calculated simply by multiplying the delta by the gearing:

Leverage = delta x *gearing*

EXAMPLE

Fleming Chinese Investment Trust warrants 36p; shares 71p
Delta = 0.80
Gearing = 1.97
Leverage = 0.80 x *1.97 = 1.58*

Using this example, an investor comparing the merits of an equal investment in the shares or warrants of Fleming Chinese would calculate that a warrant investment would be likely to change by a multiple of 1.58 of that same investment in the shares. For example, a 10 per cent rise in the share price would imply a 15.8 per cent rise in the warrants, a result which can be worked through:

10 per cent rise in the share price of 71p = 7.1p
Delta = 0.80, so warrant price moves by (7.1p x *0.80) = 5.68p*
5.68p / 36p = 15.8 per cent rise

Computing the leverage is a tremendously powerful predictive tool which helps to provide an accurate insight into the likely movement of a warrant. Most investors using gearing as a proxy for leverage will overestimate the likely change in the warrant price for a given share price movement – an error which tends to exacerbate the natural tendency for prices to overshoot. In bullish market conditions when prices are rising, investors will tend to be too optimistic about the potential for warrant prices to rise, and will buy them up to unrealistically high levels. During bearish periods, investors will tend to overestimate the likely declines, providing opportunities for better-informed investors able to form a more accurate view.

COMPUTER MODELLING

Complex algebra is also prone to error, and anyone intending to progress much beyond the CFP will find life much easier with a computer. Even relatively complicated mathematical models can be transferred quite easily into a spreadsheet which will then provide quick results. Modern spreadsheet models can run through hundreds of calculations in the blink of an eye. Another benefit of spreadsheet analysis is that it allows you to ask 'what if?' questions, enabling you to see the outcomes from various changes in different variables. Implied volatility can, for example, be reached in this way through the process of trial and error, which may be simpler for occasional use than re-arranging the formula. Moreover, the ability to 'play' with the variables in a spreadsheet can be an excellent educational method, as the cross-relationships and interaction between different variables become familiar through constant illustration.

Much of the analysis detailed in the last three chapters lends itself readily to spreadsheet analysis, at once removing much of the drudgery of calculation and achieving a degree of sophistication which manual techniques are unlikely to match. Little data input is involved: the price of the shares and the warrants, plus the terms of conversion, is usually all that is required. More effort is required to design the model, and again it is too easy to concentrate on aesthetically pleasing formulae or to over-elaborate the calculations, without paying sufficient heed to the usage. The best models tend to be those which are developed on an *ad hoc* basis to meet analytical needs.

It is difficult to identify many common strands between spreadsheet or other computer models, since there are as many variations as there are computer modellers. Most address the need not only to analyse the basic data for single warrants, but also to incorporate those findings into a more general model estimating the market curve and including parameters for the general level of market sentiment. It is a recurrent downfall of the less sophisticated models that the actual market valuation is ignored, with the result that technical predictions bear little relation to subsequent price movements.

THE *WARRANTS ALERT* COMPUTER MODEL

The *Warrants Alert* newsletter uses an adjustive market-related technical model which simplifies a complex string of calculations to arrive at a compound 'cheapness' indicator for all UK equity warrants. The different processes combined in the model fall neatly into eight stages, as follows:

Stage 1: Data input

The model requires the one-off input of the exercise price, final expiry date, and number of shares exercisable per warrant (usually one), and then the regular input of the variable data. On each occasion when the spreadsheet is updated the latest date, warrant prices, underlying share prices, and exchange rates (for those warrants denominated in overseas currencies) must be entered.

Stage 2: Calculation of the basic measures of warrant value.

Once the initial data is in the program it is a simple matter for the computer to calculate the basic measures required for evaluation, namely:

1 parity ratio
2 premium
3 break-even point
4 CFP
5 gearing
6 implied leverage
7 risk rating
8 historical volatility (extracted from data stored in the model)

Stage 3

The third stage is to amalgamate the results obtained above into a compound indicator according to a standard set of weightings. If gearing is considered important, for example, then it will achieve a high relative weighting, whilst a subsidiary and less important factor such as volatility will achieve a lower weighting. This is clearly a critical part of the evaluation process, and three points need to be made about the weightings which are assigned.

First, while the set of weightings will be standard among all warrants, they may be changed over time and altered by experience. Should subsequent performances show, for example, that warrants with a high parity ratio are being overvalued, then the weighting assigned to the parity ratio may be reduced, and vice versa.

Second, and in a similar way, the weightings may be altered to suit market conditions and aims. In bullish market conditions and when the intention is to seek warrants which may produce some large short-term gains, then the weighting assigned to gearing might rise; conversely, during less positive periods when investors are more concerned with hedging then the parity ratio and CFP may be of greater importance.

Third and finally, the *Warrants Alert* model actually incorporates three different sets of weightings, designed to eliminate anomalies which may arise from a single set applied to a broad range of warrants with widely differing technical positions.

Stage 4

The model next calculates an average of the three weighted compound indicators, and compares this result with a similar average calculated for the market as a whole. This is an important step because it places all warrant valuations firmly into the context of the market and the prevailing investment conditions. If the compound indicator for an individual warrant has a higher rating than for the market as a whole, then that warrant is relatively cheap, and vice versa.

Stage 5

A process of iteration is used for the model to 'guess' at a warrant price which will be more consistent with the average market weighting. If a warrant appears relatively cheap, then the model will guess a higher price (within defined tolerances), and the model will automatically recalculate all of the primary variables to reach another weighted compound indicator based upon the price guessed.

Stage 6

At this point the weighted compound indicator is adjusted again according to an 'augmentation/diminution' factor which takes account of the fundamental position of the underlying security. Should the equity have a strong image, a low dividend payment, a good recent performance record, positive fundamental prospects, and a high level of likely investment demand, then the indicator may be adjusted upwards. Conversely, a high income investment trust with a dull capital gains record will generally be downgraded. Again, there are some warrants which always look cheap on technical grounds – they are simply not favoured by the market. It is important to recognize this phenomenon and to incorporate it into the augmentation/diminution factor: if the subsequent price performance differs systematically from the unadjusted result, then the error can be eliminated at this stage.

Stage 7

The iterative process of estimation and recalculation continues, and each guess will become progressively more accurate until the model reaches a valuation which is consistent with the average market rating, subject to the augmentation or diminution incorporated at Stage 6. This is the fair price calculated by the model, and it may be compared with the existing market price to gauge whether the warrant is currently undervalued or overvalued on technical grounds.

Stage 8

The model finally checks the result achieved against an adapted Black-Scholes valuation, again adjusted to the market. Should the Black-Scholes result differ markedly from that derived from the standard model, then the technical position may be scrutinized more carefully.

The final result is a spreadsheet which takes up 1.2 megabytes of memory, uses 85,000 separate cells, and which undertakes around 400,000 different calculations each time a full market review is sought. And it works. No model is infallible, of course, but the results of the *Warrants Alert* model have proved consistently encouraging over a 70-month period. Over this time the newsletter has

selected a list of undervalued and overvalued warrants from the model each
month, and the 'undervalued' warrants have outperformed the 'overvalued'
warrants in no fewer than 59 out of the 70 months to date. This is a success rate
of 84 per cent.

This computer model has a very firm anchor in reality, but where many fail is
in the design which is centred around some esoteric notion of absolute analytical
worth. When considering such models it is useful to remember the 'GIGO'
theory: garbage in, garbage out. If a computer model is programmed with unrealistic parameters and expectations then it is not likely to produce sensible
answers – the worth of a computer model cannot exceed the understanding of the
person who wrote it. What it can do is to automate the number-crunching part of
the analytical process, sort a huge amount of data into a coherent structure, and
provide valuable suggestions for your consideration. As such it has a very important role to play in modern warrant evaluation.

THE PERFECT WARRANT-CASH MIX

In addition to selecting the most attractive warrants it is possible in theory to calculate a mix of cash and warrants which will always equal or better the performance of the equity – whether it rises or falls. This is the 'perfect warrant-cash
mix' which may be calculated for every warrant. In order to make this calculation it is necessary to estimate leverage, something which is most readily
achieved using either the delta and gearing, or the linear regression analysis
described for the scatter graph in the previous chapter. Once the slope of the line
of best fit is calculated, then the number of warrants per share necessary for the
perfect warrant-cash mix is ascertained very simply by dividing 1 by this slope:

$$Holding\ of\ warrants\ per\ share = \frac{1}{slope}$$

EXAMPLE

Imaginary Investment Trust

Line of best fit = y = 0.487 x –13.152

$$Holding\ of\ warrants\ per\ share = \frac{1}{0.487}$$

$$= 2.053.$$

*This means that the perfect warrant-cash mix involves the investor buying
2.053 warrants instead of one share. To express this relationship as a percentage, consider the alternative to a share worth 100p. According to the line*

of best fit formula, the warrant price should be:

$x = (0.487 \times 100) - 13.152$
  $= 35.548p$

and multiplying this by the holding of warrants per share gives the amount to be invested as a percentage:

$35.548p \times 2.053 = 72.99\%$

In other words, an investor seeking the perfect warrant-cash mix would invest £730 in warrants for every £1,000 normally invested in the shares, keeping the remaining £270 in cash. For as long as the line of best fit remains a reliable indicator of the relationship between the share price and the warrant price, then this warrant-cash mix will always at least match or better the equity investment, no matter what the performance.

This outcome, which seems almost too good to be true, may be proved by longhand calculation of various equity performances (see Table 5.2).

Share price (p)	Warrant price* (p)	Value of £1,000 invested in shares (£)	Value of £730 invested in warrants (£)	Cash (£)	Warrant + cash mix (£)
0	0	0	0	270	270
10	0	100	0	270	270
20	0	200	0	270	270
30	1.46	300	30	270	300
40	6.33	400	130	270	400
50	11.12	500	230	270	500
60	16.07	600	330	270	600
70	20.94	700	430	270	700
80	25.81	800	530	270	800
90	30.68	900	630	270	900
100	35.55	1,000	730	270	1,000
110	40.42	1,100	830	270	1,100
120	45.29	1,200	930	270	1,200
130	50.16	1,300	1,030	270	1,300
140	55.03	1,400	1,130	270	1,400
150	59.90	1,500	1,230	270	1,500
175	72.07	1,750	1,480	270	1,750
200	84.25	2,000	1,730	270	2,000
250	108.60	2,500	2,230	270	2,500
300	132.95	3,000	2,730	270	3,000

Figures are for 1,000 shares and 2,053 warrants
* As derived from the line of best fit equation

Table 5.2 Equity holdings and warrant-cash mix

In this example the warrant-cash mix outperforms the straight equity holding in the three lowest categories (ironically, when the warrants are valueless), and then matches the equity investment pound for pound thereafter. In practice, of course, the investor will not leave the cash abandoned, but will secure a return on it from a deposit account or some other interest-bearing instrument such as gilts, implying that the perfect warrant-cash mix will actually outperform an ordinary equity holding at all levels. This is a remarkable conclusion.

As with most theoretical conclusions which offer a rose without a thorn, there are drawbacks with the empirical application of this approach. The precise workings outlined above are only valid for the linear line of best fit, and once the actual movements of the share and warrant prices move away from this line, then the conditions are violated and the warrant-cash mix becomes imperfect. In practice it is an unusual warrant which will not stray from this line, although there may be some warrants which are a long way 'into the money' and with a zero premium which may exhibit a near-perfect relationship. More generally, this calculation may be of use as a rough guide to investors seeking guidance on suitable investment amounts for hedging purposes, although you should be wary of interpreting the results too literally.

VALUING THE WARRANTS MARKET AS A WHOLE: THE PERFECT MARKET MODEL

Of course the models presented for selecting the best warrants and calculating the perfect warrant-cash mix presuppose that individual warrants can represent good value, but what of the market as a whole? There is an interesting theoretical argument which suggests that the average CFP can be used as the basis for valuing the warrants market as a whole. The argument is derived from the premise that markets work efficiently and that the returns on different investments will be equalized through the process of supply and demand. In this simplified world investors are rational, there is no uncertainty, and there are only three types of investments – bonds, shares and warrants. Bonds offer an interest yield, shares offer a mix of dividend yield and capital gain, and warrants offer only capital gain.

In this world, investors will seek to maximize the return on their capital, and by moving funds to the most attractive instrument the expected returns will be equalized. This means that:

Bond yield = Share dividend yield + Capital return = Warrants' capital return

Using this simple formula it can be seen that the rational investor will invest in shares in preference to bonds if the bond yield minus the dividend yield will be more than compensated for by the expected capital gain on the shares. Hence, if the bond yield is 9 per cent per annum, and the dividend yield is 2.5 per cent per annum then the rational investor will place funds into shares if he expects a capital return of over 6.5 per cent per annum.

The next step is to compare this expected capital return with the CFP for warrants. The two should be equalized, but if the average CFP is less than the bond yield minus the dividend yield, then warrants are undervalued, and vice versa. In the example cited, a CFP below 6.5 per cent will indicate that warrants are under-valued relative to shares and bonds, and should be the preferred investment.

The engaging simplicity of this model is really its downfall. Empirically, uncertainty is of prime importance, and this affects the returns required by investors. Investment in warrants is prey to considerable risk and uncertainty, and this means that investors require a greater return than implied in the model above. Furthermore, it is not possible to incorporate this risk premium into the model as a constant factor, for the simple reason that it is not constant. It is investor confidence which probably determines the overall level of the warrants market in relation to the equity market, and that is notoriously difficult to mea-sure. There have been some attempts to construct a 'market buoyancy index'* based upon the shape of the warrant market curve, but it is not clear whether this has any predictive value.

CONCLUSION

Armed with the battery of analytical tools outlined in the last three chapters, you should now be able to sort the wheat from the chaff in the warrants market. That said, it is unlikely that one warrant will stand head and shoulders above the rest as an outstanding investment opportunity. More likely, you will be able to form a 'shortlist' from which warrants may be selected according to other criteria such as risk preference.

It is always important to be practical in your approach, however sophisticated. Investment is a practical business, so if a certain type of analysis works for you and satisfies your needs, then stick with it. If you find that some analysis fails regularly, then discard it, no matter how highly it may be recommended by a the-oretician. The equations, graphs and models presented in these last three chap-ters are intended to provide a broad palette for the art of warrant analysis. You can choose which elements are likely to be most expedient for your own pur-poses.

Should you find that some ideas tax your understanding, this need not be a cause for dismay. Indeed, analysis can become too sophisticated, and compli-cated equations can obscure the more important fundamental aspects of warrant valuation. A sound practical understanding of the way in which warrants work is

* See Downes & Elven, *Japanese Equity Warrants – a Clear and Comprehensive Guide*, Eurostudy, 1990

far more important than a technical mastery of the Black-Scholes formula. Keen market observers can often be far quicker to spot price anomalies than analysts buried deep in mounds of algebra. Too often warrant analysis seeks to identify the best opportunities for taking advantage of market imperfections by undertaking analysis which assumes a perfect market – an irony which is lost on many theoretical experts. Simple supply and demand is important, and short-term opportunities are most frequently created by a sharp movement in the underlying stock. Technical analysis can be good for estimating the medium- to long-term potential of warrants, but you should beware of pursuing technical analysis at the expense of fundamental analysis. As stressed at the beginning of this section, the two should always work hand-in-hand, as indeed should complex analysis and plain common sense.

"Fortunes can be made from warrants, but the omnipresent risk/reward trade-off means that this potential is tempered by the risks involved."

6

RISK

The risk with warrants is that you can lose your investment. All of it. Equally, investment in warrants carries the potential for large gains – this is the risk/reward trade-off which exists for every investment. The higher the potential returns, the higher risk you must assume. This is an inescapable fact, but what you can do is choose where you stand on the risk spectrum. Risk, like love, is a four-letter word. Some people would rather avoid it, while others actively seek it out and embrace the opportunities which it implies. At least warrants offer the advantage of quantifiable risk – something which is doubtful with some other instruments such as futures. With warrants you cannot lose more than your original stake, and you need not risk as much capital as you would with straightforward investment in equities. As optimists have pointed out, the down-side loss is limited to 100 per cent, whereas the upside potential is infinite. You can lose your shirt, but choose the right investment and you can renew your entire wardrobe.

This chapter explains why warrants carry more risk than shares, what implications this carries for the way in which you invest, how you can measure and choose your level of risk, and how you can reduce it. An understanding of risk is important in tailoring investments to suit individual portfolios and aims.

THE RISK SPECTRUM

Figure 6.1 is probably the most simple yet the most important graph in this book. It indicates very simply that there is a trade-off between risk and reward. The more risk you are prepared to take, the greater the likely rewards within your grasp. Stated another way, if you are seeking large profits then you will have to assume a higher level of risk. This is a key lesson which should never be forgotten when dealing in speculative markets, and warrants are well along the risk-reward spectrum.

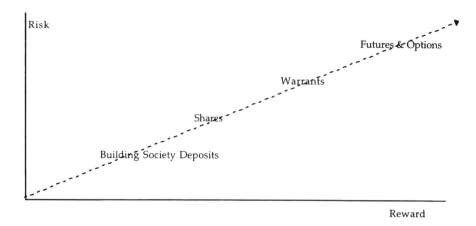

Figure 6.1 The risk spectrum

WHY WARRANTS CARRY MORE RISK THAN SHARES

Most derivative instruments – forms of finance derived from underlying securities – carry a higher level of risk than shares, and warrants are no exception. It is this feature which makes them exciting for speculative investors, and which makes the potential rewards so enticing. As the introductory remarks made quite plain, warrants stand further along the risk/reward spectrum than ordinary shares, for a number of reasons.

To begin with, warrants are further removed from the underlying assets and profits of the company. Equities derive their value directly from these factors, but warrants have no direct claim, relying instead for their value upon the price of the shares. Warrants are much nearer the Stock Exchange floor than to the shop-floor: there is a less tangible link to the company itself, and more influence which may be attributed to the financial markets. And as all investors know, markets can be fickle. The result is that warrant prices can often move for reasons barely related to fundamental, identifiable factors – their value may be regarded as more nebulous. The value of warrants has a weaker foundation than the value of shares since they are further removed from the underlying assets of the company or trust involved, and the risk is that the warrants may perform poorly even when the company is doing well. This is where technical analysis of warrant prices becomes important.

The 'time value' built into the prices of most warrants means that the ruling prices may have a tenuous relationship with the actual realizable exercise value of warrants. Almost all warrants have a premium – an extra amount which investors must pay for investing in the warrants instead of the shares – and this premium represents a built-in expectation of gain. Unless this expectation of gain is met, the value of the warrants will fall. If a warrant with one year of life remaining is trading on a premium of 20 per cent, for example, and the shares rise by 15 per cent over the course of that year, then the warrant price will fall, since the whole of the premium will evaporate ahead of the final expiry date:

Widget plc warrants, one year remaining, share price 100p, exercise price 100p, warrants 20p (20 per cent premium).

Final expiry – Widget plc shares up 15 per cent to 115p, exercise price 100p, warrants worth 15p each – a 25 per cent decline.

It is this built-in requirement for the shares to rise which can, on occasions, cause the warrants market to underperform the market as a whole. In 1994, for example, when the UK stockmarket was fairly stagnant (the FT-SE 100 Index fell by 10.3 per cent), the UK warrants market fared much worse, dropping by 19.9 per cent. This was due in part to gearing, in part to the high overseas element, where emerging markets in particular fell more sharply, but it was also due to the erosion of time value. Markets which stand still are no good for war-rant investors, and this is why the thrust of analysis must always be on finding strong growth prospects.

For a precise measurement of this risk, it is helpful to consider the break-even formula (see Chapter 3) which measures the annual percentage rise in the equity required for a warrant-holder to recover the current warrant price. This is the annual growth of the equity required for the warrant-holder to avoid a loss, and it is a very useful indicator of risk. Clearly, the higher the break-even point, the higher the risk inherent in the warrant.

In the example above the warrant still retains some value since it is 'in the money', but the price of the warrant may be composed entirely of premium, in which case it will have no intrinsic value. In this case the shares have to rise in order to exceed the exercise price by the final expiry date, or the warrants not merely lose some value – they will expire worthless. The extent of intrinsic value may be measured by the parity ratio, which is perhaps the most important factor in determining the risk for short-dated warrants. The lower the parity ratio, the higher the risk involved. Warrants with a parity ratio below 1.0 (i.e., they are 'out of the money') and a short time to expiry must be regarded as a very high-risk proposition. While shares will only fall to zero if the company concerned is forced into liquidation, warrants will fall to zero even if the company fares well and the shares go up, but not by enough to reach the exercise price. The risk attached to warrant trading is most starkly revealed when warrants fail to achieve any intrinsic value by their final exercise date and expire worthless. This happens in a minority of cases, but it does happen.

Following the break-even point and the parity ratio, the third key factor is gearing, which neatly encapsulates the risk/reward trade-off. Gearing, which is normally considered to be a positive feature, means that warrants will post far greater rises than the underlying shares in a bull market. It also implies the reverse. The higher the gearing, the higher the potential rewards, the higher the potential losses, and the higher the risk. The risk with a highly geared warrant is that a relatively small decline in the value of the shares may lead to a large percentage fall in the attached warrants.

Volatility is incorporated into risk analysis for a similar reason. Largely because of the gearing effect, the majority of warrants are more volatile than their underlying shares, and this volatility can result in large and sudden declines in warrant prices. The increased risk of a sharp downturn can deter some warrant investors, particularly the inexperienced or conservative investor who may panic in the face of a sudden price fall.

Finally, the risk of loss in the event of takeover (see Chapter 2) should be mentioned here. With some warrants it is possible to lose the premium if exercise is forced early in the event of takeover – an additional risk which can assume great importance if the company is seen as a bid target and the warrants lack time value protection. This is the one risk factor which cannot be quantified, since the additional risk is dependent upon the unknown threat to ownership rather than any technical properties of the warrants. Interestingly, this risk factor is also unrelated to rewards: there is no extra benefit accruing to warrant-holders *vis-à-vis* shareholders if the company is not taken over. As such this risk is discriminatory, if not downright unfair. Whereas warrant investors should be prepared to accept the other risks, this is nonsensical and it is a relief to see almost all new warrant issues carrying time value protection in the warrant particulars to eliminate this unjustified risk.

RISK MEASUREMENT

Much of this book is taken up with warrant analysis which seeks to measure the potential rewards from warrant investment and to identify those warrants which offer the greatest potential rewards. As suggested in the introduction to this chapter, though, those potential rewards must always be held in proper perspective and placed in the context of risk. Fortunately, warrants offer the benefit of quantifiable risk, and once the risk is quantified, then investment and portfolio management techniques may be used to manage the level of risk to suit the demands of the individual and to suit the prevailing circumstances. The risk of a warrant may be measured in terms of the following factors:

$$Risk = (w*1/parity\ ratio + \mathsf{x}*gearing + y*volatility + z*break\text{-}even\ point)$$
$$where\ w, x, y\ and\ z\ are\ constants.$$

The risk factor is calculated from a weighted formula related positively to gearing, volatility and the break-even point, and negatively to the parity ratio. This measurement does not incorporate the protection of time value in the event of takeover, *nor does it measure the risk associated with the underlying stock*. It is purely a technical evaluation.

Warrants	Parity Ratio	Gearing (times)	Volatility (%)	Break-Even (%)	Risk Rating*
United Energy	0.30	6.0	93.09	782.35	1
North American Gas	0.83	55.3	105.81	63.71	2
Cementone	0.60	3.3	47.38	93.21	3
Pacific Horizon Trust	0.89	22.3	132.62	45.36	4
WMGO Group	0.63	2.5	89.76	14.36	5
Creston Land & Estates	0.70	2.6	56.32	25.03	6
The Ex-Lands	1.22	1.3	19.74	21.64	7
Paribas French 'B' warrants	0.83	6.4	71.67	10.70	8
Raglan Property Trust	1.18	2.7	27.20	41.36	9
Ivory & Sime Enterprise	0.84	6.6	42.36	10.08	10
Perpetual Japanese	0.81	2.2	42.61	10.96	11
HTR Japanese Smaller Cos	0.77	2.4	25.63	7.55	12
The Turkey Trust	1.05	2.3	50.63	7.17	13
Pantheon International	0.76	3.7	28.90	7.44	14
Kleinwort Euro Privatisation	0.81	3.2	40.94	4.20	15
Syndicate Capital Trust	0.83	2.7	33.57	10.90	16
Saracen Value Trust	0.90	4.3	44.31	5.16	17
Anglian Water	1.07	6.2	48.70	2.78	18
Herald Investment Trust	0.97	2.3	36.68	4.94	19
Kleinwort Emerging Markets	1.11	1.9	23.91	4.00	20
Mithras Investment Trust	1.10	2.6	15.99	3.20	21
Govett Asian Smaller Cos	1.31	2.9	39.01	3.04	22
BTR 1997	1.30	4.2	59.56	0.32	23
First Philippine Inv Trust	1.66	2.4	37.59	1.28	24
Pilkington	1.53	2.6	46.37	1.20	25
Fidelity European Values	1.68	1.9	7.55	2.10	26
Gartmore Emerging Pacific	2.08	1.9	35.81	0.41	27
German Smaller Companies	2.05	1.9	20.99	2.04	28
York Waterworks	2.44	1.6	15.62	1.39	29
Navan Resources	5.43	1.2	33.01	0.00	30

* 1 = highest risk; 30 = lowest risk

Table 6.1 Risk Ratings, June 1995

Table 6.1 illustrates the outcome with a ranked list of thirty warrants, beginning with the highest-risk warrant, United Energy. With these warrants the risk of losing your entire investment is very real: indeed the shares must rise by a multiple of 3.3 times (in under seven months) for the warrants to achieve any intrinsic value. Put another way, the shares have to rise at an annual rate of over

782 per cent before the warrant-holder can begin to make a profit. This seems demanding, to say the least. At the other end of the table, Navan Resources warrant holders have no premium to lose, the warrants are well 'in the money' (share price 163p, exercise price 30p), gearing is low, and the volatility is moderate. Of course the warrant is likely to fall if the shares drop, but it would take a catastrophe for investors to suffer very heavy losses.

CHOOSING YOUR LEVEL OF RISK

The benefit of risk measurement is that you can choose a warrant to suit your own preferences. Among investment trust warrants in particular, there may be a number of similar trusts with similar management teams investing in the same region, and you can select warrants according to their individual characteristics. This is also illustrated well by the multiple series of BTR warrants which offer differing features. A short-term speculator content to assume a relatively high level of risk will choose the 'out of the money' 1998 warrants for their high gearing of 10.4 times, whilst a conservative investor might choose the 1997 series which are well 'in the money' and which boast a break-even point of less than 1 per cent per annum. In practice, many investors will be unsure of their preferences and will compromise.

Selecting individual warrants in view of their risk characteristics in this way is the first and simplest method of controlling risk, but it is also rudimentary. What happens, for example, if a risk-averse investor discovers a warrant which he believes to be enormously undervalued on fundamental and technical grounds, but which also carries a high level of risk? It would make little sense to ignore this warrant entirely, and there are ways in which high-risk warrants may be incorporated into an overall low-risk strategy.

EGGS, BASKETS AND PORTFOLIOS

There are many sophisticated procedures for controlling the overall level of risk, but one of the most important principles is best expressed by the familiar adage: don't put all of your eggs in one basket. If you drop the basket, you break all of your eggs, and however good your analysis and your advice may be, everyone drops the basket at some time. Warrant analysis is perhaps as much an art as a science, and whereas a good analyst would certainly claim to outperform the market average over a reasonable period of time, no one could reasonably claim a 100 per cent profits record. You cannot win all of the time, and you should not expect to do so – you will only be disappointed. The clever and realistic traders hope to win more than they lose, and to ensure that the losses, when they occur, are not too great. Should you make the mistake of placing all of your funds in one warrant, then one error of judgement or a simple slice of bad luck could mean that your investment capital is decimated.

A better approach is to control your risk by investing in a portfolio of warrants, placing no more than 20 per cent of your total warrant capital in any one issue. This approach means that a bad loss can be sustained from one or two warrants without an overall adverse result, and that one or two high-risk warrants may be included in an otherwise conservative portfolio. The benefits of each point are illustrated neatly by the two portfolios constructed by the *Warrants Alert* newsletter in 1990 and 1991. The first of these, a 'Recovery Portfolio' recommended in September 1990, consisted of the warrants listed in Table 6.2.

Warrant	Price(p) Sept 1990	Price(p) Sept 1991	Change %
Abtrust New Dawn 'B'	16	18	+12.50
Beta Global Emerging	16	30	+87.50
BTR 1993/94	67	46	−31.34
Drayton Asia Trust	23	25	+8.70
Lucas Industries	20	27.5	+37.50
Martin Currie European	28	29	+3.57
SPRAIT	100	121	+21.00
WPP Group	50	5	−90.00
Average change			**+6.18%**

Table 6.2 The 1990 'Recovery Portfolio'

Here the outstanding feature is the dreadful performance of WPP Group warrants, which damaged the overall result considerably. Nevertheless, the portfolio still managed a modest net gain over the period, the losses on WPP and BTR warrants being more than compensated for by gains from the other six warrants.

The '1991 Portfolio', recommended in January 1991, had a rather different outcome, and serves to illustrate the other point mentioned above. This portfolio comprised five selections, three of which offered good gearing and CFPs below 10 per cent, and two of which were more highly rated (see Table 6.3). These were included because they were recovery situations and could provide a good return if the market moved ahead smartly. The additional risks inherent in these warrants were considered worth taking in the context of a portfolio.

The most interesting warrant in these selections proved to be Airtours, which was selected in spite of a demanding CFP of 23 per cent at the buying price of 12p. The shares at this point were 169p, and they needed to reach 200p by the final expiry in February 1992 or the warrants would expire worthless. This made them an extremely high-risk proposition, and they would not have made a sensible choice for any investor choosing a single warrant in which to invest. In all but the most bullish of circumstances it is very difficult to justify the purchase

Warrant	Price(p) Jan 1991	Premium (%)	Gearing	CFP (%)	Price(p) Sept 1991	Change (%)
Airtours	12	25.44	14.1	22.99	420	+3,400
BTR 1994/95	50	35.48	6.2	7.47	101p	+102.0
Merlin Internat'l Green	18	66.20	3.9	6.91	20	+11.11
River & Merc Smaller Cos	18	40.48	4.7	8.67	31p	+72.22
Trust of Property Shares	11	157.45	4.3	12.59	24p	+118.2
Average change						**+740.7%**

Table 6.3 The 1991 Portfolio

of a highly geared warrant well 'out of the money' and with a short time to expiry, even if it is low-priced. In a portfolio, however, there may be a place for such a warrant – if its inclusion is balanced by some lower-risk investments. Using such a strategy the portfolio can provide a handsome return if the high-risk warrants take off, as above, but with some degree of protection if they fail. In this 1991 Portfolio, for example, the return would still have averaged +41 per cent even if the Airtours warrants had crashed to zero.

This section is not intended as a rigorous exploration of portfolio management, but there is a third benefit which carries considerable theoretical appeal and deserves a mention. This is the element of Darwinian selection. The evident fact that the best-performing warrants grow in value and the worst-performing warrants shrink in value means that the best-performing warrants become a larger proportion of the portfolio. For example, consider a portfolio containing two warrants – one which grows at 15 per cent per annum, and one which falls at 15 per cent per annum. Your first thought may be that these changes will cancel each other out, but Darwinian selection ensures a better result after the first year:

Portfolio – year 0

Good warrant	50p	50% of total portfolio	grows by 15% per annum
Bad warrant	50p	50% of total portfolio	falls by 15% per annum
Total	**100p**		

Portfolio – year 1

Good warrant	57.5p	57.5% of total portfolio	grows by 15% per annum
Bad warrant	42.5p	42.5% of total portfolio	falls by 15% per annum
Total	**100p**		

Portfolio – year 2

Good warrant	66.125p	64.7% of total portfolio	grows by 15% per annum
Bad warrant	36.125p	35.3% of total portfolio	falls by 15% per annum
Total	**102.25p**		

Portfolio – year 3

Good warrant	*76.04p*	*71.2% of total portfolio*	*grows by 15% per annum*
Bad warrant	*30.71*	*28.8% of total portfolio*	*falls by 15% per annum*
Total	**106.75p**		

Portfolio – year 4

Good warrant	*87.45p*	*77.0% of total portfolio*	*grows by 15% per annum*
Bad warrant	*26.1p*	*23.0% of total portfolio*	*falls by 15% per annum*
Total	**113.55p**		

Portfolio – year 5

Good warrant	*100.6p*	*81.9% of total portfolio*
Bad warrant	*22.2p*	*18.1% of total portfolio*
Total	**122.8p**	

This growth in the portfolio comes about because the intrinsic quality of the portfolio has improved over time, given the consistent price changes. And as Professor John Pick has observed*, this property of the portfolio is enhanced by the presence of warrants *vis-à-vis* shares, since the gearing element makes the changes relatively large. If portfolio investment is sensible for shares, then it must be sensible for warrants.

HEDGING TO REDUCE RISK

Having discovered why warrants carry a greater risk than shares, how to measure that risk, and how to control that risk within the context of a portfolio, it may come as a surprise to learn that investment in warrants need not be more risky than in shares at all. In fact it can be less risky. The hedging approach to warrants can reduce risk, and often makes sense in difficult market conditions or where the investor is relatively risk-averse. Strategies using a combination of warrants with some form of fixed-interest securities can be used to match the potential return on equities while providing a guaranteed minimum return.

Warrants offer great advantages to a wide range of investors, and not just those with a speculative approach. For much of the time the benefits of gearing are expressed in terms of the greater exposure provided for any given investment. This 'aggressive' approach can lead to much greater gains in the warrants when the shares perform well, but the value of the warrant investment can fall heavily if circumstances are not favourable. Figure 6.2 illustrates the case of the the Fleming Chinese Investment Trust. As the warrant is well 'out of the money', it is intrinsically worthless unless the shares rise by approximately 7.75 per cent

* 'The XYZ of Warrants', *Futures & Options World*, April 1990.

per annum to the final expiry date in ten years' time. At growth rates above this level, however, the gearing effect comes into play and provides a much greater return on the warrants than from an equity investment of the same size. Figure 6.2 shows the direct linear relationship for the shares contrasted with the higher annual returns available from the warrants at high rates of growth.

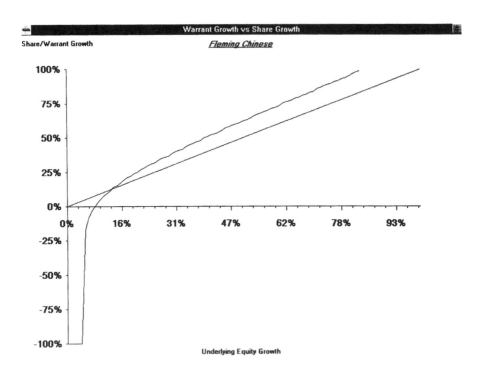

Figure 6.2 Fleming Chinese Investment Trust – projected annual growth rates for shares and warrants
(source: Warrants Alert Workbench)

At an optimistic share growth rate of 15 per cent per annum to final expiry (see Figure 6.3) the warrants grow by 297.09 per cent, at at an annual rate of 17.25 per cent. At the other end of the scale, a more modest yet respectable annual rise of 4 per cent in the shares is not sufficient to take them over the exercise price and leaves the warrants worthless (see Figure 6.4), which is a chilling reminder of the risk involved.

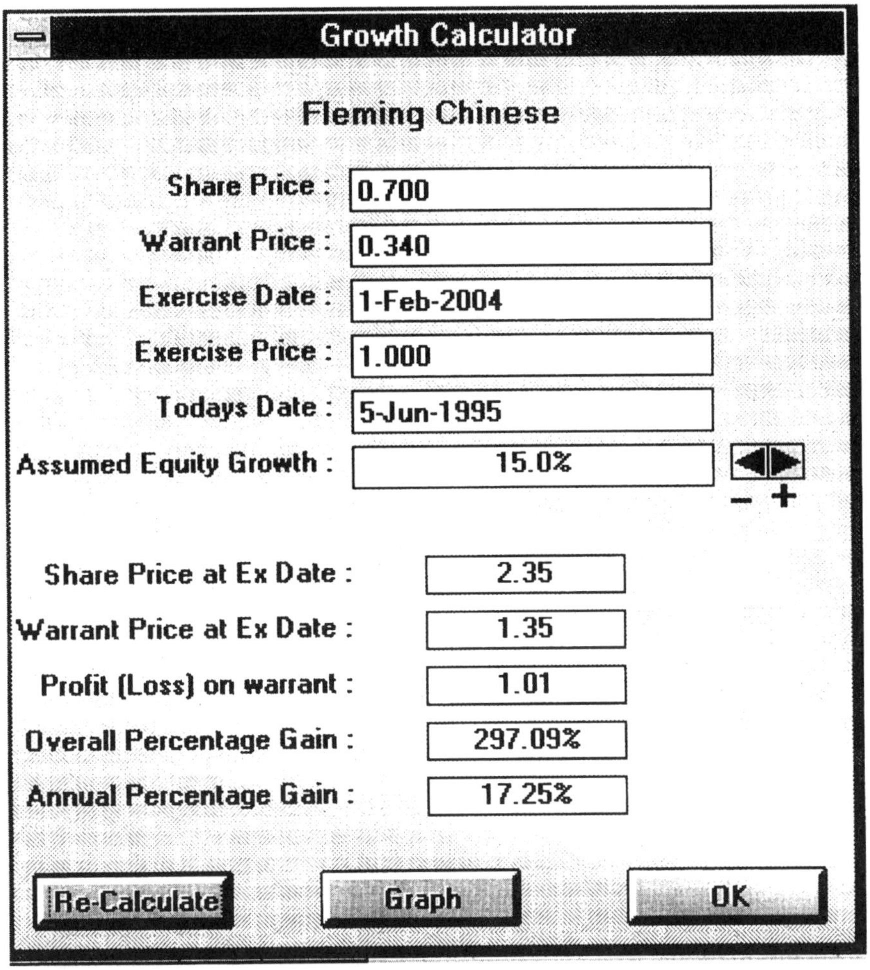

Figure 6.3 Fleming Chinese Investment Trust – illustration of 15 per cent annual growth rate
(source: Warrants Alert Workbench)

Investing your normal investment sum directly into warrants instead of shares is, however, just one approach, and a more cautious investor may interpret the gearing benefit of warrants in another way. By investing in warrants instead of shares the investor can achieve rights over the same amount of equity using much less capital. In our example, the investor can gain rights over £1,000 worth of Fleming Chinese Investment Trust plc shares with an investment of just £486 in the warrants:

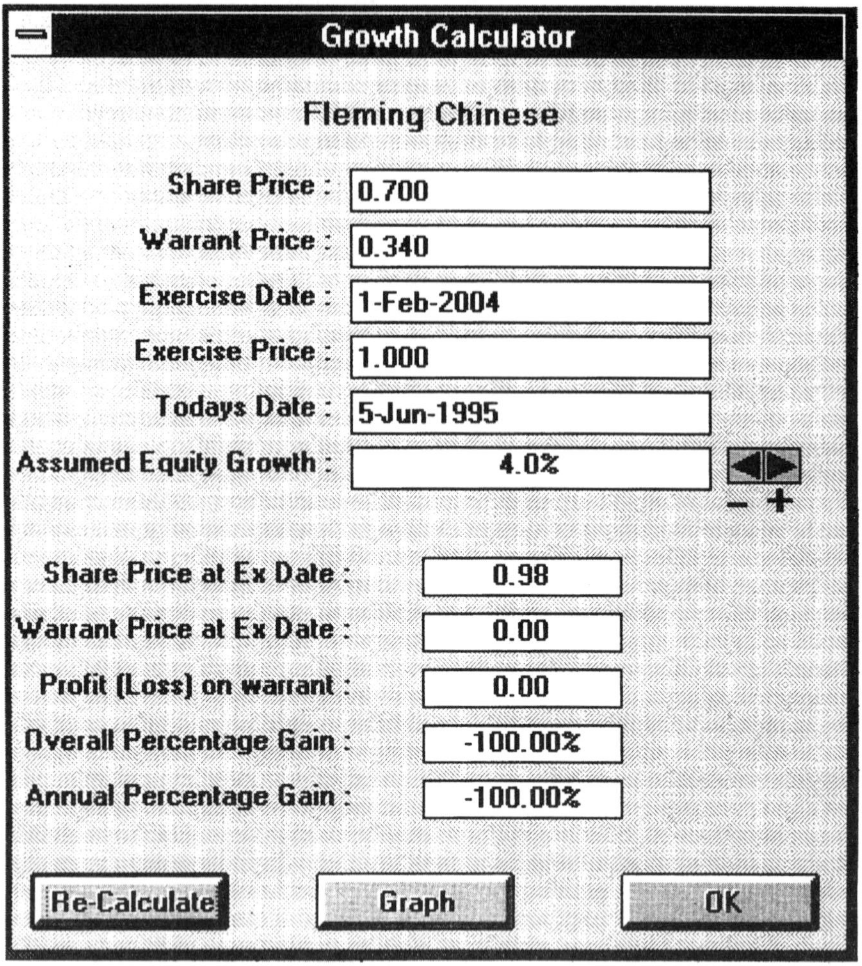

```
┌──────────────────────────────────────────────────┐
│ ━                 Growth Calculator                │
├──────────────────────────────────────────────────┤
│                 Fleming Chinese                     │
│                                                     │
│         Share Price :  │0.700              │        │
│       Warrant Price :  │0.340              │        │
│       Exercise Date :  │1-Feb-2004         │        │
│       Exercise Price : │1.000              │        │
│        Todays Date :   │5-Jun-1995         │        │
│  Assumed Equity Growth : │     4.0%        │  ◄►     │
│                                             ─ +      │
│                                                     │
│   Share Price at Ex Date :    │   0.98   │          │
│  Warrant Price at Ex Date :   │   0.00   │          │
│   Profit (Loss) on warrant :  │   0.00   │          │
│   Overall Percentage Gain :   │ -100.00% │          │
│    Annual Percentage Gain :   │ -100.00% │          │
│                                                     │
│  ┌Re-Calculate┐    ┌   Graph   ┐      ┌    OK    ┐  │
└──────────────────────────────────────────────────┘
```

Figure 6.4 Fleming Chinese Investment Trust – illustration of 4 per cent annual growth rate
(*source: Warrants Alert Workbench*)

> *£1,000 worth of shares = £1000/70p share price = 1,429 shares*
> *1,429 multiplied by warrant price of 34p = £486*
>
> *or*
>
> *£1,000 / gearing factor of 2.059 = £486*

The remaining £514 can then be invested for income in gilts or some other high-yielding instrument, providing a guaranteed return and a hedge against a fall in the equity. Not only is the potential loss on the warrants limited to £486, but the interest payments on the remaining £514 ensure a small profit over the period. If interest rates are 8 per cent per annum, then the £514 invested in gilts becomes £1,001 over the eight years and eight months period to the final expiry of the warrants, thereby ensuring that the capital is secure no matter what happens to the warrants. At high rates of growth the equity outperforms the warrant/gilt mix (because of the re-invested dividends), but the latter has the advantage of a minimum return. This minimum return is the 'safe' investment in gilts which returns £1,001 whatever happens to the equity. Using this hedging strategy this minimum return is built in and it is not possible to lose your entire investment as it is with the equity. At the high postulated growth rate of 15 per cent per annum the value of a £1,000 investment in the shares rises to £3,358, while the warrant/gilt mix is worth £2,931.

In this way the gearing benefit of warrants may be used as part of a lower-risk investment policy. According to circumstances, investors can choose an appropriately aggressive or defensive approach, and the choice is not a black and white one. Using your own risk preference as a guide, you can vary the amount invested in warrants and fixed-interest securities: ultimately it is your choice and you must feel comfortable with your own investment strategy, whether it be speculative or hedged. Clearly the hedging mechanism is worth considering, and there are a number of circumstances in which this approach makes a great deal of sense. In particular:

1 When interest rates are high the warrant/gilt mix allows the investor to take advantage of the high risk-free return from fixed-interest securities whilst keeping one hand in the market via warrants.
2 When the equity is a high-risk proposition or when the warrant is a long way 'out of the money'. By investing a much smaller sum, the hedging approach can limit the amount it is possible to lose. An investor who discovers a 'long-shot' warrant which is likely to expire worthless, but which could produce some massive gains if a certain event occurs (such as an oil find, a gold strike, or a big order) may not wish to commit much capital, but may equally wish to have a small stake.
3 More generally, highly geared warrants will allow the hedging policy to be pursued with only a small amount of risk capital. Investment in highly geared warrants can therefore become suitable for an investor seeking to achieve high speculative returns from a small portion of his portfolio set aside for risk purposes. Many warrant investors enjoy the process of speculative investment with a relatively small amount of money which has been set aside for 'playing the market'. The hedging approach, where the majority of capital is safe, can be suitable for the casual investor who sees speculative investment as a hobby.
4 Hedging can be an attractive way of adjusting your level of risk over the market cycle so that your warrant/gilt mix varies with market sentiment. During bullish market conditions you may wish to increase the proportion of investment in warrants; during bearish conditions the proportion in warrants can be reduced.

WHAT FUNDS TO USE

Whether warrants represent a peripheral hobby or part of a serious investment programme, the possibility of loss must be an important consideration. In brutal terms, warrants are high-risk instruments, so don't use money you can't afford to lose. Granny won't thank you for gambling her life savings away if you hit a rough period. Warrants are more risky than ordinary shares, and they are by their very nature highly speculative, volatile instruments. They may be difficult to trade, they may fall sharply in value, and their value may in fact fall to zero.

If this risk warning sends a shiver down your spine, then perhaps warrants are not for you. Certainly if you have little spare money, and your savings are necessary rather than discretionary, then you should not risk them by investing in warrants. Conversely, if you have some surplus funds gathering dust and little in the way of interest, then the warrants market can provide an excellent forum for an investment adventure. Excitement and stimulation are virtually guaranteed, profits are not. Fortunes can be made from warrants, but the omnipresent risk/reward trade-off means that this potential is tempered by the risks involved.

It bears repetition that the amount you invest will depend entirely upon your individual circumstances and preferences, and it is impossible to generalize about how much an investor should put into warrants. There are some basic guidelines which may be followed, however:

1 What is my expertise?
2 What is my risk preference?
3 What is my overall investment position?

First, your level of knowledge and experience is a key factor which is too often overlooked. All experienced market practitioners have a large store of tales about novices who rush into markets with more enthusiasm than skill, only to rush out again minus their capital. It is clearly foolish to commit a large sum of money to warrants if you barely know what they are, but equally there are a handful of market experts specializing in warrants who would never invest in anything else. The more you know, the more funds it is reasonable to invest. It is important not to over-estimate your abilities, and to remember that warrants boast characteristics which can make them especially suitable for small-scale investment. The gearing element means that you can get a reasonable exposure with a relatively small investment.

Second, will you be investing in the highly-geared 'go-go' warrants which carry a commensurately high level of risk, or is your preference for 'in the money' warrants with break-even points below 5 per cent per annum? It is common sense that the former policy should restrict the size of individual investments, possibly relying upon very small stakes as part of a warrants/gilt mix. In this case the funds should be pure 'risk capital', and imply no hardship should the funds be lost entirely. The investor aiming for more moderate warrants need not adopt such a bridled approach, and may apply less stringent criteria to the funds which may be invested.

Third, the funds available for investment should be considered in relation to the size and structure of the individual's overall investment portfolio. As a rule of thumb, a private investor might wish to devote 5 per cent to 10 per cent of his overall investment portfolio to a derivative such as warrants, or up to 20 per cent if you are adventurous and your emphasis is on capital gain. This is a flexible estimate though, and there is no reason why the percentage should remain constant. The relative exposure to warrants may be increased during bullish market periods, and reduced again when the prospects appear less promising.

At the final reckoning, it's your choice. You can, within reason, choose your level of investment and your level of risk. The rewards are, of course, less certain.

"The better your dealing skills, the more chance you have of making profits. And in many ways, it is the dealing process which is the final proof of the pudding."

7

DEALING IN WARRANTS

To the uninitiated, dealing in securities can be a frightening experience. To others it can be intimidating, baffling, frustrating, or just plain infuriating. Or it can be simple and rewarding. As with so many things, the key is to know what you are doing and to use the system to your advantage. The better your dealing skills, the more chance you have of making profits. And in many ways, it is the dealing process which is the final proof of the pudding. Whilst assessing warrants can be an interesting academic exercise in its own right, the majority of analysts and investors undertake analysis with a view to investing and securing a good return. There is no better way to vindicate the results of analysis than to deal successfully and emerge with a nice profit.

The general rules outlined in this chapter apply to most forms of warrants, although the specific comments and examples are again drawn exclusively from the UK equity warrants market. This market is most suitable for domestic private investors, since the warrants can be bought and sold in exactly the same way as ordinary shares. Around 250 equity warrants have a full listing on the London Stock Exchange, and they are freely traded in precisely the same way as the underlying shares. Investors do not need a special account to deal in warrants, nor should any additional dealing charges be incurred unless the warrants are settled through the Euroclear/CEDEL settlement systems. The only additional paperwork required is for investors to sign a warrants 'risk warning notice' which all stockbrokers are obliged to keep on file. The Stock Exchange introduced this form as more investors, some of whom may lack understanding, have been lured by the promise of large profits.

THE INTRODUCTION OF ROLLING SETTLEMENT

In 1994 the London Stock Exchange introduced what was known as 'rolling settlement', or 'T+10' in the jargon of the trade. Whereas previously investors had been able to work on a two-week account system, they now had to pay for purchases ten days after each trade took place. This 'trade plus ten' system has obvious attractions in making the market more efficient and accelerating settlement procedures, but there was one major drawback for speculators. Using the old two-week account system it was possible to buy shares at the start of the account and sell them later in the same account period for settlement on the same date without the necessity to incur a cash outlay. This encouraged some degree of speculation in shares which is now impossible unless speculators are able to trade in and out of a stock successfully within a single day. The result is that some activity is being displaced into other instruments which still provide a large exposure but for a smaller cash outlay. Of course the gearing property of warrants makes them suitable for this purpose, and there is no doubt that some speculators have turned to warrants as a way of ameliorating what they see as the harsh impact of the introduction of rolling settlement. Moreover, the rolling settlement period has recently been made even shorter, now T+5, and the necessity to be able to call on cash reserves quickly may drive more investors towards geared instruments which make the most of that cash which is effectively tied up.

STOCKBROKERS

Your stockbroker is usually the main link between you and the stockmarket, and as such he has an important role to play. Dealing charges do of course vary between stockbrokers, as does the level of expertise, and it is worth having one who has some knowledge of the warrants market. Warrants are not as simple as shares, so find a stockbroker who understands them. The level of ignorance is surprisingly high, and investors dealing through an inexperienced broker or some other organization such as a bank could be at a significant disadvantage.

In this case, the word 'stockbroker' is used very much in its singular sense. There are good stockbrokers in small, mediocre firms, and there are bad stockbrokers in large prestigious firms. Equally, since warrants knowledge is quite specialized, expert brokers are to be found in some unexpected quarters.

Those lucky enough to find a really good stockbroker will not only find it easy to deal in warrants, but should also reap the benefits of some good advice. First, a stockbroker who deals in warrants on a regular basis will know exactly which warrants you are referring to when you make an enquiry. It has been known for less experienced stockbrokers to confuse different sets of warrants, an error which can be critical when dealing in warrants issued by a company such as BTR, which has four separate issues currently on offer: the 1994/95 series; the 1995/96 series; the 1997 series; and the 1998 series. Needless to say, the four issues have different characteristics and trade at considerably different prices. A mix-up could be costly. You want to be sure and confident that your broker will carry out your instructions efficiently and speedily – this can be important in fast-moving markets and when dealing in volatile securities. Most stockbrokers can be expected to execute your order swiftly, unlike some banks and other institutions which rely upon a chain of commands before your order reaches the market.

More frequently, the difference between a good stockbroker and a bad stockbroker is in the information which they can provide. Too often, a telephone call to your broker about warrants will be met with the oral equivalent of a blank stare. If you enquire after the conversion terms of a particular warrant, will your broker be able to tell you instantaneously? If you wish to find warrants attached to a trust investing in Japan, can they suggest some? If you give your broker instructions to buy some warrants and the spread is unusually wide, will he warn you before you deal? Does your broker follow prices closely, and will he telephone you if an apparent short-term opportunity arises? Will your broker be able to advise you on new warrant issues? Will your broker warn you if the market is thin and the warrants are traded infrequently? These are some of the questions which you should bear in mind, and to which you should seek answers.

The third area in which your broker can make a difference is in the dealing procedure itself. Here, experience can be vital. If your broker is hurried, inexperienced, or 'execution-only', he may accept the price quoted by the market-maker, even if the spread is unusually wide. An experienced broker will know what the acceptable spread is, and might have some idea of the position of the market-maker's book. This key knowledge may enable him to deal 'inside' the quoted price, buying for you a penny or two cheaper, and perhaps fetching a penny or two more when you sell. Of course a gain of this size can be pronounced when dealing in relatively low-priced warrants, and can on occasions make the difference between a profit and a loss. To return to the example of BTR, the 'normal' spread on the 1998 warrants, which are actively traded, is around 1.5p. However, during turbulent market conditions, or when market makers' books are out of line, the quoted spread can be as wide as 4p. An experienced broker will recognize this and seek to deal at a keener price: in fast-moving markets the value of an experienced broker can be considerable in securing the best possible price for your transactions.

These practical benefits of dealing through a specialist warrants broker are important, and they should outweigh any small differences in dealing charges. Some stockbrokers offer cheap 'execution-only' services which offer excellent value for the competent investor wishing to deal in blue-chip shares, but the warrants market is too uncertain for such a service to be efficient, and investors will miss out on too much useful service to make the commission savings worthwhile.

So how should you go about finding a good warrants stockbroker? One way is to make a shortlist of brokers (either in your area, or from a list available from the Stock Exchange) and then to write or phone and ask a few questions about warrants. This will weed out the ignorant or unwilling, and might unearth a real warrants enthusiast who follows the market closely. Specialist stockbrokers can be specifically geared to dealing with warrant investors, and they are eager to deal on your behalf – there is no danger of your being treated as a 'second class' client. It can require some laborious effort to find such stockbrokers though, and it may be easier to take advantage of the stockbroker selection service offered by the *Warrants Alert* newsletter. They maintain a register of specialist warrant stockbrokers and will introduce investors to them free of charge.

DEALING SPREADS

The main cost associated with trading in warrants is not usually the stockbrokers' commission as one might expect, but the 'spread' between buying and selling prices. As such it is a subject of some importance and regrettably some concern. The trend in the City of London since the 'Big Bang' reforms in 1987 has been for the spreads to narrow on large blue-chip shares, but to widen on smaller company shares and other lesser-traded instruments. Warrants have unfortunately been afflicted by this widening of spreads.

In simple terms, the spread is the market-makers' profit. The market-maker bids for stock at the lower price and offers it at the higher price, the difference between these being his reward for holding stock and ensuring a liquid market. This is understood by most investors and accepted as a necessary evil, but not when the spread becomes excessive. Many investors hold the view that spreads are far too wide, and that this represents a serious disincentive to investing in warrants. Furthermore, few investors will appreciate the fact that individual market-maker's spreads are usually wider than the dealing spread which is quoted, as this is an amalgamation of the best which the several competing market-makers have to offer. For example, in Figure 7.1, which shows the dealing spread for Perpetual Japanese Investment Trust warrants, there are six market-makers competing to produce the best price. In this case the dealing spread shown in the central strip is 38.5–40p: the figures are produced by taking the best selling price, which comes from SG Warburg, whose spread is 38.5–41.5p, and the best buying price, which comes from UBS, whose spread is 37–40p.

In practice, trying to record the extent of spreads is not as simple as it sounds. Although most comment is conducted in terms of 'the' spread, this is not a figure carved in granite, and it can be subject to considerable variation. Not only does the spread change as the status, price and number of warrants alter over time, but it can also vary with market conditions and the state of the market-makers' books. As different market-makers move their prices, so the difference between the best bid and best offer can change. On occasions this dynamic interchange can produce some strange results, such as a 'choice' price. For example, in Figure 7.2, the market-makers differ in their prices, with the result that SG Warburg are prepared to buy First Philippine warrants at the same price as BZW are prepared to sell. The warrant effectively has no dealing spread: it is 32–32p.

```
PJIW.L                                      Cls            11:18
   S                                                      REUTER
SEAQ GBp PERPTL JAP WTS              36-38
NMS 3      PL 9     SS 0.5                        GMT 14:22
                              Net +2½      H 39½   L 38
Vol 45                                           News
Last ↑39½  D 38    D                              1/1

              WARB      38½-40      UBS.
BZWE    38-42       5+5   09:47  SBRO   38-42      5+5   09:36
CAZN    37-41       5+5   09:57  UBS.   37-40      5+5   08:08
KLWT    38-41       5+5   09:56  WARB   38½-41½    5+5   09:56
```

Figure 7.1 SEAQ Level 3 screen for Perpetual Japanese investment trust warrants
(source: Reuters)

```
FPIW.L                                      Cls            15:58
   S                                                      REUTER
SEAQ GBp 1S PHILIPPINE WT           32½-33
NMS 1      PL      SS 0.5                         GMT 15:12
                              Net -0¾      H 33½   L 32
Vol                                              News
Last ↓32     32½     32¾    33½                   1/1

              WARB       32C        BZWE
BZWE    30-32       2.5+2.5 15:58  WARB   32-34      5+5   14:47
JCMM    31½-34½     5+5     15:42
```

Figure 7.2 SEAQ Level 3 screen for First Philippine investment trust warrants
(source: Reuters)

The other problem in defining the spread, beyond these inter-market-maker fluctuations, is that skilful dealing can often take place inside the quote spread anyway. Market-makers are obliged by the Stock Exchange to publish prices at which they are prepared to deal, and as such the prices quoted on screen are necessarily conservative. When actually dealing on the telephone the market-maker may be prepared to offer a better price to secure a deal – something which happens with surprising regularity in warrants which suffer from an apparently wide spread. In the example illustrated in Table 7.1, five out of the eight deals in Perpetual Japanese Investment Trust warrants were executed inside the spread quoted at the time of the transaction.

On the other side of the coin, there are times when it is not possible to transact the deal you wish at the quoted price. It is part of the market-makers' obligation that they must deal at the screen price, but only up to the screen size which is also displayed. In Figure 7.1, the screen size is 5,000 warrants for all six market-makers, and in Figure 7.2, it is 5,000 warrants for two market-makers and

Date	Time	Price of Deal (p)	Size of Deal	Spread at time of Deal
1 June 1995	13:29	36.5	3,200 warrants	36–38p
31 May 1995	09:33	36.5	3,000 warrants	35–37.5p
30 May 1995	15:51	36.5	6,000 warrants	36–38p
26 May 1995	10:23	38	5,000 warrants	36–38p
25 May 1995	12:44	37.5	5,000 warrants	36–38p
23 May 1995	10:30	40.5	4,000 warrants	39–41p
22 May 1995	15:39	40	7,500 warrants	39–40p
22 May 1995	08:48	39.5	3,000 warrants	39–39.5p

Table 7.1 Small deals published for Perpetual Japanese Investment Trust warrants

2,500 for BZW. If you wish to deal in more warrants than this screen size, then it is usually possible, but not necessarily at the price quoted. If a market-maker will have to look around for stock to balance his books if you make a large purchase, he will normally ask you to pay a higher price to reflect his position. Equally, if you wish to sell a large number of warrants, then the market-maker will have to adopt some risk in taking your warrants on to his book, and he will offer you a lower price. This is why a good stockbroker is so important: sometimes you will deal at the quoted spread, sometimes you will be able to deal inside, and on other occasions you may only be able to deal outside the spread.

For these reasons the prices shown in Table 7.2, collected in May 1995, should be treated as a guide only. The percentage spread is calculated on the offer price, so it should show how much the warrant has to increase for a buyer to break even if the spread remains constant. For simplicity, stockbrokers' commissions are ignored.

Warrant	Bid–Offer Prices	Spread (%)
Aberdeen Trust	60–65p	7.7
Aberforth Smaller Cos	86–88p	2.3
Abtrust Scotland	8–11p	27.3
Anglian Water	71–74p	4.1
Baillie Gifford Japan	33–35p	5.7
British Assets Trust	15–17p	11.8
BTR 1998 series	33.5–35p	4.3
City of Oxford	6–8p	25.0
Energy Capital	20–23p	13.0
English & Scottish Investors	41–44p	6.8
Fidelity European	89–91p	2.2
First Ireland Investment Co	23–25p	8.0
Fleming Chinese	33–36p	8.3
French Property Trust	10–11p	9.1

Warrant	Bid–Offer Prices	Spread (per cent)
Greycoat	10–15p	33.3
Hambros Asian	17–18p	5.6
Hanson	16.25–16.75p	3.0
HTR Japanese Smaller Cos	31.5–33p	4.5
Ivory & Sime ISIS	22–27p	18.5
Kleinwort Emerging Markets	58–61p	4.9
Melrose Energy	4.5–6p	25.0
Mercury Euro Privatisation	28.5–29.5p	3.4
Mercury World Mining Trust	20–21p	4.8
Martin Currie Pacific	44–47p	6.4
NorthAmerican Gas	0.5–2p	75.0
Overseas Investment Trust	173–175p	1.1
Pacific Horizon Trust	1–2p	50.0
Perpetual Japanese	40–41p	2.4
Pilkington	70.5–72.5p	2.8
Raglan Property	9–12p	25.0
Scottish Asian Investment	700–740p	5.4
Taiwan Investment Trust	32–33p	3.0
TR Far East Income	51–53p	3.8
Utility Cable	14–15p	6.7
Yorkshire Tyne Tees TV	326–330p	1.2

Table 7.2 Dealing Spreads

What is perhaps most striking about Table 7.2 is the lack of consistency: spreads range from 1.1 per cent for Overseas Investment Trust warrants right up to 75.0 per cent for North American Gas warrants. This means that it is not particularly meaningful to calculate an average spread. The size of the spread is related principally to the size of the issue and frequency of deals. A large, actively traded warrant will stimulate a much keener price from market-makers, as they will be prepared to accept a smaller profit per deal and will be facing competition from several other market-makers. This explains why the spread is quite reasonable on most of the blue-chip warrants such as BTR 1998 (4.3 per cent); Hanson (3.0 per cent); and Pilkington (2.8 per cent). Lesser-traded warrants such as Energy Capital (13.0 per cent) Ivory & Sime ISIS (18.5 per cent) have commensurately higher spreads. The same is true of the more esoteric warrants, including most of those traded in US dollars. The spread also tends to be much higher as a percentage on low-priced warrants, such as Melrose Energy (25.0 per cent).

With spreads varying so widely, it is sensible to be aware of the spread before you deal, and this information is provided for most warrants by the *Teleshare* price service. Alternatively, you can ask your broker for the bid-offer prices in warrants which you are considering buying. Should you be investing for the long-term the spread is more likely to be an irritation rather than an obstacle to dealing, but short-term traders will generally find that trading profits are more difficult to generate from the smaller, narrowly traded warrants and may wish to concentrate on the larger active warrants.

Finally, it is interesting to note that the wider spread on warrants compared with many shares is to some extent compensated for by the commission payments. This is because the commission is related directly to the absolute costs of the investment, not to the exposure gained. An investor preferring the narrower spread on the shares would have to invest a greater sum and therefore pay more commission to gain the same exposure as that offered by a geared warrant.

EXAMPLE

Buy 5,000 shares BTR plc at mid-price 339p, spread 1 per cent.
Cost at 341p = £17,050 + £300 commission = £17,350 = 2.4 per cent over 339p mid-price.

Buy rights to 5,000 BTR plc shares through 1998 warrants at mid-price 34.25p, spread 4.3 per cent (see Table 7.2).
Cost at 35p = £1,750 + £35 commission = £1,785 = 4.2 per cent over 34.25p mid-price.

TRADING DIFFICULTIES

In addition to the spread, there are other factors which can make trading in warrants difficult. For the large majority of warrants there is a normal, organized market and market-makers quote prices in the normal way. In a minority of cases, however, trading occurs on a matched-bargain basis. Your stockbroker may post your offer to buy or sell at a specific price on a Stock Exchange electronic noticeboard, and if there is another party interested in dealing at this price then he will make contact with your broker. Investors must be aware that their bargain may not be matched for some time, and that in these cases you may not be able to buy and sell exactly when you wish.

The sort of warrants which suffer from this predicament fall into three main categories – those with few warrants outstanding, those with a very low market capitalization, and those which are concentrated in the hands of a few large holders. For obvious reasons these issues suffer from a lack of liquidity, so if there is a market-makers' quote it may be an indicative price only.

You may decide to leave these warrants alone – an entirely justifiable choice. But that is, of course, exactly what most people do, and for this reason there can be some bargains waiting for those who trawl these little-explored backwaters. Price anomalies can be most startling in conditions where there is a 'liquidity divergence' between the shares and warrants: i.e., where the freely traded shares respond quickly to news and the warrants lag behind. This does happen, and it can yield some profitable opportunities for investors who follow these warrants closely.

EUROCLEAR AND CEDEL

While the majority of warrants listed in London are dealt and settled (i.e., paid for) through the usual Stock Exchange rolling settlement system in exactly the same way as ordinary shares, some of the more esoteric warrants follow a different path. The Stock Exchange system is not designed to cope with cross-border or cross-currency dealings, so warrants attached to investment trusts registered overseas or those originally attached to instruments such as Eurobonds are usually settled through Euroclear or CEDEL. This is also the case with most warrants denominated in a foreign currency such as US dollars or Deutschmarks. When dealing in Euroclear/CEDEL warrants you can buy and sell through your stockbroker as normal, but the settlement is not arranged in the same way.

Euroclear and CEDEL are central settlement systems which operate with a five-day rolling settlement system now also adopted by the London Stock Exchange. Euroclear and CEDEL are 'paperless' depositary systems where the definitive warrant certificates are held on your behalf. Some of the larger stockbrokers will have Euroclear or CEDEL accounts, in which case they can hold them for you, but if not, then your broker will have to arrange for your warrants to be held by a collecting agent. This is administratively simple, but there is a sting in the tail. Unfortunately, the collecting agent will charge your broker a fee which he will pass on to you, and this is likely to be a minimum of £25 when you buy, £25 when you sell, plus a further 'holding' fee of around £25 per quarter. This is a serious added cost, and these charges make it uneconomical for the small investor to deal in these particular warrants unless the expected gain is very substantial. This problem is compounded further by the spreads on these warrants which tend to be much wider than for the ordinary Stock Exchange warrants, as shown above.

Investors should be generally wary of Euroclear/CEDEL warrants because of the additional costs associated with dealing – both from the spread and the holding charges. As a general rule, it is only likely to be worth dealing in these warrants if you are trading in fairly large size (over £10,000). Table 7.3 lists these warrants.

In addition to these standard Euroclear/CEDEL warrants there are also some 'hybrid' warrants which may be dealt in a different way. They are not subject to punitive additional charges, but they may require special settlement terms from some stockbrokers.

Anglian Water
The Baring Chrysalis Fund
The China Investment Company
The China Investment & Development Fund
Czech & Slovak Investment Corporation
Deutschland Investment Corporation
Fidelity Japan OTC & Regional Markets Fund
Genesis Chile Fund
Hungarian Investment Company
The Indonesia Equity Fund
IS Himalayan Fund
The Japanese Warrant Fund
JF Indonesia Fund
JF Japan OTC Fund
Korea Liberalisation Fund
The Malaysian Equity Fund
The Morgan Stanley Japanese Warrant Fund
Pilkington
The Prospect Japan Fund
Schroder Japanese Warrant Fund
Schroder Korea Fund
Shanghai Fund (Cayman)
SHK Indonesia Fund
South America Fund
The Spanish Smaller Companies Fund
The Thai Development Capital Fund
The World Trust Fund

Note: this table should be taken as a guide only. Investors should check with their stockbroker if in doubt.

Table 7.3 Warrants settled through Euroclear and CEDEL

LIMIT PRICES

As should be clear from the above, the warrants market can be a fickle place. Unlike the market for a large share issue such as ICI, in which thousands of trades every day ensure a near-perfect market and a very keen price, warrant markets can be much less ordered. You may not be able to deal at the price you want, prices can be volatile, and spreads can vary widely. Against this background, it makes good sense to take the simple precaution of stating a limit price when dealing, especially if you are dealing 'blind', without checking the price first. This is especially important when dealing through postal services or through a bank, both of which can take some time to process orders.

A limit price is the maximum price at which you are willing to buy, or the minimum price at which you are prepared to sell. There are two main ways of using limit prices, the first of which may be termed 'precautionary' as above. This is when an investor wishes to deal at what he believes to be the ruling price, but wishes to protect against a sudden move in the price before his order is executed. Investors dealing through good stockbrokers who deal instantaneously will not usually need to use limit prices in this way, although they may wish to incorporate a limit into their phrasing as follows:

Investor: What is the price for Widget warrants?
Stockbroker: 24p to 26p.
Investor: OK – sell 10,000 at 24p or better.

This means that the stockbroker will not sell at a price lower than 24p, but will advise you if there has been a sudden drop in the price.

The second use for limit prices may be termed the 'invigilatory' approach, where the investor does not wish to deal at the current price, but will wish to deal if the price reaches a certain point (usually not too far away). For example, an investor wishing to act on a recommendation at 25p, but finding the price marked up to 30p before he could deal, might wish to leave a limit order on to buy at 25p. In this instance the order will be executed in the price falls back, but not if it stays the same or moves further up. A good stockbroker should be happy to monitor prices on a client's behalf and to accept limit price orders – provided the limit has a realistic chance of being met. Investors using banks or 'execution-only' services are likely to find this difficult or impossible.

DEALING SIZE

Many private investors wonder whether warrants are really suitable for them, fearing that it might be necessary to invest large sums of money. This is emphatically not the case. The minimum level of investment is determined principally by the need to avoid commissions swallowing up too large a proportion of the initial investment. Based upon the present level of stockbrokers' commissions, the minimum practical level of investment needs to be around £750 per transaction, and £1,500 to be reasonably efficient:

EXAMPLE A:

£375 investor

Buys 1,500 warrants	*@ 25p*
Consideration:	*£375*
Stamp Duty:	*£2*
Commission:	*£25*
Total:	*£402*

Effective purchase price 27p

EXAMPLE B:

£750 investor

Buys 3,000 warrants	*@ 25p*
Consideration:	*£750*
Stamp Duty:	*£4*
Commission:	*£25*
Total:	*£779*

Effective purchase price 26p

EXAMPLE C:

£1,500 investor

Buys 6,000 warrants	*@ 25p*
Consideration:	*£1500*
Stamp Duty:	*£7.50*
Commission:	*£26.25*
Total:	*£1533.75*

Effective purchase price 25.6p

Indeed, far from requiring an unusually large level of investment, the properties of warrants can make them most appropriate for smaller investment units. The gearing benefit means that a small investment in warrants can achieve a relatively large equity exposure, so in a case where an investor might normally invest £5,000 in shares, an outlay of £1,500 might be appropriate for warrants.

While this level of investment is generally acceptable for most speculators investing directly into warrants, there is a problem which the industry has so far failed to address, with one notable exception. The most popular method of issuing warrants in the first instance is to provide them as a free attachment to the equity, usually on the basis of one warrant for every five or ten shares. With warrants also having a lower price than the shares, this can leave a large number of enfranchised holders with holdings too small to be meaningful and interesting, but also too small to sell without losing a large proportion in commission:

EXAMPLE

Investor holds 5,000 shares at 100p = £5000. Company issues warrants on a 1-for-10 basis, trading starts at 25p. Warrant holding = 500 warrants at 25p = £125.

In January 1991 Hanson plc made a highly creditable attempt to solve this problem by offering to sell small holdings for a fixed fee of £10, but this approach has regrettably not been followed by many other companies. The sad fact that many investors are effectively locked into their small warrant holdings is unsatisfactory for two reasons. First, it fails to provide a meaningful benefit to those holders, who merely hold their warrants until expiry and then exercise them, and second, it reduces the possible liquidity of the market. Were there to be some general mechanism through which holders could sell these small amounts, liquidity would improve and spreads would narrow.

At the other end of the spectrum, larger investors may find it very difficult to deal in size in many warrants. The market capitalization of the entire UK equity warrants market is marginally under £1.3 billion at the time of writing. Most warrants suffer from small market capitalizations because of the smaller number in issue and the lower price. These factors combine to produce many warrants with market capitalizations beneath £5 million, which makes them impractical for anything but small-scale investment. Funds of any size may need to restrict active investment policies to the larger blue-chip warrants such as BTR and Hanson. Dealing interest in smaller issues can provoke sharp price movements, particularly in the lesser-traded warrants which may not attract very much attention most of the time.

This may become more of a problem as new warrant funds emerge (see Chapter 13), but in some respects it represents a benefit to the well-informed private investor dealing in relatively small size. Many funds will stick with the larger 'covered' index and equity warrants, leaving the Stock Exchange market clear for the private investor to have a real influence.

WHEN TO BUY

Just as investors buy differing amounts of warrants for many different reasons, so the reasons for buying at any specific time vary also. Nevertheless, all investors will wish to time their investments so as to maximize the profits, and there are some guidelines which may be followed.

Medium-term and long-term investors will generally buy when their analysis points to some good buying opportunities. Whatever the chosen criteria (CFPs below 10 per cent; gearing over five times, new issues with over ten years to run etc), there will be certain times when funds are available and the analysis points to some sound value. On the assumption that this analysis has been sophisticated enough to incorporate some expectations of the likely gains from the shares and warrants, then it will include a market view and will be sufficiently predictive to issue a 'buy' signal which may be acted upon. There is an element of tautology in this argument, which essentially boils down to 'if you have decided something is cheap, you buy it', but the implication is interesting – namely that the underlying analysis is the sole determining factor. Since all relevant factors are already included in the analysis, it is the analysis which has all the answers.

For an analytical approach to be this compelling, it would need to pay considerable heed to overall market trends. Warrants have proved themselves to be highly sensitive to changes in the overall market indices, so some attention must be paid to whether the bulls or the bears have the upper hand. Warrant analysis can be very good for selecting the best warrants in the market, but if the whole market is going down then simple outperformance may not be good enough.

Long-term investors may not attach so much importance to fluctuations in the FT-SE Index, but for short-term investors this can be a critical determinant of success or failure. So too can be the relationship between the warrant and its underlying security. As mentioned elsewhere, short-term anomalies arise, and quick profits can sometimes be made by identifying these opportunities which typically occur when markets are moving quickly. Short-term speculators should be particularly alert when the market suddenly moves upwards with a jolt, since the liquidity divergence between frequently traded shares which respond quickly and lesser-traded warrants which are slower to react can throw up some excellent openings. The warrants market is far from perfect, and it is easily caught by surprise.

Imperfections can also be evident in the field of new issues. In the first few days of trading, a new warrant will often trade in a very broad band as it struggles to find the right level. This is particularly true of the commercial issues where there are few benchmarks from similar company warrants. For this reason it can pay the investor to keep a very close eye on the new issue market and to take advantage of any timely misalignments which occur. In this case, as with the liquidity divergence, the beneficiary must buy when the window of opportunity opens.

These brief comments have suggested some special factors which influence the timing of purchases, but they are not intended to suggest that good analysis and short-term opportunism are in any way exclusive. Quite the reverse is true. An analytical base is required to interpret the short-term signals properly. For example, if a warrant lags behind a share price increase, is it likely to catch up, or is it simply correcting a previous overvaluation? Technical analysis can be quite indispensable in providing the answer.

In conclusion, it is fundamental and technical analysis which must be seen as the prime determinants of timing, even when used in conjunction with apparent short-term anomalies. Investors should also keep a weather eye on the general state of the market, which is the most important external factor.

HOW LONG TO HOLD WARRANTS

A common question asked by less experienced investors is 'how long should I hold warrants before selling?', a question which has no real answer. There is no set time which is right: it depends entirely upon the time perspective of the individual, the specific aims for that investment, the current technical and fundamental position, the state of the market, and the past performance of the individual warrant. The key is to treat each case on its merits, and to apply basic rules of common sense.

If, for example, an investor is buying a warrant because the price has failed to react to a sharp rise in the share price over the last week, then he is likely to have a very short time horizon. Should the investor be proved correct, and the warrant price catches up with a rise of 10 per cent, then the investor may well take a small profit within a few days.

Conversely, there are circumstances in which a 10 per cent rise within a few days may act as a signal not to sell, but to buy more. If an investor buys a warrant because he likes the long-term prospects of the company, and then the market enters a bullish phase and pushes the shares and warrants up, this may reduce the CFP and make the warrants appear even more attractive as a long-term investment.

In short, one of the advantages of warrants over other speculative instruments is that they offer a good deal of time flexibility, so it makes no sense at all to impose an arbitrary time limit on investments.

WHEN TO SELL

Some investors will buy warrants with the express intention of holding them until final expiry, but the majority of investors who are prepared to trade warrants will face the perennially difficult question of when to sell. Again, analysis is the key for those who can devote the necessary time towards monitoring their warrant positions. For other investors who are unable to maintain regular calculations, there are two simple rules which bear repetition here. The first one is to cut your losses. Investors have great difficulty in accepting losses, since they prove we are all fallible, but it can often make a great deal of sense to take a small loss rather than run the risk of it turning into a large loss. Partly, of course, this approach depends upon the reason for the loss. If the warrant has simply fallen along with the market, then the initial reasons for purchase may still be valid. If, however, there is a more fundamental reason which has undermined the original analysis, then take a small loss and re-invest where the prospects look better. No one can win all of the time, and this way the majority of capital is saved to fight another day.

The other side of the coin is that investors should try and take large rather than small profits, although positions should not be allowed to run and run in the face of common sense. If the profit continues to increase, then let it, but if it starts to turn sour then close the position. There is little more disheartening than watching a large paper profit slowly evaporate. With this in mind, it is sometimes useful to have a target price. The original analysis at the time of purchase may well provide some clues as to the magnitude of the gain expected, and this can be used to calculate a target price. Once this target price has been exceeded then the investor should think about taking profits (not least because the attainment of the target can be satisfying). If the price continues to run higher then the warrants should continue to be held beyond the target price, but the investor might sell if the price breaks down through the target price, or the price declines for three consecutive sessions, whichever happens sooner.

EXAMPLE

Investor buys warrants at 35p. Target price 50p.
Day 1:   35p
Day 2:   35p
Day 3:   37p
.
.
.
Day 29:   48p
Day 30:   50p
Day 31:   50p

Day 32:   55p
Day 33:   54p
Day 34:   58p
Day 35:   57p
Day 36:   55p
Day 37:   52p   **SELL**

Using this approach the investor is not able to sell at the peak, but this is rarely a realistic possibility in any case. The investor has achieved a profit in excess of his target, and he has sold before a real downtrend has been established – a very reasonable outcome.

A different but equally valid approach where larger profits are concerned is to sell half of any holding when it reaches a 100 per cent profit. This may sound optimistic, but the gearing advantage of warrants means that they can double in a short space of time during strong market conditions. The half-sale technique recovers the initial stake and allows the rest of the investment to run for 'free'. This is a slightly more cautious approach than the one above, but some investors find this to be a useful and appealingly simple rule. And it is a rule which can be applied surprisingly often during bullish periods – investors with the right stock-broker, aware of dealing spreads, able to avoid trading difficulties, and with the right timing can find themselves forging a new meaning to the phrase 'double dealing'.

"For the companies issuing warrants, the exercise of warrants is of great importance, since the exercise monies provide additional capital. Equally for investors, the exercise rights are of key importance, because it is these rights which give the warrant value."

8

EXERCISING WARRANTS

The subscription rights attached to warrants are a considerable source of worry to many warrant-holders. When can I exercise? Do I have to? How much do I have to pay? What if I don't have enough capital to pay the full amount? What happens if I forget to exercise my rights? Do I have to exercise all of my warrants at once? Where do I send the money? These are all common questions, none of which require complex answers.

Exercising a warrant means paying the subscription price to convert your warrants into shares. In doing so the intrinsic value of the warrant is 'realized' and the warrant ceases to exist, as it will upon its final expiry if not exercised. For the companies issuing warrants, the exercise of those warrants is of great importance, since the exercise monies provide additional capital. Equally, for investors, the exercise rights are of key importance, because it is these rights which give the warrant value. This does not mean, however, that all warrant investors will necessarily wish to take up their rights when the opportunity arises. Investors may have frequent opportunities to exercise subscription rights, but this is an option, not an obligation. This distinction is of critical importance. The exercise rights belong to the investor, and the issuing company cannot enforce the conversion of warrants into shares if the terms are unfavourable. It is this property of warrants which prevents them from acquiring a negative value. In the event of the exercise price being higher than the prevailing share price, the holder will decline to exercise and his loss is limited to the original investment in warrants.

The explanation of the exercise process in this chapter relates to UK equity warrants only, and the procedure may differ considerably for other forms of warrants. Indeed some 'covered' warrants issued solely for the purpose of financial convenience may only be nominally exercisable and not in practice. You should always consult your stockbroker, the issuer, or the registrar if you are in any doubt. As this chapter explains, your investment may disappear if you overlook your exercise rights.

WHEN WARRANTS MAY BE EXERCISED

The question of when to exercise a warrant has two distinct elements – when you may exercise, and when you should. The first point is covered by the subscription terms of the warrants which specify the subscription price and the date or period when the subscription rights apply. For UK warrants most have what is known as European-style exercise terms which most often specify an annual date, for example:

The Overseas Investment Trust plc warrants each carry the right to subscribe for one ordinary share at 202p on 31 December in any year to 1998 inclusive.

Alternatively, there may be a subscription period which offers some flexibility:

Group Development Capital plc warrants each carry the right to subscribe for one ordinary share at 55.51p during the 28-day period following publication of the annual report and accounts in the years 1995 to 2006 inclusive.

Further, a few warrants have what are known as American-style exercise terms and are continuously exercisable throughout their life:

Hanson plc warrants each confer the right to subscribe for one share at 287p at any time up to 30 September 1997.

The variety of terms in the market means that is is always important to check the exact wording of the rights before dealing and to keep an accurate record of them prior to exercise or sale. The practice in the UK to prefer discrete exercise periods to continuous exercise, which is more common in America and Japan, has grown largely from arbitrary precedence, although it does have some specific benefits. A single exercise date each year is preferable for its administrative simplicity. For companies, this allows the finance director an accurate 'snapshot' picture of the likely exercise pattern, and allows him to plan for the capital which will be raised. Equally, a single exercise date each year makes life much easier for the registrars, who arrange the conversion into new shares. And for investors the principal advantage is again simplicity. It is easier to make a choice once a year than it is is to monitor the share and warrant price continuously. Furthermore, with discretely exercisable warrants, companies are usually obliged by the terms of their warrants to remind warrant-holders of their rights. This must be laudable, as UK equity warrants are distributed to a broad range of investors, and are usually offered on a scrip basis to shareholders who may have no experience or understanding of warrants. This is rather different from many overseas warrants which are in the hands of more sophisticated investors. This requirement to inform warrant-holders of their subscription rights in advance is usually encapsulated in the warrant particulars, and it is fairly standard. The usual practice is for the company to send a reminder notice to warrant-holders between eight weeks and four weeks before the exercise time. However, this service is not performed by companies with continuously exercisable warrants, and warrant-holders should never rely on reminder notices being sent. Investors should keep a note of the relevant exercise dates and plan accordingly.

The main drawback of discrete exercise periods is that they are less efficient. They do not allow warrant-holders to exercise at their convenience, and many warrants fall to a temporary discount shortly before the final exercise date. This is because the time value has evaporated, there are sellers who do not wish to exercise their warrants, and buyers who need to be compensated for the additional complication of buying the equity via the warrants (see Figure 8.1).

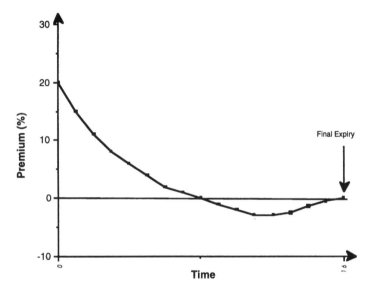

Figure 8.1 Warrants discount ahead of final expiry

WHEN WARRANTS SHOULD BE EXERCISED

Intermediate dates before final expiry

Whilst the conversion terms of warrants provide the dates on which a warrant may be exercised, the question of whether those rights should be taken up depends upon the individual circumstances surrounding each warrant. Remember, warrant-holders are not obliged to take up their rights to convert their warrants into ordinary shares. When the opportunity to exercise arises, warrant-holders have four choices. They may:

1 Exercise all of their subscription rights
2 Exercise some of their subscription rights
3 Sell all or part of their holding in the market
4 Do nothing

Each case must be decided on its merits, but there are some general principles and rules which may be applied as guidelines. The first of these relates simply to the share price and the exercise price. The warrants must have an intrinsic value for the holder to have any incentive to exercise his rights:

Condition 1:   Share price > exercise price

EXAMPLE A

Condition fulfilled

Widget plc warrants exercise price 100p; share price 120p; warrant-holder exercising his rights will be paying 100p for each share worth 120p in the market.

EXAMPLE B

Condition violated

Grommet plc warrants exercise price 100p; shares 80p; warrant-holder exercising his rights will be paying 100p for each share worth 80p in the market.

This rule is common sense. As long as the exercise price is exceeded by the share price, then the warrant-holder can buy the shares more cheaply via the warrant than he can in the market. The warrant-holder will actually lose money if he exercises his rights in violation of this rule, as he will be paying more for the shares than they are worth in the market.

As explained in Chapter 3, though, intrinsic value is only one element of the warrant valuation, and the next step is to incorporate the warrant price including any premium which may exist:

Condition 2:   Share price – exercise price ≥ warrant price

EXAMPLE A

Condition fulfilled

Widget plc warrants exercise price 100p; share price 120p; warrant price 18p. Warrant-holder exercising his rights can buy shares at 100p and sell them in the market at 120p – a profit of 20p per warrant against a market price of 18p.

EXAMPLE B

Condition violated

Grommet plc warrants exercise price 100p; share price 120p; warrant price 25p. Warrant-holder exercising his rights can buy shares at 100p and sell them in the market at 120p – a profit of 20p per warrant against a market price of 25p.

This is perhaps the most important point to understand, and it is a simple restatement of the premium. Warrants should be exercised when they are trading at a discount, or when they reach the final expiry date and it is not advantageous to sell in the market. When a warrant is exercised, its intrinsic value is realized, but any premium is lost. For this reason it is rarely sensible to exercise a warrant ahead of its final expiry date – intermediate dates or periods are generally characterized by a warrant price commanding significant 'time value' which will be forfeited by exercise.

That said, the 'premium rule' should not be applied too rigidly: it is a guide, not a hard and fast rule. Discretion should be used in marginal cases, especially as the costs of dealing are ignored in these simple guidelines. A warrant-holder who wishes to own shares in the company may find it sensible to exercise subscription rights even if a small premium exists. The costs of selling warrants in the market and then buying shares with the proceeds can be substantial when the dealing spread and commissions are included. Much depends upon whether the warrant-holder really wants the shares or not. It also depends upon whether the capital is available for exercise. When a warrant is exercised, you must pay the subscription price in cash, and for some warrant speculators holding a relatively large number of highly geared warrants a large amount of capital may be required:

EXAMPLE

Widget plc shares 350p, each warrant carries the right to subscribe for one share at 300p, warrant price at expiry 50p.

Holding of 10,000 warrants worth £5,000. Holder will have to pay £30,000 to exercise all of his warrants.

Final Expiry

The final expiry date of warrants is slightly different from the intermediate dates. Referring back to the four choices for warrant investors at the time of exercise, option four is to do nothing. This is often the most valid choice at intermediate dates or periods ahead of the final exercise date, but rarely so at the final date. This is because warrants which have not been exercised by the final expiry date become worthless. For this reason, if the warrant has any intrinsic value then the holder *must* take some action before the final exercise date, either selling in the market or taking the necessary steps to exercise the subscription rights. It is only if a warrant has no intrinsic value and is also worth nothing in the market that the warrant-holder should let the warrants lapse. Some warrants do expire worthless, particularly after periods of general market weakness, but the majority of warrants are normally 'in the money' at final expiry, and action should therefore be taken.

In theory and in practice, the premium attached to a warrant will disappear as it approaches final expiry, falling to zero on the final exercise date. This means that the 'premium rule' is of little relevance at the time of final expiry, and the decision whether to exercise or to sell in the market is influenced more heavily by fundamental considerations. At final expiry the primary decision is whether you want the shares or not. In practice, the warrant speculator will not usually wish to be concerned with exercise, and will sell holdings in the market before final expiry. Some warrant traders may deal in warrants extensively, but never exercise one. In contrast, longer-term investors and those warrant-holders who are already shareholders (who may have received the warrants as part of a scrip issue) will tend to take up their subscription rights. This is a generalization of course, but experience shows it to be valid in most cases.

The decision whether to exercise or to sell in the market does not have to be black and white. While most warrant-holders wishing to take up their exercise rights will usually decide to take up all of their rights, you do not have to exercise all of your warrants. There are circumstances in which it can make sense to take up some rights and sell the balance of your warrant holding in the market. This is true if a large amount of capital is required, or if the warrant-holder wishes to maintain the size of his holding. The gearing aspect of warrants means that a speculator can achieve rights over a large amount of equity with a relatively modest investment, but this also means that the speculator is unlikely to exercise all of his warrants even if he likes the company and the shares. A sensible compromise is to maintain the size of holding as follows:

EXAMPLE

Investor holds 10,000 Widget plc warrants, price 50p. Each warrant carries the right to subscribe for one share at 150p; share price 200p. Size of warrant holding = £5,000, but £15,000 capital required to exercise rights from all 10,000 warrants, taking equity holding up to £20,000. Holder decides to exercise a quarter of his warrants and sell the rest in the market. Cost of exercising 2,500 warrants = 2,500 × 150p = £3,750. Receipts from sale of 7,500 warrants in the market = 7,500 × 50p = £3,750. Result is that size of holding is maintained at £5,000, but now through 2,500 shares at 200p instead of 10,000 warrants at 50p.

Similarly, if the warrants have been successful and the investment has grown beyond the size of your normal investment unit, then partial exercise offers a sensible way to take profits:

EXAMPLE

Investor holds 10,000 Widget plc warrants, bought at 30p, current price 50p. Each warrant carries the right to subscribe for one share at 150p; share price

200p. Original cost of warrants £3,000, current value £5,000. Holder decides to take his profits by exercising 1,500 of his warrants and selling the rest in the market. Cost of exercising 1,500 warrants = 1,500 × 150p = £2,250. Receipts from sale of 8,500 warrants in the market = 8,500 × 50p = £4,250. Result is that holder takes £2,000 profit and returns to original holding of £3,000, now through 1,500 shares at 200p each.

THE RULES IN PRACTICE

Some investors may consider the simplicity of these guidelines to be an affront to their intelligence, but the remarkable pattern of exercise in some cases bears testament to the need for them. It is a constant source of amazement that a small number of warrants seem to be exercised each year when the holders could have realized more money by selling their warrants in the market. For example:

The Overseas Investment Trust plc warrants each carry the right to subscribe for one ordinary share at 202p on 31 December in any year to 1998 inclusive.

On 31 December 1989 the holders of 22,117 warrants exercised their rights. On this date the shares were 280p and the warrants were trading at 136p (a premium of 20.7 per cent).

The 22,117 warrants each realized 78p of value upon exercise (market price 280p – exercise price 202p), yet they could have been sold in the market for 136p each.

These warrants are probably exercised by ill-informed investors who do not know the full conversion terms, who do not understand the way in which warrants work, or those who have misunderstood the documents which they have been sent. There is one legitimate reason for exercise under these conditions, however – namely if the investor is a reluctant warrant-holder and holds a very small number of warrants which would attract prohibitive dealing costs if sold through the market. For example:

EXAMPLE

Widget Investment Trust warrants 25p each, shares 257p, each warrant carries the right to subscribe for one share at 240p. Usually the warrant-holder wishing to dispose of the warrants would sell in the market, and buy shares with the proceeds if required. But if the warrant-holder has 200 warrants, value £50, this may not be the best course.

Option 1: sell in market. Spread 8 per cent, brokers' minimum commission £15, receipts £33.

Option 2: exercise warrant rights. Realize 17p value per warrant = £34.

Even in this artificial case, the relative gain from exercise is very small, and the decision will depend more upon whether the small warrant-holder likes the shares or not. Furthermore, empirical evidence does not support the proposition that such a rational approach is behind the exercise patterns described above. For example, the 51 warrant-holders who chose to exercise their rights to subscribe for 26,385 shares in the F&C Pacific Investment Trust plc in June 1990 (realizing 101.5p against 115p in the market) had an average holding worth around £600. With this size of holding it would have been more profitable to have dealt through the market.

HOW TO EXERCISE A WARRANT

The actual process of exercise is not difficult, and instructions are issued for holders to follow. The procedure is explained on the reverse of the warrant certificate which you will receive after purchase, along with the terms of the subscription rights. Part of the certificate will usually consist of a form called the 'Exercise Notice' or 'Notice of Subscription' to be completed in the event of exercise and submitted to the company's registrar, whose address will be provided. Figure 8.2 gives an example. The form itself will usually comprise four parts.

Part 1 requires the holder to state the number of warrants to be exercised. As explained above, this will not necessarily be the entire holding represented by the certificate.

Part 2 of the exercise form relates to the subscription monies – the payment of the exercise price for each warrant the holder wishes to convert into shares. The holder will need to enclose a cheque for this amount, which is simply the exercise price multiplied by the number of warrants being exercised, as shown in the example above. This exercise price is payable in full on subscription, but there are no further charges.

Whereas parts 1 and 2 of the warrant form are standard and universal, part 3 is to be found on most but not all warrant certificates. It involves acceptance of the shares which will be allotted to you as a result of your exercise. For the majority of warrant-holders this means simply completing your name and address (or if the space is left blank, the shares will be sent to the holder at the address on the warrant register), but it is also possible to renounce your holding in favour of a nominee. In this case the nominee must accept the new shares by completing his name and address and signing the form of nomination which forms part of this section. This can be useful if the warrant-holder wishes to give shares as a gift to another family member, for example, and it has one other important use.

The form of nomination is used when the warrants have changed hands shortly before exercise is due, and the new owner of the warrants wishes to exercise his subscription rights. At this point the new holder will not be in receipt of the warrant certificate, so special arrangements must be made for exercise. The new holder must inform his stockbroker of his intention to exercise, and the form of nomination will be used to ensure that the shares are allotted to the new owner.

Part 4 of the form, finally, requires the holder to sign and date the form. In the case of joint holdings all must sign. In the case of a corporation this form must be under its Common Seal or under the hand of some officer or attorney of the corporation duly authorized in that behalf.

Once these sections are completed the warrant-holder should send the certificate together with the remittance in respect of the warrants being exercised to the registrar named on the certificate. Where a single date is specified, investors intending to exercise must ensure that the registrar receives the exercise notice no later than this date. Registrars will usually accept notices on or within 28 days prior to the relevant subscription date. Once lodged, the exercise notice is irrevocable, save with the consent of the directors. The warrants will then be cancelled and new shares issued within 14 days after the relevant subscription date. In the event of a partial exercise a fresh certificate will also be issued for the balance of warrants remaining exercisable.

WHAT HAPPENS IF A WARRANT IS NOT EXERCISED

In the event of a warrant-holder missing the exercise period and failing to take any action, then the warrants will become valueless and the investment is lost. Some (but not all) companies provide a 'rescue' service for negligent warrant-holders and within seven days following the final exercise date the company may appoint a trustee who, provided that the net proceeds of sale are likely to exceed the costs of subscription (i.e., if the warrant has intrinsic value), will exercise the remaining subscription rights, sell the new shares in the market, and distribute the net proceeds *pro rata* to the warrant-holders so entitled. This practice is by no means universal though, and you should never rely upon the company to exercise subscription rights on your behalf. It is your option, not the company's.

The action taken by some companies to exercise 'forgotten' rights on behalf of investors is not entirely altruistic. It benefits the negligent warrant-holders, of course, but it also benefits the company. If the warrants are not exercised and allowed to lapse then the company will not raise the full amount of capital expected. The exercise of rights serves to raise this capital:

Widget plc 1,000,000 warrants in issue; share price 200p; exercise price 150p. Holders of 900,000 warrants take up rights, paying £1,350,000 in exercise monies to Widget plc. Widget appoints trustee to exercise remaining 100,000

EXERCISE NOTICE

When completed this Warrant Certificate with the Exercise Notice signed and completed should be submitted, together with the payment referred to below to Phantom Registrars Ltd, Registrar House, High Street, Anytown.

To: Widget plc ("the Company")

I/We the registered holder(s) of the Warrant(s) comprised in the attached Warrant Certificate hereby give notice of my/our wish to exercise _____ [see Note (1)] of such Warrants and to subscribe for Ordinary Shares in accordance with the Particulars of the Warrants endorsed on the said Warrant Certificate.

I/We enclose my/our cheque for £ _____ [see Note (2)]in favour of Widget plc, being payment of 100p in respect of each of the Warrants specified above.

(Please complete either Section A or Section B)
Section A

I/We agree to accept the fully paid Ordinary Shares of the Company to be allotted pursuant hereto subject to the Memorandum and Articles of Association of the Company. I/We hereby authorise and request the entry of my/our name(s) in the Register of Members in respect thereof.

I/We hereby authorise the despatch of (i) a Certificate in respect of the Ordinary Shares of the Company to be allotted to me/us; (ii) a Warrant Certificate in my/our name(s) for any balance of my/our Warrants remaining exercisable; and (iii) a cheque for the balance of any subscription moneys (if £2 or more) in respect of any overpaid subscription moneys, by ordinary post at my/our risk to:

Name _____   [see Note (3)]

Address _____

_____

Section B (Form of Nomination)

For use by Warrant holders wishing to nominate some other person(s) as the allottee(s) of all or some of the Ordinary Shares.

I/We renounce my/our rights to _____ of the Ordinary Shares of the Company to be issued pursuant hereto to the person(s) who is/are named in and who sign(s) the Form of Acceptance (Section C).

Siganture(s) of Warrant holder (s)

_____   _____

_____   _____

In the case of joint holdings all Warrant holder(s) must sign. In the case of a corporation this form must be under its Common Seal or under the hand of some officer or attorney of the corporation duly authorised in that behalf.

Dated this   **day of**   **199**

Figure 8.2 Warrants exercise notice

Section C (Form of Acceptance)

I/We accept the rights to the Ordinary Shares renounced by the person(s) who has/have completed Form B above, subject to the Memorandum and Articles of Association of the Company and hereby authorise and request the entry of my/our name(s) in the Register of Members in respect of such Ordinary Shares and the despatch of a Certificate thereof by ordinary post at my/our risk to the address first written below:

Dated this   **day of**   **199**

Surname _____

Forenames in Full _____

Address in Full _____

_____

Surname _____

Forenames in Full _____

Address in Full _____

_____

Surname _____

Forenames in Full _____

Address in Full _____

_____

Signature(s)

_____   _____

_____   _____

Notes

(1)   Please insert here the number of Warrants being exercised. If no number is inserted, all of the Warrants comprised in the attached certificate will be treated as being exercised.
(2)   Please complete. The amount payable is the Subscription Price per Ordinary Share multiplied by the number of Warrants being exercised. If in doubt as to the current Subscription Price please enquire of the Registrars. Payment must be made by a cheque drawn on a bank in Great Britain.
(3)   If this space is left blank, the Share Certificate, Warrant Certificate (if any) and cheque (if any) will be despatched by post at the risk of the person(s) entitled thereto to the registered address of the (first-named) holder.

Figure 8.2 (Continued)

rights. 100,000 shares sold in market at 195p, 150p per warrant goes to Widget plc and 45p per warrant to the negligent warrant-holders. Result is that Widget plc raises an additional £150,000.

DILUTION OF NET ASSET VALUE

Finally, the warrant-holder exercising his subscription rights should be aware that this process of exercise could influence the value of the shares being subscribed for. The issue of new shares to satisfy the exercise of warrants will dilute the existing equity base, something which is of particular concern to investment trust shareholders. The share price of most investment trusts is strongly related to the net asset value, so *any reduction in the net asset value will usually have a detrimental effect on the share price.* If the new shares are issued at a price lower than the prevailing net asset value per share, then 'dilution' will take place, as follows:

EXAMPLE

Widget Investment Trust plc, 5,000,000 shares in issue, net assets £6.25 million; net asset value per share 125p. 1,000,000 warrants exercised at 100p. Company receives £1 million in exercise monies; net assets £7.25m; spread over 6,000,000 shares = net asset value per share 120.8p.

The importance of dilution is very often overestimated, although it can be substantial in cases where the net asset value per share is a long way above the exercise price. It is possible to calculate the percentage dilution as follows (full exercise of all warrants and 1-for-1 conversion terms are assumed):

$$Dilution = \left[\frac{\frac{(Net\ assets + exercise\ monies)/}{(Number\ of\ shares + number\ of\ warrants)}}{Current\ net\ assets\ per\ share} - 1\right] \times 100$$

Using the example above,

$$\left[\frac{\frac{(£6.25m + £1m)/}{(5\ million\ shares + 1\ million\ warrants)}}{£1.25} - 1\right] \times 100$$

$$\left[\frac{£7.25m\ /\ 6\ million}{£1.25} - 1\right] \times 100 = -3.33\%$$

"Covered warrants offer some remarkable opportunities which are not readily available elsewhere in the warrants market."

9

COVERED WARRANTS

The covered warrants market, which was little more than a sideshow in the UK when the first edition of this book was written in 1991, has subsequently expanded enormously, hence the complete revision and extension of this chapter. More investors are now considering covered warrants as a part of their portfolios, and issuers are displaying some renewed interest in attracting private investors to their realm.

Covered warrants were first developed in the 1980s in response to institutional demand. Such is the periodic clamour for warrants that in spite of the considerable growth of the equity warrants market, institutional investors have not found their demand to be satisfied by the existing company issues which tend to have small market capitalizations. Nor have institutions felt that the enormous benefits of warrants as financial instruments have been spread widely enough. For these reasons the standard UK equity warrants market is supplemented by 'covered' warrants issued by third parties. These are sometimes related to specific equities, but more often now they refer to sector baskets, market indices, or to other financial indicators such as currencies or interest rates. This is a burgeoning sector of the warrants market, and although private investors may prefer to stick with the equity issues, no survey of warrants markets could be complete without an explanation of this increasingly popular element.

This versatile instrument is slowly winning across some private investors in the UK. The retail side is already important in France and Germany, and in the latter, investors can deal in large numbers of covered warrants through the Stock Exchanges. As large corporate warrants such as Lucas, Hanson and BTR expire from the listed market in the UK, so we expect more investors to move across to the covered market which offers a wide range of warrants on UK blue-chip companies. The covered warrants market has already proved itself highly adaptable to meet the needs of investors, and as the market develops so there is a possibility that the London Stock Exchange may be prepared to admit covered warrants to the fold.

WHAT ARE COVERED WARRANTS?

The first key difference with covered warrants is that it is not the company which issues the warrants, rather it is a finance house. In basic terms, covered warrants are rights created by a third-party issuer, usually a major financial institution. They draw their name from the fact that they are in theory covered by purchases of the underlying security in the market: at least, the issuer undertakes to cover the issue of shares as specified in the offer documents. In practice these documents are of critical importance, since covered warrant issues can vary widely in their specifications.

To begin with, where the warrants relate to the shares of an individual company, that company may or may not have authorized the issue. Their compliance is not necessary. Unlike the standard equity issues where the company issues new shares in return for the subscription monies when warrants are exercised, the shares which are granted to holders of covered warrants upon exercise are simply bought in the market by the issuer to 'cover' their commitment. The subscription money is paid to the issuer, and the company is not involved in any direct manner. It does not benefit from what is a purely financial transaction between two private parties – the issuer and the investor. Covered warrants are synthetic derivatives created for the issuer's clients, although speculation in the warrants can have an effect on the underlying share prices. Therefore covered warrants are created in response to a request or demand among investors for a geared position in a specific sector or market.

Second, the holder of a covered warrant is not necessarily entitled to the delivery of the underlying security upon exercise. In most cases this is the practice, but in some circumstances the holder will simply be paid the cash value of the underlying security. This is most obviously the case where the warrants confer rights over instruments other than ordinary shares – for example market indices. The issuer cannot 'buy' and deliver an index.

Third, the term 'covered warrants' can sometimes be a misnomer. In practice, covered warrants may be fully covered, partially covered, or even not covered at all. In the case of a fully covered warrant the issuer will beneficially own all of the underlying securities to be issued in case of exercise, or else will own a sufficient number of warrants issued directly by the company to subscribe for those shares. In the latter case, the covered warrants issue is clearly a repackaging of a company issue, altering the subscription terms or the currency to meet the demand from institutions. Where the issuer has partial cover or no cover there is an obligation to deliver the securities or cash in lieu.

In some respects covered warrants resemble traded options. The maturity tends to be shorter than for most company warrants, at two or three years, and as the underlying shares are already in issue there is no dilution upon exercise. Another similarity is that a considerable proportion of covered warrants are 'put' warrants – i.e. they carry the right to *sell* the underlying security at a fixed price.

This is a facility which ordinary warrants cannot offer, and the additional flexibility is certainly one factor which has stimulated the growth of this market. Both put and call warrants on market indices are very popular, although there is some reticence regarding the former – largely due to a lack of understanding.

The covered warrants market is a rapidly expanding, but under-utilized derivatives market. It provides investors with another tool to improve portfolio performance, particularly at a time when the UK listed warrants market has become increasingly conservative.

THE EMERGENCE OF COVERED WARRANTS

The first covered index warrants in London were launched in 1986, but it was not until 1989 or 1990 that the market began to attract attention. Covered warrants came to the fore at this time in response to institutional demand, and there was some hectic activity as investment houses such as Salomon, Morgan Stanley and Bankers Trust jostled for position. The speed with which new warrants arrived was impressive, issues being made as soon as the demand had been identified and the issuer had found a cost-efficient way of covering the possible commitment. As one would expect, the issue of covered warrants is highly dependent upon specific demand, which has already picked up from troughs in 1991 and 1994, but the onset of another bull market would almost certainly see covered warrants being issued at a furious pace. Even in the relatively quiet conditions of 1995, there were 56 new equity and basket covered warrant issues in London between March and June, which compares with 12 new issues in the listed market over the same period.

There is some degree of uncertainty in the market, however. In early 1995 Kidder Peabody withdrew from the market for covered warrant issues (although provision was made for existing holders to sell in an orderly manner), and in the second quarter of 1995 the takeover of SG Warburg by Swiss Bank Corporation may have some implications for separate Warburg issues in the future. Nevertheless, it seems as though covered warrants are a fast-growing sector of a fast-growing market, and their future as a growing element of trading in London seems assured in the near term. Covered warrants are already far more important in other European countries such as Germany, where the 'retail' private investors' side is important, and they are even being issued in some emerging markets. The first covered warrants were issued in Malaysia to some enthusiasm in June 1995.

Already the number in issue is large. It is difficult to say just how many actually exist, since some are essentially 'private' issues which are not actively traded; some do not have Stock Exchange listings; many have numerous tranches; and the pace of issues on the international markets is furious. Bloomberg, for instance, recorded 13 issues over the course of a week in 1995 (see Table 9.1), and their coverage is far from comprehensive, excluding most of the warrants listed in London.

9 June	Citibank AG issues calls and puts on 6-months DM LIBOR
9 June	Dresdner Bank is lead underwriter for calls on Dyckerhoff
9 June	SBC issues calls and puts on SBC technology basket
9 June	BZ bank Zurich issues calls on Stillhalter Vision AG
8 June	Société Générale issues calls on French insurance basket
8 June	SBC issues calls and puts on DTB-bund-future due September 1995
7 June	SBC issues calls on Look-Back put warrants on S&P 500 Index
7 June	Creditanstalt issues call warrants on Mayr-Melnhof Karton AG
7 June	BT Effecten issues call warrants on BT Japan OTC 50 Index
7 June	Merrill Lynch issues call warrants on German bank basket
7 June	Société Générale issues call warrants on German bank basket
6 June	Bankers Trust issues call warrants on Portugal Telecom
5 June	Salomon Brothers issues call warrants on Swiss Bank shares

Source: Bloomberg

Table 9.1 Covered warrant issues listed by Bloomberg during a week in 1995

Suffice to say that the market is large enough to provide most investors with some warrants of interest, or at least a close proxy for what they are looking for. If not, and if you are a large enough investor, you can effect an issue by liaising with one of the issuing finance houses. An estimate of the number of covered warrants traded in London at the time of writing is perhaps 800 to a thousand, with the total number worldwide in excess of 5,000. This is why serious warrant investors should sit up and take notice of this market.

WHAT TYPES OF COVERED WARRANT EXIST?

Covered warrants are far from homogeneous, and largely because they are created in response to specific demands, the terms can be highly individual and varied. A number of different types exist to cater for a wide range of differing preferences, providing investors with an opportunity to hedge positions on a market sector, index or company or to obtain a geared position on an underlying security.

Call warrants

The holder of a call warrant, on exercising, has the right to buy the underlying instrument at the exercise price (or, more often than not, the cash equivalent). All listed equity warrants are call warrants, as distinct from put warrants.

Put warrants

The holder of a put warrant has the option to sell the underlying instrument at the exercise price (or, again, receive the cash equivalent). Put warrants have an inverse rather than a direct relationship with the value of the underlying instrument, gaining in value as the underlying instrument falls and vice versa.

EXAMPLE:

Put warrant carries the right to sell Stock A for 100p.
Stock price 100p; warrant price (all premium) 15p.
Stock price falls by 25 per cent to 75p; right to sell at 100p now worth 25p.
Warrant gains 66.66 per cent.

American-style

Most covered warrants have American-style exercise periods. This type enables the holder to exercise the covered warrant at any time up to final expiry.

European-style

The European-style exercise period is almost exclusively the domain of the listed warrants market. These terms enable the holder to exercise the warrant on specific dates in the future.

Single-stock warrants

These are warrants issued on a single security and are similar to standard, listed warrants. Single-stock warrants confer the right to buy a share (or receive the intrinsic value cash equivalent) at a fixed price in the future, and these have become quite popular on FT-SE 100 blue-chip companies in particular. At the time of writing, warrants exist in London for Abbey National, Argyll Group, ASDA Group, BAA, Barclays, British Airways, British Gas, British Petroleum, British Steel, BT, BTR (two series), Cable & Wireless (two series), Cadbury Schweppes, Commercial Union, Enterprise Oil, Glaxo-Wellcome (three series), Grand Metropolitan, Guinness (three series), Hanson (three series), ICI, Lucas Industries (two series), Marks & Spencer, National Westminster Bank, Pilkington, Royal Bank of Scotland, RTZ, Shell Transport, Smithkline Beecham, Standard Chartered Bank, TI Group, Vodafone, and Zeneca. A number of warrants are also available on large overseas companies such as Bayer, Broken Hill Proprietary, Carrefour, Daimler Benz, Ericsson, Hong Kong Telecom, KPN, Michelin, Philips Electronics, Skandia, STET, Swiss Re, Telebras, Telmex, Volkswagen, and Volvo.

Terms of subscription are usually straightforward, and typically take the form of the example below:

EXAMPLE

PARIBAS BRITISH AIRWAYS

Launch Date:	*23 November 1993*
Type:	*American-style call*
Expiry:	*23 November 1995*
Exercise period:	*22 December 1993 to 23 November 1995*
Exercise price:	*423p*
Exercise rights:	*exercisable for cash or stock*
Warrants per share:	*1*
Size of issue:	*6,500,000*
Minimum size:	*100 trading, 50,000 exercising*
Market-making:	*Paribas*
Reuters page:	*PCMW*
Listing:	*London*
Restrictions:	*no special restrictions*

What these single- stock warrants offer is a simple way for investors to gain geared exposure to leading blue-chip companies. The argument for investment trust warrants, that it is possible to form a sensible judgement about the course of a stable, conservative underlying security and then back your judgement using a more exciting instrument, also applies to single stock covered warrants. Issues are rarely made on smaller companies for two principal reasons, namely that the demand for a specific smaller company is unlikely to be sufficiently great, and second, the issuer has to consider the ease with which he can cover his position. With large blue-chip shares this is not difficult.

For many investors, and those entering the covered warrants market for the first time in particular, these warrants will be the obvious choice. There is a huge amount of fundamental research available on the underlying companies, they are actively traded so the price moves frequently, and novice investors will have little difficulty in understanding the terms. There is nothing complex about the majority of single-stock issues, and they represent a viable alternative to listed equity warrants.

Basket warrants

Basket warrants are issued on a group of shares. Usually the basket focuses on a particular sector, and this is especially valuable in a market where leading stock-brokers' analysts are usually organized on a sectoral basis. Often they will form opinions about the value of their sector as a whole, allowing clients to switch between sectors at favourable times. This can be a profitable approach, since companies within a sector often move very much in tandem according to the pre-vailing trends. A string of natural disasters will hit the insurance sector. News of lower interest rates boosts the building sector. Strong retail sales figures help the high street stores. Regulatory changes affect utilities. Furthermore, these sector warrants could be considered almost as specialist mini-investment trusts. In deriving value from a number of shares, albeit with some unifying factor, the risk is spread. Instead of relying on the skills of a manager to select the best performing shares within his remit, however, the baskets approximate to 'tracker' funds which remove this subjective element. Within a basket each underlying share will have its own separate weighting to allow calculation of the value of the basket itself. Very often this is no more complex than allowing for one share per company in the basket. A typical example is given below:

EXAMPLE

SALOMON BROTHERS REGIONAL ELECTRICITY COMPANIES (REC) BASKET IV

Issuer:	*Salomon Inc*
Issue size:	*10 million*
Exercise type:	*American-style calls*
Strike price:	*£25.84 ('at the money' at the time of issue)*
Launch date:	*26 April 1995*
Expiry date:	*26 April 1996*
Listing:	*Luxembourg*
Basket composition:	*1 share each of Eastern Electricity, London Electricity, Southern Electricity, and Yorkshire Electricity*
Description:	*Four warrants are exercisable into one REC basket at the strike price. The issuer will be entitled to deliver the cash equivalent of the REC basket in lieu of physical shares.*
Settlement:	*Euroclear 7 days*
Minimum size:	*10,000 (trading and exercise)*
Restrictions:	*standard UK and US selling restrictions apply*

Basket warrants are a useful instrument for investors prepared to take a view on a sector but perhaps lacking sufficient in-depth knowledge to select an individual company which may provide the best performance. They also carry a lower risk than single-stock warrants, and the selection is good. For UK company sectors, warrants are available on food retailers, builders, composite insurance, drinks, drugs, regional electricity companies, engineers, investment trusts, oil stocks, pharmaceuticals, retail distributors, smaller companies, support services, UK/US growth, and water. These are perhaps fairly run-of-the-mill, but when listing the overseas baskets the market suddenly takes on a far more exotic and esoteric flavour. Consider the baskets for Argentinean blue-chips, Australian insurance stocks, Mexican construction stocks, European airlines, French financial institutions, German mechanical engineers, Korean blue-chips, Peruvian stocks, Singapore shipbuilders, South-east Asian banks, Swedish capital goods, Taiwanese finance stocks, and US technology stocks. Truly, the covered warrants market offers something for everyone.

Index warrants

For investors who simply wish to take a position on a market generally, without any preference for individual companies or sectors, index warrants are available for hedging or speculation. They are usually given a range of 'strike' prices and are often issued in tranches of calls and puts, making them similar in composition to traded options. Exercise is for cash, as the issuer cannot deliver an index. As with the stock and sector warrants, there is a wide choice on most major market indices, including the Nikkei 225 and Nikkei 300 (Japan), the CAC-40 Index (France), the DAX (Germany), the FT-SE 100 and FT-SE MidCap (UK), the S&P 500 (US), the BCI (Italy), the JSE Industrial (South Africa), the OMX Index (Sweden), the BOVESPA (Brazil), and the IPC (Mexico). The range is global, and it is possible for investors in most circumstances to find a proxy for the exposure required.

One point which is important to note from the terms below is that the minimum dealing size is much higher than for most other forms of covered warrants. Index warrants are principally intended for use by institutions to hedge market positions, and few private investors will find these instruments to be the most suitable.

EXAMPLE

SG WARBURG NIKKEI 300 INDEX

Issuer:	*SG Warburg OTC plc*
Underlying:	*Nikkei 300 Index*
Launch date:	*2 March 1995*
Issue size:	*20,000,000 warrants per tranche*
Exercise:	*American-style*
Expiry:	*2 September 1996*
Tranche A:	**call warrant exercisable at 249.23**
Tranche B:	**call warrant exercisable at 274.15**
Tranche C:	**put warrant exercisable at 249.23**
Index reference level:	*249.23 (level at time of issue)*
Entitlement:	*One warrant entitles the holder to receive the cash equivalent of one index.*
Trading:	*minimum dealing size 10,000 warrants*
Listing:	*Luxembourg*
Selling restrictions:	*not to be offered to US investors*

Currency warrants

To obtain a position on a certain currency against another investors could use one of the many currency warrants that are available in both put and call formats. At the time of writing Citibank is the issuer which leads this sector of the market, offering a range of warrants on cross rates including DM/CHF, DM/FRF, DM/ITL, US$/ITL, JP¥/ITL, DM/JP¥, GB£/FRF, JP¥/FRF, US$/CHF, US$/DM, US$/FRF, US$/JP¥, and of course US$/GB£. In these cases, where it is the ratio between two instruments which is underlying the warrant, the warrant is at once both a call and a put, since if one side of the ratio rises, the other must fall. Thus, one of the warrants on offer is a US$ (call) / GB£ (put), and can be viewed either way. The warrant will gain in value if the dollar strengthens against sterling, or if sterling weakens against the dollar. The result is the same.

Warrants with additional terms

Investors need to watch carefully for any extra terms which may be imposed on covered warrants. There is a whole armoury of special terms including 'knock-out' warrants, 'look-back' warrants, 'outperformance' warrants, 'AIR corridor' warrants, 'down and out' warrants, 'up and out' warrants, 'capped call' warrants, and a host of other strangely named issues with strange terms. It is always crucial to check the conversion terms for these special conditions, although they are usually evident from the title of the warrant. Some affect the valuation of the warrants critically; others peripherally. Outperformance warrants, for example, enable investors to profit from anticipated differences in the relative performance of two instruments. The payoff is expressed as the percentage performance of one instrument minus the percentage performance of the other multiplied by a fixed notional amount. The AIR corridor warrants are 'accrue income in range' warrants which provide the means to capitalize on a static market. Here, the warrants accrue a fixed return for every business day the instrument trades within the specified range until exercise. Knockout warrants have an upper or a lower level imposed, and should the warrant breach that barrier then it immediately expires worthless. Such warrants are unsuitable for all but the most experienced investors, and it is hard to see why investors would use them when there are so many ready alternatives without such damning clauses.

THE ADVANTAGES OF COVERED WARRANTS

Apart from the general advantages attached to warrants, as outlined in Chapter 2, covered warrants have a number of specific advantages which can make them more attractive than listed equity warrants. In general these are well appreciated by institutional investors, hence the immense range and size of the market, but they are less well understood by private investors who have been sheltered from this market in the UK by zealous regulatory bodies.

Dealing size

Institutions, like most other investors, need to be able to deal in appropriate size in the instruments of their choice, and the standard UK equity warrants market is simply not large enough to accommodate the dealing requirements of substantial trusts and funds. This is why covered warrants have been issued, and the ability to deal in large size is without question one of their two primary attractions. Whereas it can be awkward to deal in more than £5,000 to £10,000-worth of listed equity warrants in many cases, larger investors should not encounter any problems investing much larger sums in single covered warrant issues.

EXAMPLE

Société Générale Zeneca covered call warrants
Trading size 100,000 warrants, at 230p each = £230,000

The issuing companies create a large, broad-based and liquid market with a good capitalization for each issue because they are intended for institutional use. This removes many of the problems that private investors have suffered when dealing in smaller capitalized warrants, and is a major plus for the covered market.

The range of warrants

As explained above, the covered warrants market is an increasingly popular method for institutions and private investors to obtain a medium- or short-term position on a market, company, sector or currency. For this reason the demand for covered warrants has increased and the number is growing swiftly.

Clearly it can make good sense to scan lists of available covered warrants in order to identify any warrants relating to special interests which you may have. Many private investors, for example, take a keen interest in gold, yet there are few ways in which they can reasonably speculate in precious metals. The covered warrants relating to gold might just provide the answer – but not before the terms of the issue have been checked thoroughly. Small investors may also need to check the dealing position.

Technical position

A major advantage of covered warrants is their strong technical position. Standard UK-listed warrants have gone through a three-year bull phase, and although prices have slipped since, the legacy of the bull run is a lower level of risk and return. As prices rose, so average gearing has dropped to an average of 3.2 times (having been as low as 2.4 times in February 1994). The covered warrant market, in contrast, provides investors with opportunities to gain exposure to more highly speculative instruments. For example, the UK-listed warrants of the Herald Investment Trust plc, a multi-media trust, provide a gearing of 2.1 times. When compared to the gearing of the SG Warburg European Multi-Media No.2 covered warrant, 13.2 times, the benefit of some exposure to covered warrants becomes clear. However, it must be noted that with the increase in gearing comes a commensurably higher level of risk.

Put warrants

The issue of put warrants enables investors to speculate in a company, sector, or market that they believe will fall in value. They can also be used to protect investors' assets by hedging against the prospect of a falling market – something which cannot be done with listed equity warrants which are calls only. For this reason covered warrants may be applied to a far broader range of investment strategies and circumstances.

Price anomalies

Covered warrant prices are priced in a different way to listed equity warrants (see 'How the covered warrants market works' below), and apparent price anomalies are not corrected by the forces of supply and demand. This means that 'cheap' warrants can persist in an undervalued position for lengthy periods of time, providing investors with more than a brief window of opportunity.

Dealing spreads

Many dealing spreads are more competitive in the covered warrants market, which is an irony when it is competing with the listed market which is supposed to form a competitive price from an aggregate of different market-makers' quotes. Issuers often specify the maximum dealing spread which they will quote, and it is essential for their credibility that the price remains competitive throughout the life of the warrant. Compare the spreads in Table 9.2 with those listed in Table 7.2.

Not all of the dealing spreads are tight, but the majority offer reasonable value for investors seeking to deal actively. This is one difference between the listed equity market, where the long-dated warrants are expected to be used for long-term investment, and covered warrants with a maximum maturity of three years. The emphasis is much more on trading in the covered warrants market, and the spreads are keener accordingly.

Warrant	Bid–Offer prices	Spread (%)
Abbey National (BZW)	54–57p	5.3
ASDA group (SBC)	26–28p	7.1
British Steel (SBC)	27–30p	10.0
Commercial Union (Société Générale)	130.2–137.1p	5.0
Lucas Industries (Société Générale)	30–31.5p	4.8
Marks & Spencer (Société Générale)	39.1–41.1p	4.9
RTZ (Paribas)	68.6–72.2p	5.0
Food Trolley series 2 (BZW)	415–422p	1.7
UK Retail Distribution (Paribas)	2204–2320p	5.0
UK Regional Electric (Salomon)	17–25p	32.0
UK Engineers (Morgan Stanley)	475–600p	20.8
UK Water basket (SBC)	342–348p	1.7
Bayer AG (SBC)	DM6.59–DM6.89	4.4
Ericsson (SBC)	SEK73–SEK75	2.7
Sandoz (BZW)	CHFr38–CHFr40	5.0
Volkswagen AG series 2 (SBV)	DM0.93–DM1.23	24.4
Blue-Chip Malaysian basket (Société Générale)	US$1.50–US$1.55	3.2
Irish Blue-Chip Basket (Morgan Stanley)	IR£12.45–IR£13.20	5.7
Peru Series 2 Basket (Société Générale)	US$0.26–US$0.31	16.1
US Technology Basket (SBC)	US$10.10–US$10.30	1.9

Table 9.2 Dealing spreads for covered warrants

Lack of dilution

Another difference between covered warrants and listed equity warrants is that there is no dilution to existing shareholders, since no new shares are issued. If the issuer of the warrant should undertake to deliver stock when warrants are exercised, then he will do so by purchasing existing outstanding stock in the market, and no new shares will be created upon exercise. Dilution is no longer a concern.

DISADVANTAGES OF COVERED WARRANTS

Whilst the range of covered warrants available is undoubtedly impressive, this is still not a market in which many private investors will be prepared to deal. The main worry is that most covered warrants are not listed on the London Stock Exchange, and that dealing is less regulated. It is normally the issuer who makes a market in the warrants, but there is not necessarily any guarantee that a continuous market will be maintained until the warrant expires. In most issues the liquidity is probably better than that for ordinary equity warrants, but it is not assured. In some cases the market has dried up, leaving the warrant-holders with little choice but to forgo the time value and exercise their warrants. The standard of service received varies considerably, and in times of market strife it is doubtful whether pricing would continue to be efficient and spreads reasonable. There is also a small risk of default, and investors should only deal in covered warrants issued by the most respectable institutions. Certainly the need to deal through a specialist dealer is paramount, and the subscription terms must always be checked very carefully. It would be foolish to deny that covered warrants have substantial drawbacks:

Relatively short expiry

Covered warrants tend to be relatively short-dated compared to listed warrants. Expiry times of less than two years, at issue, are not uncommon, and three years is the maximum maturity in this market. This increases the risk of holding the warrants, because the share, basket, or market may enter a bear cycle and the warrants may not have a long enough expiry time to return to previous values. For medium- and long-term investors this is a considerable problem which they are unlikely to overcome.

Difficult to track

As covered warrants are not usually fully listed on the London Stock Exchange it can be difficult to track your investments. Covered warrant prices are not published in the *Financial Times* or any other newspaper, they are not on the *Market-Eye* system, nor are they available on the *Teleshare* service. This is probably the greatest challenge to new investors in the covered warrants market, and until recently it was simply not possible for private investors to track a portfolio of covered warrant investments without the considerable expense of a Reuters screen. Now the problem has been eased slightly and British investors can gain easy access to prices using the *Covered Warrants Alert Price Line*, a premium rate telephone service which provides quick coded access to a wide range of covered warrant prices. This is not entirely satisfactory, however, since the service carries a limited number of prices, it is updated only once a day, and of course it costs money to use.

Issuers are aware that this difficulty must be addressed if they are to attract substantial numbers of private or 'retail' investors to deal in the market. Understandably, investors are reluctant to invest blindly, where they cannot track prices on a daily basis. For some time SG Warburg placed monthly advertisements in the *Financial Times* displaying the recent prices of covered warrants issued by them, but this proved rather expensive and was halted. The screen-based Reuters system is the main route to obtaining indicative prices for covered warrants, as the issuers have contributor pages on which they list their prices, most of which are updated in real-time (see Figure 9.1). These prices, it should be stressed, are

```
 Function   Screens   Format   Quotes   SetUp
 12:18 11JUN95 LN SWISS BANK CORPORATION                    UK08594          SBCEDGB1
                          UK Warrants
 London (+44 171 711 2281)   Zurich (+41 1 239 3313)   Trading (+44 171 711 3505)

 Instrument   (M'ply) A/E C/P Maturity Strike Spot Cur Bid Offer Telekurs
 ASDA PLC                A C 08-DEC-97     75    87 GBP   26    28 328350
 BARCLAYS PLC            A C 08-DEC-97    650   676 GBP  125   132 328341
 Brit Aero Part Cert     A C 15-JUN-95      0   528 GBP  533   538 245516
 British Gas plc         A C 10-NOV-97    300   312 GBP   52    56 308803
 British Petroleum       A C 10-NOV-97    450   443 GBP   76    81 308792
 British Telecom plc     A C 10-NOV-97    400   395 GBP   51    54 308781
 BTR plc                 A C 10-NOV-97    325   339 GBP   62    67 308797
 BRITISH STEEL plc       A C 08-DEC-97    175   166 GBP   27    30 328331
 Enterprise Oil plc      A C 10-NOV-97    400   407 GBP   70    75 308795
 FTSE Warrant    0.3171  E C 18-MAY-95   3154  3313 GBP 48.0 50.5 239993
 FTSE Warrant            A C 16-JUN-95   3200  3334 GBP  127   139 251058
 Glaxo plc               A C 10-NOV-97    625   739 GBP  183   190 308804
 GUINNESS PLC            A C 08-DEC-97    500   470 GBP   71    76 328294
 UK Drinks Basket        A C 13-JUN-96  18885 17396 GBP  803   844 158773
 UK Electrical Basket    A C 11-AUG-95  20439 19420 GBP  220   232 271987
 UK Pharmaceutical Bas   A C 13-JUN-96   3788  5413 GBP 1622  1707 244667
 UK Water Basket         E C 28-NOV-96   2042  2212 GBP  342   348 325597
 ICI Warrant             A C 18-APR-97    760   789 GBP  140   146 363012

 SBC Main Index <SBCINDEX> Equity Derivative Index <SBCED1> Pg Fwd <SBCEDGB2>
```

```
 ing to HP LaserJet 4/4M Plus PS 600 on      SBCEDGB1              REUTERS
 RG          LPT1: ...              Cancel
 Reuter
 Graphics
```

Figure 9.1 SBC Reuters page SBCEDGB1 for covered warrant prices
(source: Reuters)

accurate most of the time but they are not regulated in the same way as Stock
Exchange SEAQ price quotes, and the issuer is not obliged to offer you the price
quoted on his screen at that time.

Your stockbroker may be able to provide indicative price quotes and dealing
advice, although it is a source of regret that too few stockbrokers serving the private investor market have seen fit to invest the funds required for a Reuters
screen. Of those which have, most will subscribe to the equity service, but many
of the covered warrant contributor pages form part of the debt package, an
expensive addition which even fewer brokers have. If your existing stockbroker
cannot offer you this service, the McHattie Group can suggest a suitable broker
free of charge through the *Which Stockbroker?* service.

Difficult to trade

Covered warrants often have minimum dealing sizes, as detailed in the examples
above, and are often traded in multiples of that minimum amount. This can cause
problems when a specific investment amount is required, although this problem

is easily surmountable with a little flexibility. Minimum dealing sizes should only present a problem with index and currency warrants. A more frequently encountered drawback may be that of currency. Many covered warrants, although traded in London, are international in nature and are traded in currencies other than sterling, which makes them less accessible to private investors. Stockbrokers can convert the currency for you, but this incurs extra charges which may be punitive when added to the other dealing charges which can themselves be high.

Extra dealing charges

Dealing in covered warrants is more difficult for stockbrokers and so extra dealing charges will be levied. These include charges for settling deals through Euroclear/CEDEL and for holding the warrants in nominee accounts, about which you have no choice. Covered warrants have bearer status and no definitive certificates are distributed. Charges for these services vary remarkably between stockbrokers, and it is always wise to check dealing charges before proceeding. Firms with their own Euroclear/CEDEL account are often cheaper than those which have to use a third party for this service, and some stockbrokers see Euroclear/CEDEL deals as an easy path towards a quick profit. For them, not their customers. A reasonable charge is £25–30 on top of normal dealing charges when buying and when selling, plus an annual holding charge of approximately the same amount. One stockbroker who shall remain nameless tried recently to charge clients an additional £80 for purchases and sales, plus a monthly holding charge of £80. Figures such as these are not common, but they may be levied by stockbrokers who view such deals as a nuisance rather than sound business. To deal effectively in covered warrants you are likely to require what may be termed a 'traditional service broker'. An execution-only stockbroking service will not generally be able to deal for you in this market.

The extra dealing charges, when reasonable, need to be taken account of, but they should not prove a great deterrent. One key implication is for the minimum efficient dealing size, which rises from £500–1,000 for listed warrants up to around £2,000–3,000 for covered warrants. That said, because the dealing spreads tend to be narrower for covered warrants, an investment of £1000 or £1500 may well incur approximately the same overall cost of dealing – i.e., dealing spread plus stockbrokers' commissions.

Rolling settlement

Settlement for covered warrants is through Euroclear/CEDEL and payment is due within five working days. This is no longer a comparative disadvantage since the London Stock Exchange switched to five-day rolling settlement recently from the ten-day rolling settlement introduced in 1994.

Difficult to exercise

Covered warrants are either physically settled in the same way as equity warrants, meaning that they are exercisable in return for physical shares, or cash-settled, in which case they may be exercised for a cash amount equal to their intrinsic value. Whilst some single-stock warrants are physically settled, the majority of basket and index warrants are cash-settled, if only because of the difficulty in delivering the underlying instrument or a proxy for it. If the holder wishes to exercise his covered warrants, a procedure must be followed:

1 In order to exercise the warrants the warrant-holder must, on any business day during the exercise period, at his own expense, deliver in writing to Euroclear or CEDEL, with a copy to the warrant agent, an exercise notice, in the form available from Euroclear or CEDEL.
2 The exercise notice must: (a) specify the number of the warrants being exercised; (b) give permission and instruction to Euroclear or CEDEL to debit the warrant holders account *pro tanto* with the warrants being exercised; (c) provide the numbers of the warrant-holder's account at Euroclear or CEDEL (whichever is appropriate) to be debited with the warrants being exercised and to be credited with the amount equal to the aggregate cash settlement values; (d) undertake to pay any applicable expenses, taxes and duties.
3 Upon receipt of the exercise notice, Euroclear or CEDEL shall verify that the person exercising the warrants is the holder thereof according to the books. Subject thereto, Euroclear or CEDEL, will confirm to the warrants agent the number of warrants being exercised and the account number specified by the warrant-holder to which the amount equal to the aggregate cash settlement values is to be paid.

In practice this cumbersome procedure is normally avoided: covered warrants are usually sold in the market and are rarely exercised. This is far simpler, has the benefit of immediacy, and of course, by selling in the market rather than exercising, the holder knows the exact price achieved. If, however, you do wish to exercise the warrant, then your stockbroker should handle the process.

Only one market-maker

Each covered warrant has only one market-maker and so there is little or no competition for prices. Investors are at the mercy of the issuer who makes the secondary market price and could move it against you. There are, however, checks and balances in the market which work to protect investors. First, many warrants have a maximum dealing spread specified at the time of launch. Second, if the market for one warrant turns sour and alienates investors, this dents the issuers' ability to offer new warrants and to continue as a credible market participant. Therefore issuers would not wish to spoil their reputations by making an uncompetitive market. Third, there is some competition between issuers. Whereas an investor seeking to buy Mithras Investment Trust listed equity warrants cannot go elsewhere if he does not like the market price and spread, there can be an element of 'shopping around' in the covered market. There are, for example, three extant issues of Guinness covered warrants all competing for business, and investors will deal in the warrant which offers the best terms overall, including the dealing spread. From observing the market over a period of two years, with both bull phases and bear phases, a market crash in Mexico and a market boom in the United States, the one market-maker system seems to function well at present.

Restrictions on dealing

Many covered warrants are issued under UK law. This can cause some complications for investors in the USA, because US law prohibits the trade of these warrants as they are not registered under the US Securities Act of 1933. Certain institutional buyers may qualify for exemption from this rule.

HOW THE COVERED WARRANT MARKET WORKS

When a covered warrant is issued, the terms are announced by the issuer who will already have researched the demand for his product before it enters what is known as the 'primary' market. The primary market is where the warrant is offered for a limited period at the issue price, before secondary trading begins. Much of the demand comes from the issuer's own client base, the principal issuers being large finance houses. In June 1995, the principal issuers for warrants traded in London were as follows, with SBC and Société Générale probably the most active over the preceding months.

SG Warburg
BZW
Morgan Stanley
Paribas
NatWest Markets
SBC
Société Générale Strauss Turnbull
Goldman Sachs
Salomon Brothers
Citibank International

Unlike the listed equity market, where prices are theoretically adjusted according to the forces of supply and demand, there is no pretence that this is the case for covered warrants. Instead, the issuers write sophisticated algorithms which specify the relationship between the share price and the warrant price over time, and computer models set the prices according to the specified algebraic notation. As a result covered warrant prices move very much in tandem with the underlying share prices. This differs from the listed market where investors will be used to situations in which a share and warrant may move in opposite directions, or at least by a different degree. On occasions warrants lag behind the shares, resulting in a price anomaly. Such anomalies do not generally occur in the covered market, but pricing is far from perfect and a completely different type of anomaly is often created, which is a difference between the software valuation and an investor's valuation. This is what creates buying and selling opportunities.

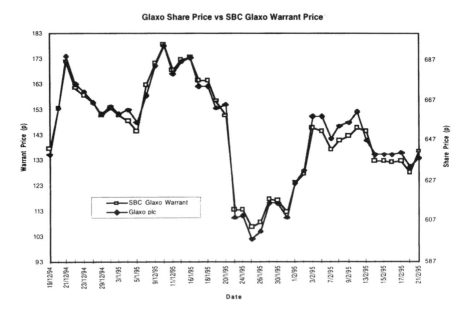

Figure 9.2 Glaxo share price and covered warrant price, December 1994 to February 1995

The one major implication of this structural feature is that fundamental research to construct a valid investment case for the underlying share or basket is of paramount importance. The technical position of the warrant becomes a secondary, accommodating factor rather than a leading indicator, since the warrant value will fall if the underlying instrument falls, and vice versa. The relationship is surprisingly direct, as illustrated by Figure 9.2.

CAN I EVALUATE COVERED WARRANTS?

Covered warrants can be treated in a similar manner to listed equity warrants when attempting to evaluate them, although as explained above the fundamental aspect of research must take precedence. Fundamental analysis of a single stock covered warrant relates to the future profitability, assets, announcements, management record, current and prospective p/e ratios, merger activity, new products and a host of other factors. Basket, index, commodity and currency warrants require a much wider view of a number of companies, a particular sector, or even a country's political and economic behaviour.

Technical analysis relates to the value of the covered warrants themselves. The calculation of gearing, capital fulcrum point and the other technical indicators for call warrants can be carried out in a similar manner as outlined in Chapters 3–5. These technical indicators can show whether the warrants are fully valued or the extent of their undervaluation.

When evaluating 'put' warrants the regular formulae need to be adjusted to provide accurate, comparable results. Calculating the gearing of a put warrant is carried out as for a call warrant, remembering to adjust the warrant price for the number of warrants required to exercise one security.

To calculate the premium of a put warrant a number of minor adjustments to the formula are required. The premium formula becomes:

$$Premium = \frac{\begin{array}{c}(Warrant\ price \times No.\ of\ warrants\ required\ for\ exercise)\\ + Underlying\ security\ price - Exercise\ price\end{array}}{Underlying\ security\ price} \times 100$$

EXAMPLE

MKT Index 'put' warrant. MKT Index = 110. Exercise price = 100. Expiry in two years. One warrant per index point. Warrant price = 30.

$$Premium = \frac{(30 \times 1) + 110 - 100}{110} \times 100$$

Premium = 36.36 per cent

More importantly, perhaps, when assessing put warrants the CFP calculation is of negligible value. The CFP is used to define the point at which the warrant will outperform the share, which is useful when evaluating call warrants, as the result provides an indication of the required capital growth in the underlying share for the warrant to perform in a similar way. If the share appreciates at a rate which is faster than the CFP then the warrant will outperform the share.

When applying the adjusted CFP calculation, shown below, to a put warrant the result indicates the annual rate of fall required in the underlying to produce an equal *loss* in the warrant value. If the underlying share exceeds the CFP, then the warrant will depreciate in value at a slower rate. The CFP is therefore of little use when assessing warrants for speculative investment, but can be used to evaluate hedging strategies.

$$CFP = \left[\left(\frac{Exercise\ price}{Share\ price + Warrant\ price} \right)^{1/y} - 1 \right] \times 100$$

EXAMPLE

MKT Index 'put' warrant. MKT Index = 110. Exercise price = 100. Expiry in two years. One warrant per index point. Warrant price = 30.

$$CFP = \left[\left(\frac{100}{110 + 30} \right)^{1/2} - 1 \right] \times 100$$

CFP = −15.48 per cent

Assuming the underlying share depreciates at this rate the resulting level of the security and the warrant after the two-year period would be 78.57 and 21.43, respectively. This represents an equal fall of 28.57 per cent. If the share fell at a higher rate, say 17 per cent per annum, the underlying share would be 75.78, down 31.11 per cent, at the end of the two-year period and the warrant would be priced at 24.22, down 19.26 per cent.

The indicator which is more useful when evaluating put warrants is the break-even point. This is the point at which the holder of the warrant begins to make a profit. The adjusted formula is as follows:

$$Break\text{-}Even = \left[\left(\frac{Exercise\ price - Warrant\ price}{Share\ price} \right)^{1/y} - 1 \right] \times 100$$

EXAMPLE

MKT Index put warrant. MKT index = 110. Exercise price = 100. Expiry in two years. One warrant per index point. Warrant price = 30.

$$Break\ even = \left[\left(\frac{100-30}{110}\right)^{1/2} - 1\right] \times 100$$

Break-even = –20.23 per cent

Assuming the underlying depreciates at the indicated rate the resulting value of the equity would be 70 and the warrant would be 30. This represents a fall of 36.36 per cent in the underlying and no change in the warrant. If the equity were to fall at a faster rate the warrant would move into profit, i.e. an annual depreciation of 30 per cent in the underlying would represent a total fall of 51.00 per cent to 53.9 and a rise of 53.67 per cent, to 46.10, in the warrant. Therefore, for the purpose of evaluating a put warrant the break-even formula is of more use than the CFP.

Index put warrants can provide something of a puzzle at first glance, but they are not in fact too different from standard call warrants:

EXAMPLE

BZW stock index 'put' warrant 30/3/93. FT-SE 100 Index = 2527.80. Exercise price = 2500. 100 warrants per index point. Warrant price = 1.37. Warrant is currently 'out of the money.'

$$Premium = \frac{\begin{array}{c}(price\ per\ warrant \times no.\ of\ warrants\ per\ index\ point) \\ +\ index\ level - exercise\ price\end{array}}{index\ level} \times 100$$

$$= \frac{(1.37 \times 100) + 2527.8 - 2500}{2527.8} \times 100$$

$$= 6.52\ per\ cent$$

Effect of 10 per cent fall in index to 2275.0.

Warrant now has intrinsic value of exercise price – index level.

Intrinsic value = 2500 – 2275

$$= 225$$

$$= 2.25\ per\ warrant\ (an\ increase\ of\ 64\ per\ cent).$$

Most investors should be able to re-work the standard warrant equations for put warrants, and they can certainly provide a valuable addition to a portfolio during bearish periods, either for hedging or for speculation.

CONCLUSION

Covered warrants offer some remarkable opportunities which are not readily available elsewhere in the warrants market, and as such they are worthy of attention. It is unfortunate that the market is lacking in structure and regulation, but as with other warrants which may be awkward to deal, the problems should not be insuperable. In fact the solutions to most of the problems posed by covered warrants are to be found repeated elsewhere within these pages. Be informed, do some analysis, get a good stockbroker, and don't risk more than you can afford to lose.

"In reality, the US warrant market is highly parochial, speculative, non-standardized, and full of quirky features which are not found elsewhere. That's why the market is a minefield for the unwary, but equally a field of great opportunities for those who have attained a full understanding."

10

AMERICAN WARRANTS

To European investors, the American warrants market looks like a minefield which they would not dream of entering without a specialist guide. The market is extremely different in scope and structure, valuations are far higher, terms are non-standardized, the companies involved are far more speculative, and the support services are hardly what one would expect from a market which is clearly developed. That said, there are a number of lessons to be learnt from the way in which companies use the market, and as the same valuation theories apply there is no reason why investors cannot analyse the warrants fairly using internationally standard criteria. There are profits on the other side of the minefield if you tread carefully, or if you leap over it.

Described in the first edition of this book as the 'jokers in the pack', American warrants are also the oldest. It was in America that warrants first emerged, as long ago as the 1920s, expanding in the run-up to the great Wall Street Crash, and then disappearing for some time thereafter. The first long-term warrants were listed on New York Stock Exchange (NYSE) in 1970, and one might have expected the market to have matured to the status of a large, highly refined, standardized, international market. Furthermore, it would be reasonable to suppose that America would provide the model for other world markets to follow. Not so. In reality, the US warrants market is highly parochial, speculative, non-standardized, and full of quirky features which are not found elsewhere. This is why the market is a minefield for the unwary, but equally a field of great opportunities for those who have attained a full understanding.

This observation is confirmed by the current composition of the market, which is biased heavily towards warrants on over-the-counter (OTC) stocks. These are not listed and traded on organized exchanges, but dealt through an inter-dealer network. The stocks are normally smaller companies which do not meet the listing requirements of the NYSE or the American Stock Exchange, although there are some larger companies which prefer to maintain their OTC status. The result is that most warrant issues are very small, and the aggregate market capitalization of the North American warrants markets is surprisingly low, certainly weighing in beneath the leading European warrant market of Germany. The market capitalization of the US warrants market according to *Value Line* is

US$2.8bn as at 26 May 1995, with average gearing of 3.3 times and an average premium of 13.1 per cent.

WHICH COMPANIES ISSUE WARRANTS

As in most developed warrant markets, a broad range of companies has tapped the warrants market for funds, from well-known blue-chips such as Chase Manhattan to lesser-known companies engaged in a wide variety of specialist industries. By investing in warrants you can take a stake in businesses as diverse as electronic casino systems, miniature racing car replicas, the development of colour patents for cosmetics, quick-service chicken restaurants, used car financing, drugs for dogs, tabloid newspapers, loans to difficult clients, loom-making, recycling of tyres, and voice recognition technology, among many others. A colourful world of opportunity presents itself on the OTC market, where most warrants trade for just a few cents each – but only for the brave. It is possible to buy warrants attached to the following companies, among others: Action Performance, Advanced Mammography Systems, Cluckers Wood, Corrections Corporation, Genetics Institute, Golden Eagle Group, The Great Train Store, Jackpot Enterprises, Lone Star Industries, Mister Jay Fashions, Nutrition Management, Princeton Dental, Pollution Research, and Xxsys Corporation. 'Only in America', it is tempting to say.

Table 10.1 gives the numbers for US warrants, listed by their exchanges.

Amex	90
Boston	126
Cincinnati	111
Mid-West	117
NASD (SIAC)	106
NASDAQ (NMS)	203
NASDAQ (Small Cap)	419
New York	25
OTC Bulletin	189
Pacific	123
Philadelphia	114

Note: due to a large number of multiple listings it is incorrect to sum this column
Source: Bloomberg

Table 10.1 US Warrants listed by exchange

Among the large number of smaller warrant issues, and those listed on NASDAQ in particular, there is an understandable bias towards start-up 'development' stage companies which have a great thirst for capital. Among these are a large number of biotechnology companies and mining exploration companies.

In both cases the majority of investors can expect to be left with little or nothing of their investment, but a small and fortunate number will strike it rich. The slant is certainly speculative when compared to the sober range of diversified investment trusts available in the UK, and in many cases it is difficult to justify taking on a second dimension of risk by buying the warrants. Where the companies are successful, however, the warrant gains can be huge.

WHY WARRANTS ARE ISSUED

US companies issue warrants for a specific and simple reason: to raise money. They treat warrants just like any other instrument of corporate finance, and use them to provide extra funds at a time when they are needed. As the Communication Intelligence Corporation said in a press release in December 1994, 'the proceeds from the warrant offering will satisfy the company's current working capital requirements and will allow CIC to fully execute its reorganization plan.' This functional approach carries two important implications which investors need to understand. The first is that maturities tend to be shorter, since the companies are seeking to raise capital in the near future for projects already in the planning stage, rather than looking ahead to expansion in the next century. Framingham Savings Bank, for example, issued warrants on 11 March 1993 with three exercise dates ending on 31 January 1996, and this is a fairly standard length of maturity – much shorter than in the UK where the intention of warrant issues is more frequently to create immediate market value. In America it is probably true to say that warrants are rarely issued for their properties as a 'sweetener' for issues which may otherwise prove unpalatable. Their popularity is not great enough for that purpose: hence their main function as a utilitarian instrument of capital-raising. Many European firms might do well to follow this example, as warrants can provide companies with a relatively painless method of capital-raising whilst apparently giving shareholders a 'free gift' and encouraging loyalty. In the UK the problem with this is that warrants are widely considered to be a marginal form of financing not held in the highest esteem, whereas in America the approach seems to be far more flexible: warrants are simply another instrument in the creative toolbox of corporate financiers. The fact that warrants are issued for a definite purpose means usually that the company wishes the maturity to be fairly short, and the average maturity for 150 leading warrants works out at about two years and one month, less than half the average maturity for UK warrants.

The second implication of this functional approach is that the conversion terms are frequently adjusted to ensure that warrants are exercised rather than left to expire worthless. Whereas warrant terms seldom change in the UK and elsewhere once they have been set, it seems quite normal and accepted to alter the terms of subscription in America to suit the purposes of the issuing company. There are many examples of companies taking this course to some extra cash, either by reducing the exercise price or by extending the maturity of the warrants:

11 August 1994: Datawatch Corporation announced that it was to reduce the exercise price of each Redeemeable Common Stock Purchase Warrant from US$7.50 to the discounted price of US$1.00 for a 70-day period (subsequently extended further to 10 February 1995).

6 September 1994: Franklin Supply Co Ltd said the company has cut the exercise price of its outstanding common stock purchase warrants from US$5.00 to US$3.125. The company said the price was cut to raise additional equity capital to repay a portion of the company's demand operating loan and for other corporate purposes.

3 October 1994: Alpharel Inc, a software supplier, announced that it had extended the exercise period of its warrants from 12 December 1994 to 12 December 1995.

12 September 1994: BPI Packaging Technologies Inc announced an amendment to the terms of its Class A warrants. The period of time to exercise the warrants was extended from 6 October 1994 to 14 October 1994. The company also reduced the exercise price of each Class A warrant from US$5 to US$4, and offered to provide warrant-holders with the option of exercising 50 per cent of the warrants held. For each Class A warrant exercised on or before 14 October 1994, at the reduced exercise price of US$4, the warrant-holder will be entitled to extend the period of exercise for a second Class A warrant for a period to 31 March 1995, at the original exercise price of US$5.

Whilst changes to the conversion terms such as these are usually in the warrant-holders' favour, it is difficult to escape the conclusion that investors are playing on a far from level playing field, but one which is constantly being tilted to favour the issuers. Because companies use the market for definite capital-raising exercises they are not afraid to manipulate the terms to receive the right amount of capital at the right time. It would seem staggering to European investors that maturities are changed and that exercise prices are frequently reduced, but the US warrants market adopts a far more flexible approach.

CONVERSION TERMS

The principal difference between American and European warrants is that US warrants are usually exercisable at any time during their remaining life. American warrants are a sufficiently distinct breed in this respect to have their form of exercise known specifically as 'American-Style', as distinct from 'European-style' exercise. The former is when warrants are exerciseable at any time up to a given date or period; the latter when specific dates or periods are provided for exercise. For investors the former is preferable for the additional ease and flexibility which it provides, although companies may find it much easier to administer the issue of new share certificates etc, when European-style exercise periods are used. The American-style exercise periods have been widely adopted by covered warrants, where the number of holders is commonly small and administration is relatively simple. This feature might suggest that the terms should be more straightforward, dispensing with the need to know of specific exercise dates or periods. This is emphatically not so. In fact many American warrants carry more interesting conversion terms which differ substantially from those elsewhere. Unlike UK warrants which generally have simple and standardized conversion terms, American warrants are both more varied and more complex. Individual companies set the terms to meet their own needs, and have less reason to set the conversion price to a round number in order to attract investors. Equally, the conversion ratio – the number of warrants needed to buy one share – is not always 1:1, and some warrants confer rights over fractions or multiples of shares. The need to check the conversion terms before dealing is nowhere more important, although overseas investors are likely to find this an onerous task. It is difficult for investors outside of America to get detailed information on US warrants, so it seems reasonable to suggest that the market is largely of domestic interest. Many warrrants have quirks in their terms:

LTV Corporation A warrants each confer the right to subscribe for 0.5582 shares of LTV common stock at an exercise price of US$16.28 per each full share of LTV common stock purchased.

3.584 Safeway warrants are exercisable into one common share.

IMRE Corporation warrants carry the right to subscribe for one share at US$2.50, but the exercise price rises by US$1.00 each year through 1998.

Houston Biotech warrants carry the right to subscribe for one share at US$5, but the strike price rises to US$10 after 30 June 1995.

Immunex Corporation warrant-holders receive one share of common stock plus US$21 upon exercise.

There is one further feature of some warrants which must not be ignored. Some warrants can be called for early redemption by the company once the warrants are a long way 'in the money'. This is a fairly common clause which is used by many companies:

TAT Technologies Ltd warrants are subject to early redemption by TAT on 30 days' prior written notice, provided that the average closing bid price of the ordinary shares exceeds US$15 for Class A warrants, and US$24 for Class B warrants, for the prior 30 business days before the notice of redemption.

Teletouch Communications warrants may be redeemed by the company at US$0.10 per warrant if the closing bid price of the common stock has been at least US$5.625 for 15 consecutive trading days.

20 December 1994: Country Star Restaurants Inc announced it is redeeming its publicly traded redeemable common stock purchase warrants on 23 January 1995. All warrants that are not exercised prior to the redemption date shall be redeemed on the basis of one share of the company's common stock for every three warrants. Each warrant is exercisable for one share of the company's common stock at an exercise price of US$4.00 per share prior to the redemption date.

This practice of redeeming the warrants early if the stock performs well effectively puts a cap on the gains available to warrant-holders, and is an insidious clause as far as investors are concerned. One of the great attractions of warrants is that the downside risk is limited to 100 per cent, whilst the potential profits are unlimited. This clause tilts the balance firmly in favour of the issuing companies, for whom it ensures that the warrants are not highly dilutive. Investors should watch out for redemption clauses and consider their risk/reward profile carefully.

THE VALUE OF AMERICAN WARRANTS

Very high valuations seem to be accorded to the majority of American warrants, which seem overvalued by international comparison. A study of 150 leading American warrants at the end of 1994 revealed an average capital fulcrum point (CFP) of 37.58 per cent, with only five out of the sample being regarded as 'good value' by the *Warrants Alert* computer model. To some degree this indicates the speculative nature of the market, since the average level of gearing was fairly typical at 2.9 times. These results indicate that American investors, or international investors interested in American warrants, need to tread carefully and to seek professional advice before investing. The pitfalls seem great, a view which is confirmed by a calculation of the average delta for a sample of 316 American warrants. The average delta worked out at 0.499, which raises the spectre of half of all American warrants being expected to expire worthless – unless rescued by an improvement in the conversion terms. This compares with a much higher delta figure of 0.672 derived from a study of 89 leading UK warrants, in spite of a weaker stockmarket performance prior to the surveys.

INFORMATION SOURCES

In view of the breadth and size of the market it is reasonable to expect a number of ancillary services to provide information to investors. It is a source of surprise that investors seem to be ill-served by much in the way of advice or analytical coverage. Newspapers, television, radio, and financial magazines appear to ignore the market, or to treat it as a sideshow for gamblers. Nor are investors overwhelmed with choice from the massive investment newsletter market. There may be well over a thousand 'tipsheets' in America, but barely any touch upon warrants. Sources of information are rare, but two which have been in existence for some time are *Value Line Convertibles** and *The RHM Survey of Warrants and Options†*. The former is a relatively expensive publication which touches upon warrants peripherally in its text but provides excellent numerical tables to guide investors. In the 5 June 1995 issue there are two elements which illustrate the Jekyll and Hyde nature of the US warrants market neatly. On the one hand, the general overvaluation of the market is recognized and the warrants section says simply 'there are no recommended issues in this group.' Conversely, the newsletter also draws attention to the fact that individual warrants can perform extremely well. In making a 'sell' recommendation for Bank of New York warrants the newsletter notes that they had risen by 836 per cent since the initial buy notice in January 1992 – an annual compounded rate of return of no less than 93 per cent. Figure 10.1 gives a price graph for Bank of New York warrants. *The RHM Survey of Warrants and Options* is more focused than the *Value Line* publication, but again it is not devoted exclusively to warrants.

The range of problems outlined in this chapter makes this lack of coverage understandable perhaps, but not defensible. The Press needs to provide much more coverage in America to ensure that investors are properly informed and protected, although in the meantime the small band of investors who have been able to attain a good understanding of the warrants market are tremendously well-placed to gain from price anomalies and opportunities created by the ignorance of others.

ANALYSING AMERICAN WARRANTS

The lack of information and advisory sources at present means it would not be surprising if analysts seeking to identify market winners and losers found the process demanding. There is some evidence, however, that the forms of technical analysis used for UK warrants can be transferred directly and successfully to the US market. A portfolio of five American warrants, comprising Elan Corporation,

---

* *Value Line Convertibles*, 220 East 42nd Street, New York, NY 10017, USA.
† *The RHM Survey of Warrants and Options*, 172 Forest Avenue, Glen Cove, New York, NY 11542, USA.

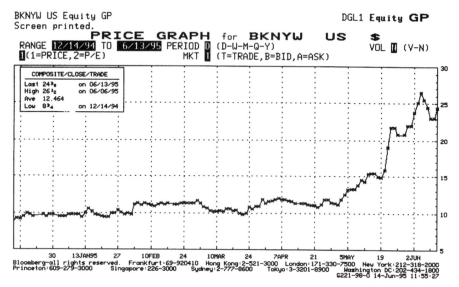

Figure 10.1 Bank of New York warrants 1994/5
Source: Bloomberg

Magma Copper, Corrections Corporation, Bank of New York, and Chase Manhattan was selected by the *Warrants Alert Fax Service* in December 1994, and the result five and a half months on was remarkable. The average gain from the five warrants reached 118.2 per cent, a result which left no doubt that the standard technical analysis applies across different warrant markets. When this is twinned with the huge amount of material available for fundamental research on American companies, there seems no reason why analysts should not be able to direct investors towards the most profitable warrants.

LEAPS

A cross between traded options and warrants, LEAPS have become an important adjunct to the US warrants market which investors will do well to consider as an alternative or a complementary investment. The acronym stands for Long-Term Equity Anticipation Securities, and these have been around for a short time only, launched in November 1990. This excellent range, available on around 120 leading blue-chip stocks plus some major market indices, enables US investors to speculate or hedge their portfolios (see Table 10.2). LEAPS are very much like traded options in the UK, with a range of strike prices and expiries, but instead of a maximum maturity of nine months, LEAPS run for up to three years – a similar maturity to covered warrants. They are generally defined as index and equity options that exceed nine months. In view of the relatively short periods to expiry for most US warrants, it seems reasonable to consider LEAPS as *bona fide* warrants for analytical purposes.

Allied Signal
American Barrick
  Resources
American Express
American Home Products
American Tel. & Tel.
Amgen Inc.
AMR Corporation
Anheuser-Busch Cos.
Apple Computer
ASA Ltd.
Avon Products
Baker Hughes
Bank of Boston
BankAmerica
BellSouth Corporation
Blockbuster Entertainment
Boeing Co.
Bristol-Myers Squibb
Campbell Soup
Centocor Inc.
Chase Manhattan
Chemical Bank
Chevron Corporation
Chrysler Corporation
Chubb Corporation
Citicorp
Coca-Cola
Columbia Gas
COMPAQ Computer
Conner Peripherals
Consolidated Stores
Dell Computer
Delta Airlines
Digital Equipment
Disney (Walt) Co.
Dow Chemical
du Pont (de Nemours)
Eastman Kodak
Exxon Corp.
Federal Express
Federal National Mortgage
  Assn.

Ford Motor
Fruit of the Loom
Gap Inc.
General Electric
General Mills
General Motors
Georgia Pacific
Glaxo Holdings plc
GTE Corp.
Heinz (HJ)
Hilton Hotels
Home Depot
Homestake Mining
Intel Corp.
International Business
  Machines
International Game
  Technology
Johnson & Johnson
K-Mart Corp.
Limited Inc.
Liz Claiborne
Magna International 'A'
Marriott Corp.
Maytag Co.
McDonald's Corp.
McGraw-Hill
Merck & Co
Merrill Lynch
Microsoft Corp.
Minnesota Mining &
  Manufacturing
Mobil Corp.
Monsanto Co.
Morgan (JP) & Co.
Motorola Inc.
NationsBank
NIKE Inc. 'B'
NYNEX Corp.
Oracle Systems
Pacific Telesis Group
Paramount
  Communications

Pepsico
Pfizer Co.
Philip Morris
Placer Dome Inc.
Polaroid Corp.
PPG Industries
Primerica Corp.
Procter & Gamble
Quaker Oats
Reebok International
RJR Nabisco Holdings
Salomon Inc.
Schering-Plough
Sears, Roebuck
SmithKline Beecham plc
Sprint Corp.
SunAmerica
Sun Microsystems
Synergen
Syntex
  Telecommunications
Teléfonos de México ADR
Tenneco Inc.
Texaco Inc.
Texas Instruments
Time Warner Inc.
Triton Energy Corp.
UAL Corp.
Union Carbide
Unisys
Unocal Corp.
Upjohn Co.
US Surgical
US West
USX-Marathon Group
USX-US Steel Group
Wal-Mart
Warner-Lambert
Wells Fargo
Westinghouse Elec.
WMX Technologies
Woolworth Corp.
Xerox

Source: LEAPS – What They Are and How to Use Them for Profit and Protection, by Harrison Roth,
Irwin 1994

Table 10.2: Company LEAPS available on American Stock Exchanges, 1995

Backpage   DGL8 **Equity O M O N**
Monitoring enabled

		O P T I O N B I D A S K M O N I T O R					
		Time	Current	Change	Open	High	Low	Prev Cls
D I S U S		18:34	$55\frac{3}{4}$	$-\frac{1}{8}$	$55\frac{3}{4}$	$55\frac{7}{8}$	55	$55\frac{7}{8}$

THE WALT DISNEY CO.

	C A L L S						P U T S				
DIS	JAN 96	Bid	Ask	Last	Volume	DIS	JAN 96	Bid	Ask	Last	Volume
1) AF	30	$26\frac{1}{4}$	$26\frac{3}{4}$			14) MF	30		$\frac{1}{16}$		
2) AH	40	$16\frac{7}{8}$	$17\frac{1}{4}$			15) MH	40	$\frac{1}{16}$	$\frac{3}{16}$	$\frac{1}{8}$	130
3) AJ	50	$8\frac{1}{8}$	$8\frac{1}{2}$			16) MJ	50	$1\frac{1}{16}$	$1\frac{5}{16}$	$1\frac{1}{8}$	5
4) AK	55	$4\frac{3}{4}$	$5\frac{1}{8}$	$4\frac{5}{8}$	5	17) MK	55	$2\frac{9}{16}$	$2\frac{13}{16}$		
5) AL	60	$2\frac{7}{16}$	$2\frac{11}{16}$	$2\frac{1}{2}$	7	18) ML	60	$5\frac{1}{4}$	$5\frac{5}{8}$		
ZDS	JAN 97					ZDS	JAN 97				
6) AF	30	$27\frac{1}{2}$	28			19) MF	30	$\frac{1}{8}$	$\frac{1}{4}$		
7) AH	40	$18\frac{7}{8}$	$19\frac{3}{8}$	$19\frac{1}{4}$	20	20) MH	40	$\frac{1}{2}$	$1\frac{1}{16}$		
8) AJ	50	$11\frac{3}{8}$	$11\frac{7}{8}$			21) MJ	50	$2\frac{3}{16}$	$2\frac{7}{16}$		
9) AL	60	$5\frac{3}{4}$	$6\frac{1}{8}$			22) ML	60	$6\frac{3}{8}$	$6\frac{3}{4}$		
WDS	JAN 98					WDS	JAN 98				
10) AH	40	$20\frac{7}{8}$	$21\frac{5}{8}$			23) MH	40	$\frac{13}{16}$	$1\frac{1}{16}$		
11) AJ	50	$14\frac{1}{8}$	$14\frac{5}{8}$			24) MJ	50	3	$3\frac{1}{4}$		
12) AL	60	$8\frac{5}{8}$	$9\frac{1}{8}$			25) ML	60	$6\frac{7}{8}$	$7\frac{1}{4}$		
13) AN	70	$4\frac{7}{8}$	$5\frac{1}{4}$			26) MN	70	$13\frac{7}{8}$	$14\frac{5}{8}$		

Figure 10.2 LEAPS for January 1996/8, the Walt Disney Co
Source: Bloomberg

One major advantage of LEAPS is that they come in two varieties: calls and puts. The latter entitle the holder to sell the underlying security at a fixed price and provide a good mechanism for speculating on a falling market or for hedging a portfolio. The range of strike prices also makes this is an attractive medium for investors. Instead of facing a fixed exercise price it is possible for investors to select an option which is 'in the money' or 'out of the money' with a commensurate level of premium and gearing, according to preference. This is best understood using an example (see Table 10.3).

	Very bullish investor buys January 1998 US$70 calls at US$5.25	Moderately bullish investor buys January 1998 US$40 calls at US$21.625	Bearish investor buys January 1998 US$60 puts at US$7.25
Scenario A: share price rises modestly to US$65 by January 1998	Calls expire worthless Loss 100%	Calls rise to US$25 Profit 15.6%	Puts expire worthless Loss 100%
Scenario B: share price rises strongly to US$90 by January 1998	Calls rise to US$20 Profit 281.0%	Calls rise to US$50 Profit 131.2%	Puts expire worthless Loss 100%
Scenario C: share price falls to US$45 by January 1998	Calls expire worthless Loss 100%	Calls fall to US$5 Loss of 76.9%	Puts rise to US$15 Profit 106.9%

Table 10.3 Illustration of strategies using Disney LEAPS

As Table 10.3 shows, LEAPS can be used to back a range of different judgements which may be formed from fundamental analysis, and of course technical analysis can still be used in conjunction with this. There seems no reason why LEAPS should not be analysed in very much the same way as warrants, using gearing, the CFP, and other indicators in precisely the same way.

Given the inherent problems of high risk and limited marketability of so many American warrants, it does seem sensible for investors to give serious consideration to LEAPS, even where the warrants market has been dismissed as speculative and frothy. Using LEAPS, investors can make a geared or hedged investment in major American corporations with the relative peace of mind that the extra maturity of warrants provides over options. Dealing spreads are also competitive.

CONCLUSION

There is a supreme irony about the American warrants market. The very lack of understanding which ought to make the market such a haven for informed opportunists is probably a contributing factor to its overvaluation. The lack of information means that overvaluations have tended to persist because investors have not sold warrants when the valuations have become too high. Opportunities for profit certainly exist, but at this time the scope seems less attractive than for most other warrant markets, and investors must take care to be well-informed. The American warrants market is the market in which the risks attached to warrants are most apparent, and investors seem to be better served overall by the LEAPS market which offers a far greater diversity of opportunity on more stable stocks, with the additional benefits of good size and put varieties.

"Warrants have become so widespread and so broad in their coverage, so pervasive and penetrating in all of the world's stockmarkets, that few active international investors will now be unaware of their existence."

11

OTHER OVERSEAS WARRANTS

W arrants are a worldwide phenomenon, and they exist in many different forms. Geographically, warrants have spread to all major financial markets around the globe, gaining in importance not only in the UK, but particularly in Asia and in Continental Europe, where considerable growth has occurred since the late 1980s. Elsewhere the most mature market is in the USA (see Chapter 10), and the largest quite plainly in Japan, where warrants, which have been around since late 1981 and exploded into life after 1986, were fuelling possibly the greatest financial boom in recent history. Warrants have become so widespread and so broad in their coverage, so pervasive and penetrating in all of the world's stockmarkets, that few active international investors will now be unaware of their existence. Some conservative investors choose to avoid them, but they cannot ignore them.

What follows is a brief description of the major international warrants markets. Although the instrument itself is fairly standard, potential investors must be aware that dealing practices and procedures may vary widely. For this reason it is essential that a knowledgeable broker or independent analyst is consulted before committing funds to volatile overseas markets. All of the data provided in this chapter is given in US dollars for ease of comparison.

THE JAPANESE WARRANTS MARKET

The Japanese warrants market is the most famous, infamous, and easily the largest warrants market in the world. And this is in spite of a late start. Japanese companies first issued bonds with warrants in December 1981, and the market started to grow rapidly after 1986. Since then the warrants have been fêted by successful investors pocketing huge profits, lambasted by other investors, and have provided something of a symbol for the profligate 1980s. Yet for many warrant investors the workings of the giant Japanese market are still a mystery.

It doesn't help that most Japanese warrants appear to have a tenuous relationship with the country of origin. Unlike the majority of UK warrants, which are issued in sterling and listed on the domestic stock exchange, Japanese warrants are generally denominated in US dollars, issued in the Euromarkets, and traded primarily in London. This sounds strange, but the reasons for this geographical displacement are quite logical, as even a rudimentary explanation makes clear.

Debt packages are issued with Japanese warrants attached as 'sweeteners' to reduce the cost of funds. Bonds with warrants attached can be launched with a lower coupon rate than that which needs to be paid on straight bonds, and furthermore, when the warrants are exercised the amount received by the company will be the amount required to pay off the bondholders. The result is a debt package which is very cheap for the companies to service – if it is launched in Europe. This low cost of issue in the Euromarkets, coupled with an absence of borrowing limits and other stringent regulations, means that the rule-bound Japanese domestic market struggles to compete. Japanese companies simply issue debt in dollars, convert the proceeds back into yen and leave the warrants to be traded separately in London – the centre of the Euromarkets. The enthusiasm of some companies has even led to them launching several warrant issues which are running concurrently.

The warrants themselves feature highly standardized terms – something which aided the enormous volume of issues considerably. Once a blueprint had been established, it was a simple matter for other companies to copy the formula for their own issues, and investors endeavouring to choose from a large number of competing issues were grateful for the simplification which made analysis far easier. Japanese equity warrants, which are bearer certificates, generally have their exercise price fixed at 2.5 per cent above either the closing equity price on the date of pricing, or the average closing price of the equity on six consecutive trading days up to and including the date of pricing of the warrants. Once issued, the warrants are usually exercisable at any time during a fixed period of between four and ten years from the date of issue. In the beginning the favoured term was five years, but most issues reaching the market since 1989 have had a maturity of four years. The average premium for Euromarket warrants is 37.8 per cent, and average gearing 10.0 times, largely because many warrants have sunk below their exercise prices. At the start of 1990 the average premium was only 18.8 per cent and the gearing 3.4 times. For most of the bull period investors could buy warrants at less than 20 per cent premium and with gearing of around four times, but both figures are now much higher as warrant prices have sunk and share prices have dropped below the exercise prices.

The boom in Japanese warrants really took place between 1986 and 1989, and it was an extraordinary ascent. In 1986 both the number and size of the new issues exceeded the total of all of the issues in all previous years, a trick repeated in terms of market capitalization in 1987 and again in 1989, which proved to be the market's zenith. Table 11.1 lists the issues by year, and Figure 11.1 lists them by month.

Amount US$ million	
1982	268
1983	300
1984	1,110
1985	1,275
1986	9,065
1987	20,349
1988	26,805
1989	62,340
1990	17,870
1991*	19.175
Total	**US$ 158,577 million**
January to November	
Source: Daiwa Europe Ltd	

Table 11.1 Japanese US$ Warrant-Bond Issues

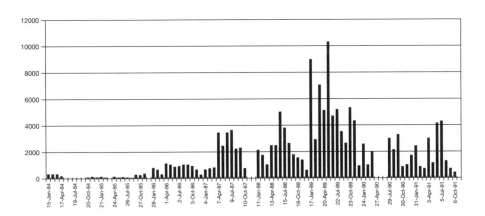

Figure 11.1: Monthly Japanese US$ warrant-bond issue amounts (US$ million)

In addition to the US dollar warrants there have also been warrants denominated in other currencies, but these are very much smaller by capitalization, as
Table 11.2 shows.

It is interesting to note the pattern of issues and to consider the relationship
with the stockmarket's appetite for warrants. The first major non-seasonal
decline in issues took place immediately after the stockmarket crash of 1987, but
the halt in issues lasted for only two months before the market continued to grow
apace in 1988. The peak in 1989 coincides of course with the peaks of the market
before the precipitate decline in 1990. Issuers have a keen eye on investor

Currency of Denomination	Amount US$ million	Number
US dollar	158,577	967
Swiss franc	10,829	273
Deutschmark	10,280	162
ECU	1,072	9
Dutch guilder	683	9
Sterling	404	6
French franc	178	1
Yen	101	1
Totals	**US$ 182,105 million**	**1,428**

Note: Individual tranches are counted separately.
Source: Daiwa Europe Ltd

Table 11.2 Japanese Overseas Warrant-Bond Issues: totals since inception

demand, and dollar issues have slackened along with the market. There are a few commentators who believe that the market has had its day, and some London market-makers have withdrawn, but the majority of market practitioners believe that the warrants market will revive if the Nikkei average can resume an upward track.

The remarkable bull run in Tokyo which sustained the market throughout most of the 1980s was of course reflected in the performance of the warrants. Extraordinary gains were made during the bull market, a time when investors threw analysis out of the window and chose warrants almost with a pin in a newspaper. The approach of most investors was little more sophisticated than that. The majority regarded Japanese warrants as the quickest way to make a fortune, and weren't too worried about maximizing their gains when they were already making fabulous profits. A glance at the gearing and the premium might be sufficient for what amounted to an orgy of unfettered speculation. Warrants were bought for the simple benefit of buying the market at a lower cost and with greater rewards. The party lasted until late 1989 and 1990, when bad losses injected a new note of realism into the market, and the profile of investors changed. Many of the speculators and casual investors are no longer prepared to participate now that the odds are not so clearly stacked in their favour, while the remaining investors are adopting a far more cautious role. There is an increasing use of warrants for hedging rather than for speculation, and investors recognize the need to be more selective. There are profits to be made, but not in the indiscriminate way that happened during the bull run of the 1980s. The need to be informed has never been greater, and for this reason there is an increasing demand for the sort of penetrating analysis which the Japanese warrants market has lacked for most of its life.

The confidence of warrant investors throughout the 1980s was backed by the fact that no warrants expired even partially worthless until 1989. Many investors were hardly aware that this was possible at the time – a level of ignorance which has since been eroded by the harsh light of reality. Now the market is in recession, both in terms of performance and size. At the end of 1994 there were 707 Japanese warrant issues outstanding, a drop of 153 (there were 87 new issues but 240 expired), or 18 per cent, over the year. For 1995 the picture is no brighter: some 259 issues are due to expire and the total number in issue is sure to drop again.

Furthermore, according to statistics from Morgan Stanley, some 84 per cent of Japanese warrants were 'out of the money' in March 1995. It is likely that over 200 warrants will expire worthless in 1995 alone, which is a sad indicator of how times have changed in Tokyo.

THE EUROPEAN WARRANTS MARKET

In line with the UK market, equity warrant issues across Europe began in the 1970s but grew modestly until the late 1980s when growth accelerated markedly. The aggregate market capitalization now places Europe firmly in second place in the world rankings. The absence of well-developed options markets in much of Europe has encouraged the issue of warrants, which are in any case better suited to the longer-term nature of European development. Warrants which last for several years are clearly more suited to situations like German reunification than options which mature after a period of months.

Within Europe, Germany is easily the largest of the European warrant markets, with around US$5 billion of major warrant issues. According to the figures for warrants in the BZW database, Italy is second and UK is third. The prominent position attained by Italy is due almost entirely to a huge tranche of warrants issued in May 1991 by the country's largest insurance company, Generali. The issue was interesting not only for its size (one warrant was offered for every four shares held), but also because of its structure and complexity. The warrant was launched well 'in-the-money', and the exercise price is linked to the interest rate on Italian treasury bills. There was some intriguing speculation that this complication was contrived deliberately in order to concentrate the warrants into the hands of the largest friendly shareholders, thereby diminishing the threat of takeover. Another interesting possibility is that since the warrants are in bearer form, as distinct from registered, a large new shareholder could use the warrants to build a stake without attracting attention from competitors or regulators. Whatever the reasoning behind the issue, the outcome was that Italy managed to catapult past even the fast-growing UK warrants market, which is ahead of Switzerland, France and the Netherlands among the six notable European warrants markets. Table 11.3 gives the European 'league table'.

	Market Capitalization US$ million
Germany	4,853
Italy	1,887
United Kingdom*	1,317
Switzerland	849
France	783
Netherlands	730
Belgium	92
Sweden	47
Austria	24
Finland	9
Total	**US$ 10,591 million**

Note: The average premium for the Continental European company warrants is 9 per cent, the average gearing is 4 times, and the average time to expiry is 2.4 years.

*Source: BZW Securities Ltd, except * Warrants Alert. This table should not be regarded as comprehensive.*

Table11.3 European Company Warrants, May 1995

There is also one warrant listed in Luxembourg, and one in Denmark, although these markets are clearly not developed. More generally, institutions will often turn to covered warrants where company issues are sparse, or where existing issues are unexciting or difficult to trade. Germany is just ahead of Switzerland as the largest and most prolific issuer of domestic covered warrants, followed by Italy and the UK, as shown in Table 11.4.

	Market Capitalization US$ million
Germany	7,113
Switzerland	6,525
Italy	1,942
UK	1,674
France	977
Total (all Europe)	**US$ 19,750 million**

Note: The average premium for these call warrants is 9 per cent, the average gearing is 7.7 times, and the average time to expiry is 1.2 years; for the put warrants the average premium is 6 per cent; average gearing is 10.4 times; and the average time to expiry is 1.2 years.

Source: BZW Equity Derivatives Group

Table 11.4 European covered and basket warrants, June 1995

THE ASIAN WARRANTS MARKETS

Perhaps the fastest-growing region for warrant issues and investment is Asia. The common perception of the Hong Kong Stock Exchange as a market which appeals to the speculative instincts of its inhabitants is well supported by the proliferation of warrants, which first appeared in the colony in 1973. The number has grown to around 262 warrants now, making Hong Kong the most important warrant market in Asia, together with Singapore and Malaysia. In Hong Kong the market exploded into life in the post-1987 Crash era, with companies rushing to raise money by issuing warrants. Indeed, such was the pace of growth that there was a danger of the market degenerating into speculative frenzy, and for this reason the market has become more regulated in an attempt to provide a reasonable structure for trading. Company issues are now limited to between one and three years of maturity, and the warrant issues must not exceed 10 per cent of each company's market capitalization. In spite of these sensible measures, the Hong Kong warrants market is still a highly speculative arena, where investors are far more concerned to 'gear up' their investments to inject some excitement than they are to use warrants for the sober purposes of hedging and portfolio investment. Liquidity is perhaps best described as 'sporadic' in many issues.

Elsewhere in Asia warrants have made an early appearance in some emerging stockmarkets, largely as a knock-on effect from the growth in Hong Kong and Singapore. Emerging markets such as Thailand, Malaysia and Korea, which are very new, are rightly concentrating on equities now, which tend to be highly volatile in any case, but have already issued a number of warrants between them (see Table 11.5). These markets are likely to turn to options markets for more speculative activity as they mature, but in the meantime warrants can be issued as demand arises. Barring another external shock such as that which shook all of the world's stockmarkets in 1987, the number of Asian warrants should increase as these fledgeling markets grow and begin to attract more international attention. Already the number of warrants listed below has grown from 205 to 429 since the first edition of this book, and the aggregate market capitalization has more than trebled from US$3.4bn to US$10.4bn.

	Market Capitalization US$ million	Number
Hong Kong	1,539	262
Singapore	3,904	70
Malaysia	3,917	62
Thailand	999	27
Korea	n/a	8
Total	**US$ 10,359 million**	**429**

Source: BZW Securities (Asia) Ltd

Table 11.5 Asian Warrants Markets, June 1995

THE GLOBAL WARRANTS VILLAGE

All of the world's major financial markets can now boast a well-developed warrants sector. Warrants have become established a fixture in Japan, in New York, in London, in Frankfurt, in Paris, in Hong Kong, in Singapore, and in a host of other world markets – and in nearly all cases the emergence has taken place over the last decade. This places the recent growth of the UK market into context, and augurs well for future development. It is not inconceivable that in order to achieve a role commensurate with London's status as a financial centre, the domestic warrants market could double or triple in size over the next decade, particularly if the capital begins to lose Japanese warrant business. It is a difficult task to predict the future for world warrant markets, but the question of growth in the UK is addressed in detail in Chapter 13.

"In addition to warrants, there are a number of alternative risk instruments – offshore warrant funds, capital shares, traditional options, traded options and futures – which may be used for the purposes of speculation and investment in the UK stockmarket."

12

OTHER RISK INSTRUMENTS

In addition to warrants, there are a number of alternative risk instruments which may be used for the purposes of speculation and investment in the UK stockmarket. This chapter attempts to explain when each of the different instruments should be used, or when some may be used in conjunction with warrants to achieve a specific aim. On some occasions two or more instruments may be complementary in managing risk, whether to increase the exposure through double or even triple gearing, or to reduce it with a hedging policy.

Offshore warrant funds, capital shares, traditional options, traded options and futures are all covered to some extent below, but the following text is not a comprehensive guide to these areas of investment. Investors should take appropriate professional advice before committing money to these high-risk niches of the investment market.

OFFSHORE WARRANT FUNDS

Beginning with the clearest alternative to direct investment in warrants, there is a wide range of warrant funds available – largely at present offshore. There is just one listed investment trust specializing in warrants, and two onshore unit trusts. The rest of the warrant funds are something of a 'hidden' market, tucked away in the *Financial Times* 'Managed Funds Service' pages and strictly limited in the advertising and marketing which they are allowed to pursue. The result is that the funds are known to market practitioners, and to the favoured clients of large stockbrokers, but to few others. It may surprise many investors to see the range of largely dollar-denominated funds available, investing principally in Japanese, European, Asian or North American warrants (see Table 12.1). The broad spread across all geographical regions, a number of fund managers and most offshore centres bears testament to the widespread influence of warrants across all major financial markets, although the lack of any funds investing solely in UK warrants bears equal testament to the limited size of the domestic market.

Registered Base	Manager	Name of Fund
UK (authorized)	Scottish Value Management	Warrants & Value
	Exeter Fund Managers	Warrant
	Hargreaves Lansdown	HL Warrant Portfolio
Ireland (regulated)	Baring International	Tristar Warrant
	GT Asset Management	GT Jap Warr & Derivatives A
	GT Asset Management	GT Jap Warr & Derivatives B
Isle of Man (regulated)	City Financial Administration	Beckman Option & Warrants
Luxembourg		
(SIB recognized)	Cresvale Group	Equity Warrant (Japan)
	Gartmore Luxembourg	Japan Warrant
	INVESCO International	Asia Tiger Warrant
		European Warrant
		Nippon Warrant
	Kleinwort Benson	Japanese Warrant Fund
	Lloyds Bank Luxembourg	Warrant
Luxembourg (regulated)	Fleming Group	Japan Warrant
		European Warrant
Other Offshore Funds	Daiwa	Japanese Equity Warrant
	HSBC Asset Management	Japanese Warrants
	Jardine Fleming Inv Management	JF Pacific Warrant
	Jardine Fleming Unit Trusts	JF Far Eastern Warrants
		JF Japan Warrant
	MBf Unit Trust Managers	MBf Pacific Warrant
	Moore Global Investment	MGI Detachable Warrant
	Morgan Stanley	Japanese Warrant Fund
	Nomura	Warrant Fund 1990
	Regent Fund Management	RL Country Warrant
	Schroders Asia	Far Eastern Warrant
		International Warrant
	Thornton Investment Management	Asian Conqueror Warrants

Table 12.1 Warrant funds, 1995

Perhaps the most famous of these funds is the INVESCO MIM Nippon Warrant Fund, rightly renowned for multiplying its assets more than 14-fold in a three-year period. The net asset value per share grew from $7.43 at its low point on 21 October 1986 to $105.36 (adjusted for share split) by 29 September 1989. This performance seems all the more remarkable when you remember that this period included the 'Crash' of October 1987, during which the assets of the fund fell by two-thirds before recovering.

The volatile performance of these funds is understandable enough in view of the gearing of the warrants in which they invest, but to compound this feature, the funds themselves may be geared using borrowings. Each fund's policy in this regard will be outlined in the prospectus. Moving one step further, there are warrants attached to some of these funds, such as Robert Fleming's European Warrant Fund, and the Schroder Japanese Warrant Fund, offering double-gearing or even triple-gearing (if the fund is geared) for those who find it attractive. The resulting investment is one which can move substantially in response to a relatively small change in the underlying net assets – both up and down.

Whether or not you opt for the extra gearing, warrant funds can make a good deal of sense for many investors who may not have the time or the interest to select and maintain their own portfolios. They can, further, provide a useful addition to a portfolio for those who are content to manage their domestic interests, but rightly fear the problems of dealing overseas. The warrant funds can provide an excellent way of investing in international warrant issues, particularly where the managers have a proven track record. Two caveats apply however. First, watch out for the charges on these funds, which can be penal. If the fund is an open-ended company (like a unit trust), then the initial and annual charges need to be checked, and if the fund is a closed-end company (like an investment trust) then the dealing charges can be expensive, especially when settlement takes place through Euroclear and CEDEL. And second, the majority of funds are denominated in US dollars, so you will have to assume a currency risk in addition to the risk of investing in what may be a highly volatile fund.

SPLIT-CAPITAL INVESTMENT TRUST CAPITAL SHARES

On the domestic front, as the investment trust industry has revived in recent years, so investors have become increasingly demanding, and split-level trusts have become popular as a means of satisfying a range of investor demands. Although such trusts first emerged in the 1960s, they have only recently come to prominence. For issuers, the split-capital structure helps to reduce or eliminate the problem of the discount which plagues the investment trust industry, and for investors the attraction is a choice of investment within a single investment trust. Modern split-capital investment trusts tend to have several classes of share, but the two most important are the income shares and capital shares. As the names suggest, each concentrates on one aspect of investment returns, the income shares ranking for all of the dividends and being repaid at a fixed par price, while the capital shares receive no income but benefit from all of the capital gains accruing to the trust in excess of the predetermined repayments due on the other classes of share. One of the prime merits of this arrangement is that it allows investors to structure their portfolio according to their income or capital preferences (which may be influenced by taxation). To this end, when trusts make proposals for conversion into split-level companies they usually include a 'mix and match' election facility. Investors preferring the income shares will benefit from a high initial yield and a known capital return, while investors preferring the capital shares can not only concentrate on capital gains, but they also benefit from gearing. If the assets of an ordinary investment trust rise by 50 per cent, then so will the shares, but in a split-level investment trust the capital shares can perform rather better:

EXAMPLE

The Imaginary Split-Capital Investment Trust plc has assets of £150 million, split between £60 million of income shares (repayable at par), £40 million of capital shares, and a capital reserve of £50 million This makes the capital shares worth £90 million. Assets grow by 40 per cent to £210 million, income shares still worth £60 million and capital shares now £150 million – a rise of 67 per cent.

In a simple case such as this, gearing is calculated as follows:

$$Gearing = \frac{Total\ asset\ value}{Asset\ value\ of\ capital\ shares}$$

And from the example above:

$$Gearing = \frac{£150m}{£90m} = 1.67\ times.$$

Unlike the gearing associated with warrants, this measure provides an reasonably accurate calculation of leverage. Returning to the example above, the capital shares moved up 1.67 times as much as the underlying assets, and could have moved down by the same multiple. Unfortunately, gearing is not quite that simple in practice, as the capital shares may command a premium or trade at a discount to the intrinsic net asset value. In a similar way as warrants, capital shares may be 'in the assets' or 'out of the assets'. They will have no intrinsic value until the net asset value of the trust is sufficient to repay all of the classes of share with prior claims upon the assets. This 'asset strike price' is similar to the subscription price for warrants.

The similarities are such that capital shares have sometimes been called warrants in disguise. Investors may wish to consider them as an alternative bull market instrument, although the range is far more limited. There are around 30 investment trust capital shares listed in London at the time of writing, six of which also have warrants attached. These are marked with an asterisk in the list below:

Aberforth Split Level
Archimedes
Contra-Cyclical
Danae*

Derby Trust
Foreign & Colonial Special Utilities*
Fulcrum
Gartmore Scotland
General Consolidate
Jos
Jove
Lloyds Smaller
M&G Dual
M&G Second Dual
M&G Income
M&G Recovery
Mezzanine Capital & Income Trust 2001
Mezzanine Capital & Income Trust 'S'
Murray Split
New Throgmorton
River & Mercantile American Capital & Income*
River & Mercantile*
River & Mercantile Geared Capital & Income
River Plate & General Investment*
St David's
Save & Prosper Linked
Schroder Split
Scottish National*
Throgmorton Dual
Venturi
Yeoman

The warrants attached to capital shares are of particular interest, since they are essentially warrants on warrants, implying a double dose of gearing. Of course this makes them highly volatile and therefore unsuitable for conservative investors. Conversely, for speculators expecting a strong performance from the underlying assets, these warrants have the potential to be among the best performers.

When analysing these particular warrants, however, the standard forms of calculation can produce rather misleading answers, since they do not take explicit account of the gearing of the capital shares. In particular, the high CFPs which tend to characterize such warrants can understate the relative potential for gain. A very different string of calculations is required to unravel the relationships between the assets, capital shares and warrants, some of which are highly complex. It is rare to find much separate analysis of warrants attached to capital shares for this reason. Instead of the CFP, for example, which compares the position of the warrants with that of the capital shares, it is often more useful to use what we may call the asset fulcrum point (AFP), which is the annual growth of the underlying assets required for the warrants to outperform the capital shares. If the AFP is 7 per cent and the assets actually grow by 8 per cent per annum to the winding-up date, then you will do better with the warrants than with the capital shares.

The calculation itself is difficult, and requires precise information from the company. Once the data is collected and checked it is easiest to construct a spreadsheet to perform the necessary functions and to provide definitive answers. When prices change it is then a simple matter to enter the new data and recalculate the AFP – a process which is laborious and prone to error when attempted without a computer.

The formula for the AFP is as follows:

AFP (fully diluted)* =

⟦ ({[no. of shares with prior claims on assets × capital repayment per share of this class]

$$+ [\frac{e}{s - w} \times s \times number\ of\ capital\ shares]$$

$$+ [(\frac{e}{s - w} \times s - e) \times number\ of\ warrants]\} \div current\ asset\ value)^{1/y}$$

$$- 1⟧ \times 100\%$$

where y = years to expiry; e = exercise price; s = capital share price; w = warrant price

This may not appear too daunting in this form, but when applied to trusts with a number of different share classes, the formula can extend to several lines. Below the formula is adapted for the largest of the split-level investment trusts, the Scottish National Trust plc†. This trust has five classes of share which rank ahead of the capital shares in the queue for asset repayments when the trust is wound up in 1998**. The debenture stock 2011 (DS) has first priority for repayment at par (100p), then the 6 per cent cumulative preference shares (CCPS) at 100p, the stepped preference shares (SPS) at 171p, the zero dividend preference shares (ZDPS) at 325p, and then the income shares (IS) at 100p. The capital shares (CS) are entitled to all surplus assets of the company after all of these payments have been made in full. Figure 12.1 shows this graphically.

---

* This takes account of the full exercise of all outstanding warrants into capital shares. As the exact claim on assets is known, it is simple to incorporate this sophistication, unlike the normal CFP calculation where it would be necessary to estimate the degree of actual dilution which would take place upon exercise. In the example above the fully diluted AFP is equal to 13.67 per cent, against 13.32 per cent if dilution is not included.

† The data used is from the company's 1990 annual report. Total assets amounted to £269,090,000, the capital share price was 34p, and the warrant price 11p.

** Unless within the preceding three months the shareholders vote to continue the company.

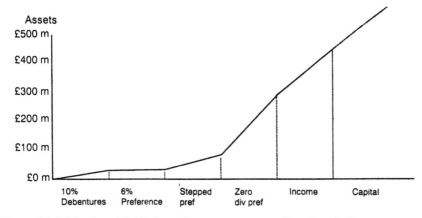

Figure 12.1 The Scottish National Trust – asset growth and capital repayments

EXAMPLE

AFP (fully diluted) =

$$[\{([25,000,000\ DS \times 100p] + [1,500,000\ CPS \times 100p]$$
$$+ [31,930,630\ SPS \times 171p] + [63,861,260\ ZDPS \times 325p]$$
$$+ [159,653,150\ IS \times 100p] + [\frac{300p}{34-11p} \times 34p \times 63,861,260\ CS]$$
$$+ [(\frac{300p}{34p-11p} \times 34p - 300p) \times 12,771,018]\} \div £269,090,000)^{\frac{1}{1998.75-1990.75}}$$

$$- 1] \times 100\%$$

$$= \{[(£25,000,000 + £1,500,000 + £54,601,377 + £207,549,095$$
$$+ £159,653,150 + £283,210,805 + £18,323,635) \div £269,090,000]^{1/8}$$
$$-1 \} \times 100\%$$

$$=[\left(\frac{£749,838,062}{£269,090,000}\right)^{1/8} - 1] \times 100\%$$
$$= (2.78657^{1/8} - 1) \times 100\%$$
$$= 13.67\%$$

In this case the annual growth rate of 13.67 per cent in the underlying assets derived from the AFP will result in the assets growing to £750 million (plus £38 million from exercise of the warrants), leaving £340 million to be distributed to the capital shareholders at the rate of 443.5p per share. This represents a compound annual growth rate of 37.9 per cent in the capital shares, matched by a 37.9 per cent annual increase in the warrants from 11p to their intrinsic value at 143.5p. Figure 12.2 illustrates this.

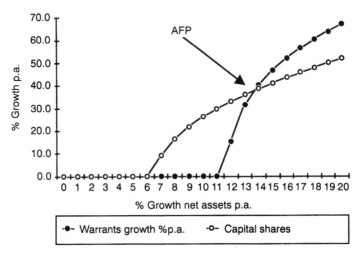

Figure 12.2: Scottish National Trust – asset growth rate and AFP

The AFP is one of a series of fulcrum points which may be calculated in respect of split-level trust performance. The others are, thankfully, simpler. Examples are provided below for the zero dividend payment point, the income share payment point, the capital break-even point, the warrants subscription price point, and the warrants break-even point.

The Zero Dividend Payment Point (ZDPP) is the annual compound rate of growth required to repay the zero dividend preference shares (ZDPS) in full:

ZDPP =

[[[(No. of shares with prior claims on assets × Capital repayment per share of this class)

+ (No. of ZDPS × Capital repayment due per ZDPS)]
÷ Current asset value]^{1/y}–1] × 100%

=

[[[(25,000,000 DS × 100p)
+ (1,500,000 CPS × 100p)
+ (31,930,630 SPS × 171p)
+ (63,861,260 ZDPS × 325p)]
÷ £269,090,000]^{1/8} – 1] × 100%

$$= \left[\left(\frac{£288,650,472}{£269,090,000}\right)^{1/8} - 1\right] \times 100\%$$

$$= (1.0727^{1/8} - 1) \times 100\%$$

$$= 0.88\%$$

Thus the underlying assets must grow at an annual compound rate of 0.88 per cent per annum to 1998 in order for the Zero Dividend Preference Shares to receive the full 325p payment per share.

The same equation may be applied for the income share payment point, with an extra line included in the equation for their fixed capital entitlement. The rate of growth required works out at 6.59 per cent.

The next stage is to move on to the capital shares, and to the capital break-even point (CBEP). This measures the annual compound rate of growth required for holders of the capital shares to recover their investment – e.g., the growth required for the assets to be sufficient to repay all prior classes of share plus 34p per capital share.

$CBEP =$

$[[[(No.\ of\ shares\ with\ prior\ claims\ on\ assets \times Capital\ repayment\ per\ share$
$of\ this\ class)$
$+ (Number\ of\ capital\ shares \times Current\ capital\ share\ price)]$
$\div Current\ asset\ value\}^{1/y} - 1] \times 100\%$

$$= \left[\left[\frac{£448,303,622\ in\ prior\ repayments + (63,861,260 \times 34p)}{£269,090,000}\right]^{1/8} - 1\right] \times 100\%$$

$$= (1.7467^{1/8} - 1) \times 100\%$$

$$= 7.22\%$$

Further along the spectrum comes the warrants subscription price point, which is the annual compound rate of growth required in the underlying assets for the capital shares to reach the subscription price for the warrants. This is exactly the same equation as above, except that 300p should be substituted in place of the market price of 34p. The result is 11.44 per cent.

And finally, there is the warrants break-even point (WBEP). This measures the annual compound rate of growth required for holders of the warrants to recover their investment – e.g. the growth required for the assets to be sufficient to repay all prior classes of share plus 311p per capital share. This equation is exactly the same as for the CBEP except that 311p (the exercise price plus the market price of the warrants) should be substituted in place of 34p (the market price of the capital shares). The result is 11.62 per cent.

This range of equations has taken a lot of space to detail, and requires a lot of effort to calculate (unless automated in a spreadsheet), but is it really worth the effort? The outcome is a range of fulcrum points, building up a picture of stepped growth (see Figure 12.3) which provides both an excellent analytical benchmark

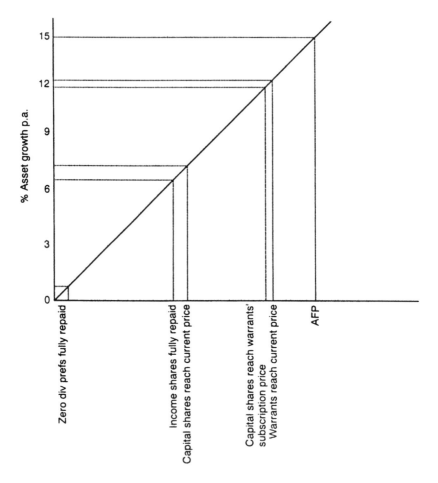

Fig 12.3: Scottish National Trust – the repayment spectrum

and a wonderful illustration of risk. As you move along the risk spectrum, so the required growth rate increases, as do the potential rewards.

At annual rates of growth between 0.88 per cent and 6.59 per cent the assets go towards repayments for the income shares; between 6.59 per cent and 7.22 per cent towards repaying the capital shares up to the current price; between 7.22 per cent and 11.44 per cent towards repaying the capital shares up to the warrants' subscription price; from 11.44 per cent to 11.62 per cent towards repaying the capital shares and warrants up to the current market price; from 11.62 per cent to 13.67 per cent towards repaying the capital shares and warrants, but with greater profits on the former; and above 13.67 per cent creating a superior profit on the warrants.

Once this repayment spectrum is completed, the investor can simply compare his expected rate of growth derived from fundamental considerations with the rates of growth required for various outcomes. An investor expecting growth of 8 per cent per annum would expect a modest profit on the capital shares, but would avoid the warrants (since the capital shares would not reach the subscription price). By contrast, a far more optimistic investor anticipating annual growth of 14 per cent would prefer the highest-risk security – the warrants – which also offers the greatest reward at this growth rate.

TRADITIONAL OPTIONS

Warrants, warrant funds, and capital shares are still wet behind the ears when compared with traditional options, which have been in near-continuous use in London since the late 17th century. They are used regularly to this day, as evidenced by the daily listings of option activity and rates in the *Financial Times*, and many market players find them to be a useful and flexible way of achieving certain investment aims. For investors concerned principally with warrants, traditional options can occasionally play a part in strategies which combine the two instruments, or as an alternative where warrants are unavailable or unsuitable.

To begin with, it is important to realise that traditional options differ substantially from warrants. They are private option bargains between two parties only, the 'giver', who buys the option, and the 'taker' or 'writer' who takes the option money and is liable to deliver the stock if required at the end of the option. This means that the options are not easily transferable, and they are not usually traded during their short lives. While they allow you to construct 'custom-made' positions, therefore, exclusivity can also be a drawback, and the inability to buy and sell traditional options freely in the market is an important limitation on their utility. Another critical restriction is the time to expiry, which is set by Stock Exchange regulations at a maximum period of approximately three months. The option is set at a 'strike price' which is the market price of the underlying security on the day of issue, and the option carries the right to buy one share at this strike price on predetermined 'declaration days'. If the option is not 'declared' on one of these days during its life, then it is deemed to be abandoned. Up to this point, traditional options sound like a feeble forerunner of warrants, but they do offer two major advantages which can make them an excellent proposition.

First, traditional options are not 'one-way' instruments in the same way as ordinary warrants, which will only benefit from rising prices. In addition to the standard call option it is possible to give money for put options which give you the right to sell shares at the strike price*, and for put and call options, or 'doubles', which give you the right to buy or sell the shares during the agreed period.

---

* This strike price will be the offer price of the security for a call option, the bid price for a put option, and the middle market price for a 'double'.

This means that using traditional options you can benefit from a rising market, a falling market, or even a fluctuating market. A put option, for example, works in the following way:

EXAMPLE

WIDGET PLC TRADITIONAL PUT OPTION

Widget plc share price spread 117–123p

Investor gives money for 10,000 put options at strike price 117p. Cost 15p each: total outlay £1,500.

Shares price spread drops by 25 per cent to 88–92p.

Investor declares his options, sells 10,000 shares at 117p and buys 10,000 shares in the market at 92p to close the position.

Profit per share = 117p–15p–92p = 10p = £1,000

Result: a 25 per cent fall in the share price produces a profit of 67 per cent from the put options.

Furthermore, it is possible in theory at least to give money for an option on almost any security listed and traded on the London Stock Exchange, whether it be a share or a warrant. The market is therefore much broader than the limited coverage offered by warrants, and it offers the enticing prospect of a geared investment in any security of your choice, with a reasonable 'at the money' strike price and several exercise periods throughout its life.

The catch lies in the premium which must be paid for the option. This varies considerably according to the nature of the underlying security, the position of the market-makers' book, his opinion of the security, and the liquidity of the market. A call or put option on a blue-chip share may cost the giver around 8 per cent of the market price, and about one and a half times that amount for a double option – a perfectly reasonable price to pay. In contrast, the market-makers may be reluctant to quote a price for an option on an illiquid low-priced warrant, and the premium may be anything from 20 per cent up to 50 per cent of the market price. As the security needs to rise (or fall in the case of a put option) by the amount of the spread plus the amount of this premium plus dealing charges before you break even, it is rarely likely to be feasible giving money for such options.

There are, however, certain circumstances in which warrant investors may like to consider traditional options, six of which are detailed below:

1 In the course of your warrant researches, you may uncover a promising fundamental position for an underlying stock, but the warrants may appear too expensive on technical grounds. Traditional call options on the underlying shares may be used for a short-term speculation – as an alternative to the warrants.

2 Few investors restrict their stockmarket interests to warrants, particularly as warrants are currently available for around 200 securities only. For companies with sound prospects but without warrants attached, traditional options may again be a viable alternative.

3 When considering warrants you may decide that your opinion is so positive that you wish to take on a double layer of gearing, and that a traditional call option on the warrant may be viable (subject to the price). This simple strategy can produce some very large gains from a relatively small rise in the shares:

EXAMPLE

Grommet plc shares 100p; warrants 40p, 'in the money' with six months remaining, no premium; call option on warrants 8p. Spreads and dealing charges are ignored.

Shares	Change (%)	Warrants	Change (%)	Options	Change (%)
100p	0	40p	0	0p	−100
108p	+8	48p	+20	8p	0
110p	+10	50p	+25	10p	+25
120p	+20	60p	+50	20p	+150
130p	+30	70p	+75	30p	+275
140p	+40	80p	+100	40p	+400
150p	+50	90p	+125	50p	+525

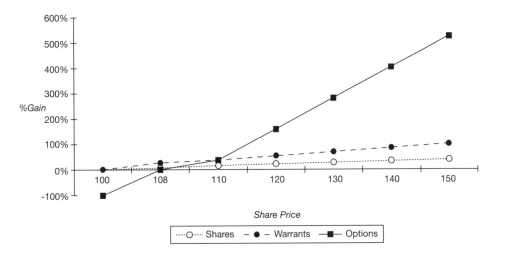

Figure 12.4 Double layers of gearing

In the example illustrated in Figure 12.4, a 20 per cent rise in the shares stim-
ulates a 50 per cent rise in the warrants and a 150 per cent in the call options.
This is an attractive return, but it must be tempered by the loss which call
option investors will incur if the shares fail to rise by 8 per cent during the
three-month period. Moreover, the increase required is understated by the
absence of dealing charges and the lack of a premium on the warrants. The
potential for large losses as well as large gains is evident, and investors should
be in no doubt that this is a very high-risk approach.

4 In a similar vein, if your researches lead you to a seriously overvalued warrant which you expect to fall sharply in the short-term, then you may try to
give money for a put option to take advantage of the anticipated decline. In
theory this could be a powerful combination, but in practice the quoted option
premiums are likely to be too high for most warrants. Nevertheless, this
approach may be adopted for the largest warrant issues such as Hanson, BTR,
Pilkington, and British Aerospace where the market-makers may be more
amenable to doing business at a reasonable rate.

5 In the same way that the gearing advantage of warrants may be interpreted in
two ways, so this is true with traditional options. Just as they can provide extra
gearing for a given outlay, so they can also provide a given level of exposure
for a much smaller sum. This feature can be useful when you wish to limit
your risk to a very small capital amount, and the traditional option route can
be the most fruitful if you have identified a warrant close to expiry, 'out of the
money', and likely to expire worthless, but with a slim chance of rocketing to
a much higher level. This may be the case for an oil exploration company, for
example, or where a bid is possible (in which case you must check the time
value protection of the warrants).

EXAMPLE

*Mythical Investment Trust plc shares 90p; warrants 8p, exercise price 100p; tra-
ditional call option on the warrants 4p; investor buys either 25,000 warrants for
£2,000 or 25,000 call options for £1,000; spreads and dealing charges ignored.*

Shares	Change (%)	Warrants	Gain/Loss	Options	Gain/Loss
85p	−5.6	0p	−£,2000	0p	−£1,000
90p	0	0p	−£2,000	0p	−£1,000
95p	+5.6	0p	−£2,000	0p	−£1,000
100p	+11.1	0p	−£2,000	0p	−£1,000
105p	+16.7	5p	−£750	0p	−£1,000
110p	+22.2	10p	+£500	2p	−£500
115p	+27.8	15p	+£1,750	7p	+£750
120p	+33.3	20p	+£3,000	12p	+£2,000
125p	+38.9	25p	+£4,250	17p	+£3,250

The use of traditional options in this way has halved the maximum loss to £1,000, but enabled the investor to retain most of the gains made if the gamble pays off. Buying the call options at 4p is not the same as buying half as many warrants at 8p. The latter move would halve the maximum loss to £1,000, but it would also halve the potential profits shown in the table.

6 Finally there is hedging. If you are a large holder in a relatively illiquid warrant, and you are worried about the onset of a period of volatility, but you do not wish to sell at a bad price and then find it difficult to re-establish your position, you can solve the dilemma by giving money for a put option:

EXAMPLE

Investor holds 10,000 warrants in Widget plc at 40p each (£4,000). Investor gives 8p for 10,000 put options (£800).

Warrants	Gain/Loss	Options	Gain/Loss	Net Gain/Loss
20p	−£2,000	20p	+£1,200	−£800
25p	−£1,500	15p	+£700	−£800
30p	−£1,000	10p	+£200	−£800
35p	−£500	5p	−£300	−£800
40p	£0	0p	−£800	−£800
45p	+£500	0p	−£800	−£300
50p	+£1,000	0p	−£800	+£200
60p	+£2,000	0p	−£800	+£1,200

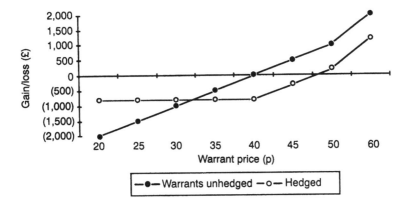

Figure 12.5 Option hedging strategy

The result in this instance is that the investor limits his potential loss over the period to a maximum of £800, reducing his possible gains by the same amount (see Figure 12.5). When the put option is exercised (at prices below 40p) the investor may close his position by buying stock in the market. Alternatively, should the decline have altered the investor's view of the warrants, he may choose to close his position by delivering his existing 10,000 warrants.

These six examples of when warrant investors may find it useful to consider traditional options are intended to outline some of the possibilities, not to present an exhaustive guide. Some alternatives, such as taking (or 'writing') option money have not been covered here, but should you wish to learn more you can either consult the relevant literature or contact your stockbroker for advice.

TRADED OPTIONS

The same applies to this brief coverage of traded options. Developed from traditional options and introduced to London in 1978, their name divulges the major advance which has been made. Traded options are negotiable and freely tradeable contracts giving the right to buy or sell securities at a fixed price within an agreed time period of up to nine months. Traded options are issued in three-month cycles so that, for example, a company may have options expiring in January, April and July. As such, the call options are essentially short-dated warrants, although the market also offers put options which add a different dimension to the trading possibilities. The ability to benefit from price falls is a major advantage which warrants cannot offer, and in bearish conditions the traded put options can be an excellent alternative to UK equity warrants. For short-term speculation the market is also more flexible in terms of exercise prices and therefore gearing. Whereas warrant investors are usually limited to one issue which has a single subscription price and one level of gearing, traded option investors can choose from a range of strike prices both 'in the money' and 'out of the money', structuring their risk to meet their preferences.

Such flexibility is a prime attraction, but investors will always meet the critical stumbling block of the time to expiry. Traded options are for short-term traders only, and do not meet the requirements of most investors seeking investments such as warrants which offer the potential for short-term gains, but which may be held over the medium- or longer-term if preferred. Apart from this drawback, you will also need a special account with your stockbroker to deal in traded options, commission rates are higher, settlement is different, and options are dealt in standard contract lots of 1,000 shares (except for Vaal Reefs, 100 shares). You do not receive a certificate, and whilst traded options carry the theoretical right to exercise into the shares, this is rarely done in practice. These features are diametrically opposed to warrants, and there is little similarity either in the composition of the two markets.

At the time of writing, LIFFE equity options are available for 71 blue-chip companies (no investment trusts), as follows:

Abbey National	Fisons	Reuters
Allied Domecq	Forte	Rolls Royce
Amstrad	GEC	Royal Insurance
Argyll	Glaxo-Wellcome	RTZ
ASDA	Grand Metropolitan	Sainsbury
BAA	Guinness	Scottish Power
Barclays	Hanson	Sears
Bass	Hillsdown	Shell Transport
BAT Industries	HSBC	Smithkline Beecham
Blue Circle	ICI	Standard Chartered
Boots	Kingfisher	Storehouse
British Aerospace	Ladbroke	Tarmac
British Airways	Land Securities	Tesco
British Gas	LASMO	Thames Water
British Petroleum	Lonrho	Thorn EMI
British Steel	Lucas Industries	Tomkins
British Telecom	Marks & Spencer	Trafalgar
BTR	National Power	TSB
Cable & Wireless	Nat West	Unilever
Cadbury Schweppes	P&O	United Biscuits
Commercial Union	Pilkington	Vodafone
Courtaulds	PowerGen	Williams
Dixons	Prudential	Zeneca
Eastern Electricity	Redland	

Of these companies, only four also have listed equity warrants in issue – namely BTR, Hanson, British Aerospace, and Pilkington. Many more have covered warrants in issue. In these cases it can be interesting to compare the premiums payable on the two instruments, and in certain circumstances they may be used together to manage the risk and reward profile of your investment. The beauty of such a combination is that it allows you to construct the most appropriate matrix of potential returns for your short-term expectations, whether this be a flat, rising or falling market. Warrants can work extremely well as long-term investment vehicles, but they cannot always provide the best short-term returns when used alone.

Consider, for example, a period of three months, over which you expected the share price to remain unchanged. Your holding of warrants might retain its value, or it might fall slightly, but it will not generate a profit if you are correct. Using a strategy called either a 'time spread' or a 'buy-write' manoeuvre it is possible to profit from a correct reading of a flat market. The time spread involves the simultaneous sale of a short-dated call option and the purchase of warrants for the same stock. In theory, the time value of the short-dated call will waste away over the three-month period as the equity fails to make any headway, while the longer-dated warrant will retain most, if not all, of its time value which is spread over a much longer period. It is this difference which the investor hopes to pocket.

The strategy works best with a call option which has approximately the same strike price as the warrants' subscription price, and where the warrants are 'at the money'.

EXAMPLE

Buy-write strategy for neutral price expectations:
Widget plc shares 400p, warrants' exercise price 400p
Buy 10,000 warrants expiring in two years' time for 50p – cost £5,000
Sell (write) 5,000 three-month 400p calls for 20p

Result (warrant price is the predicted price – the degree of movement will depend upon your estimation of leverage):

Shares	**Warrants**	**Profit/Loss**	**Calls**	**Profit/Loss**	**Net Change**
350p	*35p*	*–£1,500*	*0p*	*£1,000*	*–£500*
375p	*40p*	*–£1,000*	*0p*	*£1,000*	*+£0*
400p	*50p*	*£0*	*0p*	*£1,000*	*+£1,000*
425p	*60p*	*£1,000*	*25p*	*–£250*	*+£750*
450p	*70p*	*£2,000*	*50p*	*–£1,500*	*+£500*

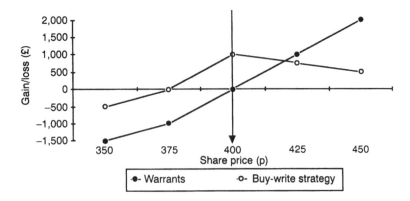

Figure 12.6 Neutral buy-write strategy

Using this buy-write strategy (shown graphically in Figure 12.6), the investor has managed to maximize his gain if the shares remain unchanged, altering the reward profile of the investment to suit his expectations. Similar combinations of warrants and options may be used for both bullish and bearish outlooks, the former accentuating gains made when the warrants rise (see Figure 12.7).

EXAMPLE

Buy-write strategy for bullish price expectations:
Sell 'out of the money' short-dated calls; buy 'out of the money' warrants
Widget plc shares 400p, warrants' exercise price 475p
Buy 20,000 warrants expiring in two years time for 25p – cost £5,000
Sell (write) 20,000 three-month 475p calls for 5p

Result (again the warrant price is the predicted price – see previous example):

Shares	*Warrants*	*Profit/Loss*	*Calls*	*Profit/Loss*	*Net Change*
375p	*20p*	*–£1,000*	*0p*	*£1,000*	*+£0*
400p	*25p*	*£0*	*0p*	*£1,000*	*+£1,000*
425p	*30p*	*£1,000*	*0p*	*£1,000*	*+£2,000*
450p	*35p*	*£2,000*	*0p*	*£1,000*	*+£3,000*
475p	*45p*	*£4,000*	*0p*	*£1,000*	*+£5,000*
500p	*55p*	*£6,000*	*25p*	*–£4,000*	*+£2,000*

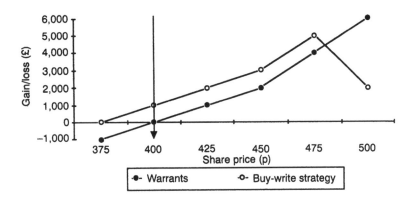

Figure 12.7 Bullish buy-write strategy

Clearly, the more bullish the investor, the further 'out of the money' he will write calls, as this strategy reduces profits once the strike price has been exceeded. This is, however, a high-risk operation, since calls a long way from the money are unlikely to command much premium and it may be necessary to write a large number of options in order to achieve substantial gains.

Finally, a bearish buy-write strategy will produce a profit if the equity falls. This may be of value when a warrant-holder wishes to retain a holding for the longer term, but wishes to protect the investment against a possible short-term decline. Figure 12.8 illustrates this strategy.

EXAMPLE

Buy-write strategy for bearish price expectations:
Sell 'in the money' short-dated calls; buy 'in the money' warrants
Widget plc shares 400p, warrants' exercise price 350p
Buy 5,000 warrants expiring in two years time for 100p – cost £5,000
Sell (write) 5,000 three-month 350p calls for 75p

Result (again based on predicted warrant price):

Shares	Warrants	Profit/Loss	Calls	Profit/Loss	Net Change
300p	40p	–£3,000	0p	£3.750	+£750
325p	50p	–£2,500	0p	£3,750	+£1,250
350p	60p	–£2,000	0p	£3,750	+£1,750
375p	75p	–£1,250	25p	£2,500	+£1,250
400p	100p	£0	50p	£1,250	+£1,250
425p	115p	£1,000	75p	£0	+£1,000
450p	130p	£2,000	100p	–£1,250	+£750
475p	150p	£2,500	125p	–£2,500	+£0

These strategies (which are only a small sample from a broad range including such schemes as 'butterfly spreads' and 'straddles') appear theoretically attractive, although it is always important to construct a reward matrix to predict the likely outcome for a range of price movements both fitting and confounding your expectations. Whereas the buy-write strategy can increase returns from a correct prediction, it can also imply heavy losses from an incorrect prediction. Care is therefore required. In practice, warrant investors are unlikely to use these strategies very often, as they require (i) a share to have both warrants and a traded options series attached, which immediately narrows the field to seven; (ii) the warrants to have the parity ratio matching your requirements. BTR's four different series of warrants (which are rather like a series of long-dated traded options, except they are calls only) offer excellent opportunities in this regard, since you will usually be able to find a warrant suitably 'in the money' or 'out of the money', but of course this is unusual. Usually there is one set of warrants only, and this can inhibit the application of these strategies.

In practice, you will very rarely find a perfect set-up. The solution to this is to undertake careful calculations to predict the likely profit or loss for a range of price movements and to calculate the risk and reward potential accordingly. The key to the successful application of sophisticated hedging strategies is the same as that for simple direct investment: be informed.

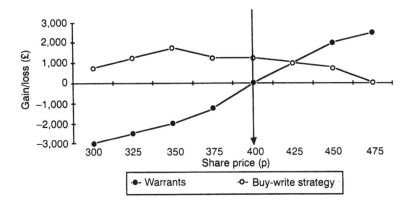

Figure 12.8 Bearish buy-write strategy

FUTURES

Nowhere is the need to be informed more starkly revealed than in the arena of futures, which are a different proposition altogether from warrants and options. The critical difference is that using futures it is possible to lose more than the amount of your original investment. Futures are therefore not for the faint-hearted, and nor are they suitable for the casual investor without specialist knowledge of this area.

The traditional view of futures tends to reinforce this caution. Trading con-tracts on actual commodities ranging from cocoa and copper to potatoes, plat-inum and pork bellies by the process of open outcry in the 'pit' is a process which mystifies many private investors. Slightly more intelligible is the financial futures market which was developed in America during the 1970s and which led to the establishment of an organized market in London (LIFFE) in 1982. Finan-cial futures are contracts which carry the right to buy or sell currencies, interest rates, exchange rates or market indices at fixed prices at certain dates in the future. These may be used for speculation based upon macroeconomic analysis, or more usually they are used for the purposes of arbitrage, hedging, cash flow management, or efficient portfolio management. As such they can have an important part to play in the management of a large, active international portfolio, but they are of doubtful relevance to most private investors who will not wish to look further than the London Stock Exchange (or LIFFE for traded options) and the other instruments described above.

"The position of the market outlined in this book, with few able analysts, little media attention, a lack of liquidity, relatively modest retail interest, and an overwhelming cloud of ignorance, could be unrecognizable by the turn of the century."

13

THE DEVELOPING MARKET

In the early 1990s, the warrants market could fairly lay claim to being the fastest-growing sector of the London Stock Exchange. The weak market conditions of 1994 slowed the market considerably, but with a resumption of a bull trend the warrants market could return to its hectic heydays for the rest of the decade. The movement towards warrants, stimulated by investment trusts in particular, is gaining in momentum, and corporate finance departments are just waiting for another bullish phase to unleash another rush of new issues with warrants attached to a receptive public. The position of the market outlined in this book, with few able analysts, little media attention, a lack of liquidity, relatively modest retail interest, and an overwhelming cloud of ignorance, could be unrecognizable by the turn of the century.

The reasoning behind this bold assertion is derived from a variety of factors representing both the demand and supply sides of the warrants market. Investors who have studied the market in detail present a picture of a multi-faceted magnet which is drawing attention from several different areas at once – from issuers, from investors, from the stockbroking community, from the media, and from collective investment schemes. The increased awareness of warrants by all of these parties is creating a virtuous circle which is self-reinforcing (see Figure 13.1). The more investors who demand warrants, the more companies who respond to that demand, the more warrant-holders are created. The more warrants in issue and the larger the number of warrant-holders, the more investors deal through stockbrokers. In turn, stockbrokers channel more resources into warrant research, stimulating more trading and interest. This interest feeds through to the media which responds to the upturn in interest with more articles and information, thereby attracting more investors and encouraging more companies to issue warrants. And as more warrants are issued and the market grows, so the market becomes suitable for collective investment schemes, pulling in yet more investors of another sort. The outcome of this web of mutually beneficial activity is a thriving market.

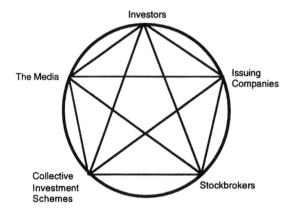

Figure 13.1 The virtuous circle of warrant activity

It is almost impossible to quantify the stimulant effects mentioned above, and equally difficult to explain all of the precise link mechanisms, but this does not invalidate the reasoning. The argument rests upon the continuation and augmentation of activity which has already started and which has led to well over 80 new issues in the last two years.

COMPANY ISSUES

There is a strong element of inertia influencing the warrants market, and this has possibly its strongest effect in corporate boardrooms. Few company directors are noted enthusiasts for innovative financing techniques, and most prefer to follow standard procedures. This natural conservatism takes some time to overcome, but the pressure is mounting on many companies to place warrants on the agenda for the first time. Inherent caution is being eroded as warrants become more common, and directors are also becoming subject to more direct influences. The most prominent of these is the momentum of the market. Quite simply, as the number of warrants grows, so it becomes easier for another company to join the congregation. Whilst it would be a brave decision to become the first company to issue warrants, it is not so remarkable to become the 249th or the 250th. Critics may dismiss the existence of a crowd mentality among such a highly sohisticated group as company directors, but this interpretation ignores the practical advances which have been made as the market has grown. The first company to issue warrants did so on its own initiative, it had to explain the benefits of warrants to a doubtful shareholder base, the terms and conditions of the warrants had to be written from scratch, the market was unsure how to value them, there was unlikely to be much demand in the after-market, and the company ran the risk of an ignorant media dismissing the exercise as some form of shady creative financing. Contrast that with the current position. Companies issuing warrants now can tread the well-worn path of precedent, cite issues from competitors or demand from investors as the origin, draw attention to the more widely understood advantages of warrants, point to real historical examples for justification, conform to the standard warrant particulars, be fairly certain of their likely value in the market, have confidence in the subsequent liquidity of the issue, and expect a positive reaction from the media. Where companies such as Hanson and BTR once had to wield their innovative corporate machetes to clear a path through the warrant jungle, the route to the market is now relatively clear. As such, it is likely to be followed by an increasing number of companies.

That said, it was undoubtedly a blow to the warrants market when BTR decided to cease future warrant issues, and the large Hanson issue is due to expire in 1997. The market would benefit enormously from one large blue-chip company deciding to issue warrants now, otherwise there is a danger that warrants could become the sole province of small, capital-hungry companies which are already speculative in nature. This is, to some degree, how the American market has matured.

THE GROWTH OF INVESTMENT TRUSTS

Important though the commercial sector is, the catalyst for the growth process has unarguably come from the increasing popularity of investment trusts. As explained in Chapter 1, investment trusts have special reasons for issuing warrants, so the two markets move hand-in-hand to some extent – a link which has provided a major boost to the warrants market since 1990. This has been the external driving force which was required to set the virtuous circle in motion, and it shows no signs of running out of steam. At the time of writing a number of the largest and most prestigious investment trust managers such as Mercury and Schroder have moved into the investment trust field for the first time, and the signs are that this sector is set for continued growth, market conditions permitting. There will come a point when the market becomes saturated though*, and it will be interesting to see whether commercial issues can resume their original position as the dominant sector. The market is used by a surprisingly small number of companies at present compared to most other countries with developed warrant sectors.

---

* This point may be some way off. There are fewer than 400 UK authorized investment trusts in total, compared with around 1,500 unit trusts.

THE INTRODUCTION OF WARRANT FUNDS

In the meantime it is a source of pleasant irony for the warrants market that it is not only gaining from the revival of investment trusts, but that it should eventually benefit from the efforts of the unit trust industry to respond. New SIB regulations which came into force in 1991 brought warrant funds into the realm of authorized unit trusts for the first time, along with property funds and futures and options funds. This was a response to the strong desire of many fund managers to provide new and innovative products to meet changing investor demands, and to the desire of the unit trust industry as a whole to re-vamp both its image and its performance. The success of offshore warrant funds (only of real interest to the most keen and sophisticated investors) provided a clear signal that warrants were among the leading securities which would attract attention, and most commentators welcomed the move to market them to a wider domestic audience. Only two warrant unit trusts have been launched so far, but more can be expected to follow.

One problem which still exists is that unit trusts usually rely upon Independent Financial Advisers (IFAs) to provide an important complement to direct marketing, and a conflict begins to emerge. The problem is that IFAs are very wary of recommending any high-risk products to their clients, fearing a loss of business if investments turn out badly. Unlike their clients, IFAs have more to lose from a poor performance than they have to gain from a good performance: a 50 per cent loss might mean the departure of their client; a 200 per cent gain for their client is unlikely to be matched by a commensurate increase in commissions. Second, IFAs have little knowledge of warrants. This is not a criticism, just a fact. It is inevitable that advisers who spend the majority of their time evaluating insurance, mortgages, pensions and collective investment schemes are unlikely to appreciate the full merits of secondary stockmarket instruments.

Education, it is to be hoped, will erode this problem. If it does, and more warrant funds are issued, the boost to warrants could be very substantial. First, there is sure to be an increase in publicity and media coverage as new investors seek to learn about warrants. Second, the existence of onshore warrant funds will provide a much wider choice for the private investor, and some realistic opportunities for investing in overseas, currency and bond warrants which are presently unavailable to most people investing relatively small amounts. Third, the existence of collective investment schemes specializing solely in warrants may be seen as a mark of maturity for the market, lending it both stature and respectability. And fourth, the stimulus provided by the new warrant funds together with their direct demand for warrants in which to invest is likely to encourage many more companies to issue warrants. There is little doubt that the development of warrant funds could have major consequences for the future growth of the market, although it is a matter of guesswork to quantify their contribution in anticipation of the event.

INVESTOR AWARENESS

Partly because of dissatisfaction with other speculative instruments such as penny shares, and partly because of the increasing sophistication of the investing public, derivatives such as warrants are currently in demand from a wide range of investors, many of whom would benefit from a managed approach. Already there is a much increased awareness of the opportunities which warrants can offer. The highly publicized issues such as Eurotunnel, Hanson, and BTR have seen to that. Furthermore, there is a direct causative link from supply to demand. When Lucas Industries issued free warrants on a scrip basis in 1990, for example, it created 20,000 new warrant-holders at a stroke, some of whom were motivated to learn more and to invest directly in other warrants. Even those who are not active investors can appreciate the increment in their holding from the 'free' warrants and may press other companies in which they hold shares to follow the same route. Cross-shareholdings can work in the same way as cross-directorships as envoys for the warrants market.

STOCKBROKERS' RESEARCH AND DEALING

In addition to demand and supply, there is also what is known as the service side. As the market grows, so related expertise emerges to service the higher level of activity. In particular, as merchant banks and stockbrokers increase their fees from corporate finance and their revenue from warrant trading, so it is likely that specialist warrants analysts will be employed. The consequent improvement in the quality of advice and research should encourage more reticent investors to enter the market with confidence, again stimulating more warrant trading. It is possible that more expert and experienced dealers may have the same effect, although this depends equally upon the market makers. They are only likely to respond with keener spreads and more efficient practices if liquidity improves along with activity.

MEDIA COVERAGE

A second service is public information. Scouring the media for articles on warrants was once a fruitless task, but in recent times the media has started to pick up on the subject, with the occasional piece to be found even in the tabloid newspapers. The *Investors Chronicle*'s 'Bearbull' column began a new speculative portfolio in 1991 which consisted primarily of warrants, and other pieces have appeared in periodicals from the specialist *Futures & Options World* to the less studious *What Investment?* Nevertheless, the amount of comment is relatively sparse, and does not compare favourably with the number of column inches lavished on competing securities such as traded options. The most wily of investors realise that this absence of coverage can work to their advantage (see Chapter 2), but for most people considering warrants for the first time the search for information is a constant hindrance. This is likely to change as the market develops and turns out more newsworthy stories. Some journalists such as Stephen Lodge of the *Investors Chronicle*, Michael Walters of the *Daily Mail*, and John Davis of *The Observer* have developed some interest in warrants and are prepared to write about them on a regular basis.

OVERALL MARKET PERFORMANCE

It is disappointing that the media has done very little to make investors aware of such astonishing warrant performances as those of Anglesey Mining warrants in 1989 (up eight-fold), and Airtours in 1991 (up nearly 50-fold), and Yorkshire Tyne Tees TV in 1993/95 (up 65-fold). Warrants perform extremely well in bull markets, impressing both investors and issuers alike, if not journalists. New investors observe the large gains and move into the market, while existing investors taking full advantage of the gearing benefit during such periods will see their returns comfortably exceed those from equities, and are likely to shift an increasing proportion of their funds into warrants. The result is an increase in demand. Similarly, the most important potential drawback for issuing companies – that of worthless expiry – recedes markedly during bullish periods, and removes a major obstacle to participation. Moreover, at times of general market optimism it is more likely that companies are planning to expand, either organically or by acquisition, and that finance directors will therefore appreciate the capital-raising function of warrants. The result is an increase in supply.

Whereas bull markets encourage the warrants market to grow, a bear market can obliterate new issue activity and investor demand. Any investor holding warrants during a period of prolonged market weakness is likely to suffer heavy losses, and earlier issues may begin to expire worthless. This is the worst-case scenario for everyone involved in the warrants market, and the impact can be severe (see the post-1973 lull, Chapter 1). Even the most virtuous of circles can be broken by a bear market, and overall market performance must be considered the most important external factor influencing the future of warrants. The harvest is dependent upon the weather.

A stable or rising market may be said to be a necessary but not sufficient condition for the warrants market to flourish, and it is important therefore to build some degree of market expectation into any model of growth. It is beyond the scope of this book to undertake a rigorous examination of general market prospects, but at the time of writing most commentators are looking towards a new bull market which could see prices surge to new all-time highs as the world economy moves out of recession. Should they be right, then the positive prognosis of this chapter may understate the actual eruption of warrant activity in the coming years.

CONCLUSION

As so much of this argument is conjecture, it is easy to fall into the trap of circular reasoning which reproduces the underlying assumptions. Nevertheless, there are some solid reasons for expecting the warrants market to grow rapidly over the medium-term. A simple extrapolation of the growth over the last five years suggests that there may be around 400 warrants listed by the year 2000. If this sounds fanciful, remember that there were only 54 warrants in issue a decade ago, and that the market had never exceeded that number at that point. Whether or not the market can retain its momentum and continue the remarkable growth experienced recently remains to be seen, but the most sensible forecast combines optimism with pragmatism. *The market will continue to forge ahead unless and until the virtuous circle is broken by an external shock such as a repeat of the 1987 'Crash'.* If this seems too vague for those with a pessimistic outlook, bear in mind the following fact; even if new warrant issues were to cease tomorrow, the existing long-dated warrants would ensure that the market was still alive well into the next century. For the foreseeable future, warrants are here to stay.

APPENDIX A

Worked Example

The worked example contained within this appendix is intended to serve as a second point of reference for anyone seeking further clarification of the equations relating to individual warrants. Using the example of the Greenfriar Investment Company, the calculations below cover intrinsic value, the parity ratio, time to expiry, the premium, the break-even point, the capital fulcrum point, the present value of the exercise price, gearing, leverage (implied gearing), high-low volatility, adjusted volatility, standard historical volatility, Giguere, the Black-Scholes formula, implied volatility, delta, leverage, and the calculation of the line of best fit using the 'least squares' method.

Greenfriar Investment Company plc

Terms of subscription:	One share at 334p on 1 April 1990 to 1995 inclusive
Share price:	288p
Warrant price:	62p
1991 High:	63p
1991 Low:	38p
Date:	18 October 1991
Interest rate:	10% per annum
Average market warrant price:	53p

Intrinsic Value

Intrinsic Value = share price – exercise price
$$= \quad 288p - 334p$$
$$= \quad -46p$$

Parity Ratio

Parity Ratio $\quad = \quad$ share price ÷ exercise price
$$= \quad 288p \div 334p$$
$$= \quad 0.862$$

Time to Expiry

Time to expiry = 1 April 1995 – 18 October 1991
$$= \quad \text{three years, five and a half months}$$
$$= \quad 3.458 \text{ years}$$

Premium

$$\text{Premium (\%)} = \frac{\text{warrant price} + \text{exercise price} - \text{share price}}{\text{share price}} \times 100$$

$$= \frac{62p + 334p - 288p}{288p} \times 100$$

$$= 37.50\%$$

Break-Even Point

$$\text{Break-Even \% pa} = \left[\left\{\frac{\text{exercise price} + \text{warrant price}}{\text{share price}}\right\}^{1/y} - 1\right] \times 100$$

$$= \left[\left\{\frac{334p + 62p}{288p}\right\}^{1/3.458} - 1\right] \times 100$$

$$= [\, 1.375^{1/3.458} - 1\,] \times 100$$

$$= [\, 1.0965 - 1\,] \times 100$$

$$= 9.65\%$$

Capital Fulcrum Point (CFP)

$$\text{CFP} = \left[\left(\frac{e}{s-w}\right)^{1/y} - 1\right] \times 100\%$$

$$= \left[\left(\frac{334p}{288p - 62p}\right)^{1/3.458} - 1\right] \times 100\%$$

$$= \left[\left(1.4779\right)^{1/3.458} - 1\right] \times 100\%$$

$$= [\, 1.1196 - 1\,] \times 100\%$$

$$= 11.96\%$$

Present Value of Exercise Price

Present value of exercise price

$$= \frac{\text{exercise price}}{(1+r)^y}$$

$$= \frac{334p}{(1+0.1)^{3.458}}$$

$$= \frac{334p}{1.3904}$$

$$= 240.22p$$

Gearing

Gearing factor = Share price / Warrant price

$$= 288p / 62p$$

$$= 4.65 \text{ times}$$

Leverage: Implied Gearing

Implied gearing $\quad = \dfrac{(2 \times \text{parity ratio}) - 1}{\text{warrant ratio}} - 1$

$$= \dfrac{(2 \times 0.862) - 1}{62p \div 334p} - 1$$

$$= \dfrac{0.724}{0.186} - 1$$

$$= 2.89 \text{ times}$$

High-Low Volatility

$$= \text{High/Low}$$

$$= 63p/38p$$

$$= 1.658$$

Adjusted Volatility

Volatility of z warrants = standard deviation {monthly prices} of z warrants

$$\dfrac{\times \text{ average market warrant price}}{\text{average monthly price of z warrants}}$$

= standard deviation {   42p (mid-Jan) $\times \dfrac{53p}{56.3p}$
45p (mid-Feb)
58p (mid-Mar)
59p (mid-Apr)
59p (mid-May)
59p (mid-Jun)
56p (mid-Jul)
60p (mid-Aug)
63p (mid-Sep)
62p (mid-Oct) }

$$= 7.056 \times 0.941$$

$$= 6.64$$

Standard Historical Volatility

$$= \left[\text{Standard Deviation for range of } \ln \left(\dfrac{\text{Price } t}{\text{Price } t\!-\!1} \right) \right] \times \sqrt{\text{(number of entries per year)}} \times 100$$

Date	Shares (p)	Warrants (p)	Price t /Price t–1	Natural Log
4-Jan-91	246	41		
11-Jan-91	238	40	0.976	–0.2469
18-Jan-91	231	42	1.050	0.04879
25-Jan-91	231	42	1.000	0.00000
1-Feb-91	233	44	1.048	0.04652
8-Feb-91	236	44	1.000	0.00000
15-Feb-91	245	45	1.023	0.02247
22-Feb-91	246	49	1.089	0.08516
1-Mar-91	273	53	1.082	0.07847
8-Mar-91	290	53	1.000	0.00000
15-Mar-91	306	58	1.094	0.09015
22-Mar-91	294	57	0.983	–0.01739
29-Mar-91	290	57	1.000	0.00000
5-Apr-91	290	58	1.018	0.01739
12-Apr-91	290	58	1.000	0.00000
19-Apr-91	290	59	1.017	0.01709
26-Apr-91	286	59	1.000	0.00000
3-May-91	285	58	0.983	–0.01709
10-May-91	285	59	1.017	0.01709
17-May-91	283	59	1.000	0.00000
24-May-91	285	59	1.000	0.00000
31-May-91	286	59	1.000	0.00000
7-Jun-91	288	59	1.000	0.00000
14-Jun-91	288	59	1.000	0.00000
21-Jun-91	288	58	0.983	–0.01709
28-Jun-91	285	58	1.000	0.00000
5-Jul-91	283	56	0.966	–0.03509
12-Jul-91	282	56	1.000	0.00000
19-Jul-91	283	56	1.000	0.00000
26-Jul-91	288	56	1.000	0.00000
2-Aug-91	288	57	1.018	0.01770
9-Aug-91	289	58	1.018	0.01739
16-Aug-91	287	60	1.034	0.03390
23-Aug-91	288	63	1.050	0.04879
30-Aug-91	288	63	1.000	0.00000
6-Sep-91	290	63	1.000	0.00000
13-Sep-91	290	63	1.000	0.00000
20-Sep-91	290	63	1.000	0.00000
27-Sep-91	290	63	1.000	0.00000
4-Oct-91	290	63	1.000	0.00000
11-Oct-91	288	62	0.984	–0.01600
18-Oct-91	288	62	1.000	0.00000

Standard deviation		**0.02758**
x √52 =		0.19890
x 100%		**19.89%**

Giguere

warrant price $= \dfrac{\text{parity ratio}^2}{4}$ x exercise price

where   *parity ratio is $\leqslant 2$*

$$= \dfrac{0.862^2}{4} \text{ x } 334\text{p}$$

$$= \dfrac{0.743}{4} \text{ x } 334\text{p}$$

$$= 62.04\text{p}$$

Black-Scholes formula

Valuation $\quad = S N(d_1) - \dfrac{e}{2.71828^{ry}} \times N(d_2)$

where

$$d_1 = \dfrac{\ln (S/e) + (r + 0.5v^2)y}{v \sqrt{y}}$$

$$d_2 = \dfrac{\ln (S/e) + (r - 0.5v^2)y}{v \sqrt{y}}$$

where S = share price; e = exercise price; $N(d)$ = normal distribution function of d; r = rate of interest; y = time to expiry in years; v = volatility; $\ln(S/e)$ = natural logarithm of (S/e).

$$d_1 = \dfrac{\ln (288/334) + (0.1 + (0.5 \text{ x } 0.1989^2)) \, 3.458}{0.1989 \, \sqrt{3.458}}$$

$$d_1 = \dfrac{\ln (0.8623) + (0.1 + 0.0198) \, 3.458}{0.36987}$$

$$d_1 = \dfrac{-0.1482 + 0.4143}{0.36987}$$

$$d_1 = 0.7194$$

$$d_2 = \dfrac{\ln (288/334) + (0.1 - (0.5 \text{ x } 0.1989^2)) \, 3.458}{0.1989 \, \sqrt{3.458}}$$

$$d_2 = \dfrac{\ln (0.8623) + (0.1 - 0.0198) \, 3.458}{0.36987}$$

$$d_2 = \dfrac{-0.1482 + 0.2773}{0.36987}$$

$$d_2 = 0.3491$$

Valuation $\quad = S N(d_1) - \dfrac{e}{2.71828^{ry}} \times N(d_2)$

$$= 288 \times N(0.7194) - \frac{334}{2.71828^{(0.1 \times 3.458)}} \times N(0.3491)$$

$$= 288 \times N(0.7194) - \frac{334}{1.4131} \times N(0.3491)$$

$$= (288 \times 0.7642) - (236.36 \times 0.6368)$$

$$= 220.09 - 150.51$$

$$= 69.58p$$

Implied Volatility (from Black-Scholes formula)

The complex mathematical workings required to derive implied volatility from the Black-Scholes formula are rather beyond the scope of this book, and the answer is more easily reached by a process of iteration in a spreadsheet model. For this reason the workings are not shown here, but the answer is 17.8 per cent.

Delta

The delta is taken from the Black-Scholes model, where delta $= N(d_1)$
In this case the figure is 0.7642.

Leverage

Leverage = delta $\times$ gearing
= 0.7642 $\times$ 4.65
= 3.55 times

Calculating the Line of Best Fit by the Least Squares Method

Where $y = a + bx$ and r = correlation coefficient

Date	Shares (p)	Warrants (p)	s $\times$ w	s^2	w^2
4-Jan-91	246	41	10086	60516	1681
11-Jan-91	238	40	9520	56644	1600
18-Jan-91	231	42	9702	53361	1764
25-Jan-91	231	42	9702	53361	1764
1-Feb-91	233	44	10252	54289	1936
8-Feb-91	236	44	10384	55696	1936
15-Feb-91	245	45	11025	60025	2025
22-Feb-91	246	49	12936	69696	2401
1-Mar-91	273	53	14469	74529	2809
8-Mar-91	290	53	15370	84100	2809
15-Mar-91	306	58	17748	93636	3364
22-Mar-91	294	57	16758	86436	3249
29-Mar-91	290	57	16530	84100	3249
5-Apr-91	290	58	16820	84100	3364

Date	Shares (p)	Warrants (p)	s x w	s^2	w^2
12-Apr-91	290	58	16820	84100	3364
19-Apr-91	290	59	17110	84100	3481
26-Apr-91	286	59	16874	81796	3481
3-May-91	285	58	16530	81225	3364
10-May-91	285	59	16815	81225	3481
17-May-91	283	59	16697	80089	3481
24-May-91	285	59	16815	81225	3481
31-May-91	286	59	16874	81796	3481
7-Jun-91	288	59	16992	82944	3481
14-Jun-91	288	59	16992	82944	3481
21-Jun-91	288	58	16704	82944	3364
28-Jun-91	285	58	16530	81225	3364
5-Jul-91	283	56	15848	80089	3136
12-Jul-91	282	56	15792	79524	3136
19-Jul-91	283	56	15848	80089	3136
26-Jul-91	288	56	16128	82944	3136
2-Aug-91	288	57	16416	82944	3249
9-Aug-91	289	58	16762	83521	3364
16-Aug-91	287	60	17220	82369	3600
23-Aug-91	288	63	18144	82944	3969
30-Aug-91	288	63	18144	82944	3969
6-Sep-91	290	63	18270	84100	3969
13-Sep-91	290	63	18270	84100	3969
20-Sep-91	290	63	18270	84100	3969
27-Sep-91	290	63	18270	84100	3969
4-Oct-91	290	63	18270	84100	3969
11-Oct-91	288	62	17856	82944	3844
18-Oct-91	288	62	17856	82944	3844
TOTALS	**11,708**	**2,351**	**660,419**	**3,279,858**	**133,483**
AVERAGES	**279**	**56**			

$$b = \frac{n\,\Sigma sw - \Sigma s\,\Sigma w}{n\,\Sigma s^2 - (\Sigma s)^2}$$ where n = number of data points; Σ = total sum; s = share prices; w = warrant prices

$$b = \frac{42 \times 660{,}419 - 11{,}708 \times 2{,}351}{42 \times 3{,}279{,}858 - 11{,}708^2}$$

$$b = \frac{27{,}737{,}598 - 27{,}525{,}508}{137{,}754{,}036 - 137{,}077{,}264}$$

$$b = \frac{212{,}090}{676{,}772}$$

$$b = 0.313$$

$$a = \text{average } (w) - (b \times \text{average } (s))$$

$a = 56 - (0.313 \times 279)$

$a = -31.434$

$y = -31.434 + 0.313x$

$r = \dfrac{n \sum sw - \sum s \sum w}{\sqrt{(n \sum s^2 - (\sum s)^2)} \times \sqrt{(n \sum w^2 - (\sum w)^2)}}$

$r = \dfrac{(42 \times 660{,}419) - (11{,}708 \times 2{,}351)}{\sqrt{(42 \times 3{,}279{,}858 - 11{,}708^2)} \times \sqrt{(42 \times 133{,}483 - 2{,}351^2)}}$

$r = \dfrac{27{,}737{,}598 - 27{,}525{,}508}{\sqrt{(137{,}754{,}036 - 137{,}077{,}264)} \times \sqrt{(5{,}606{,}286 - 5{,}527{,}201)}}$

$r = \dfrac{212{,}090}{\sqrt{(676{,}772)} \times \sqrt{(79{,}085)}}$

$r = \dfrac{212{,}090}{822.66 \times 281.22}$

$r = \dfrac{212{,}090}{231{,}348}$

$r = 0.917$

Database of UK Equity Warrants

Aberdeen Trust plc

Category   Other Financial
Activities   Fund management
Address   10 Queen's Terrace, Aberdeen, AB9 1QJ
Telephone   01224-631 999
Conversion terms   One ordinary share at 50p at any time up to 30 September 1999
Number in issue   199,648 warrants and 7,722,002 'A' warrants (both have the same conversion terms)
Number of market-makers   Two for the ordinary warrants, three for the 'A' warrants
Warrants listed in FT   No

Aberforth Smaller Companies Trust plc

Category   Investment Trusts
Activities   Investment in small UK quoted companies
Address   14 Melville Street, Edinburgh, EH3 7NS
Telephone   0131-220 0733
Conversion terms   One ordinary share at 100p on 31 March 1992 to 2003 inclusive; time value protected
Number in issue   11,241,943
Number of market-makers   Six
Warrants listed in FT   Yes

Abtrust Emerging Economies Investment Trust plc

Category   Investment Trusts
Activities   Investment in emerging markets
Address   99 Charterhouse Street, London, EC1M 6AB
Telephone   0171-490 4466
Conversion terms   One share at 100p on 31 January 1995 to 2008 inclusive; time value protected
Number in issue   10,000,000
Number of market-makers   Eight
Warrants listed in FT   Yes

Abtrust European Index Investment Trust plc

(formerly Abtrust New European Investment Trust plc)

Category   Investment Trusts
Activities   Investment to closely track the FTA Eurotrack 100 Index
Address   99 Charterhouse Street, London, EC1M 6AB
Telephone   0171-490 4466
Conversion terms   One ordinary share at 100p on 31 May 1993 to 2000 inclusive; time value protected
Number in issue   6,839,880
Number of market-makers   Six
Warrants listed in FT   Yes

Abtrust Latin American Investment Trust plc

Category   Investment Trusts
Activities   Investment in Latin America for long-term growth
Address   99 Charterhouse Street, London, EC1M 6AB
Telephone   0171-490 4466
Conversion terms   One share at 100p on 31 October 1996 to 2009 inclusive; time value protected
Number in issue   4,000,000
Number of market-makers   Four
Warrants listed in FT   Yes

Abtrust Lloyd's Insurance Trust plc

Category   Insurance
Activities   Investment in Lloyd's insurance market
Address   99 Charterhouse Street, London, EC1M 6AB
Telephone   0171-490 4466
Conversion terms   One ordinary share at 100p during the 30-day period commencing one day after the posting of the annual report and accounts and interim results in 1995 to 2008 inclusive; time value protected; estimated final expiry 30 October 2008
Number in issue   6,000,000
Number of market-makers   Three
Warrants listed in FT   Yes

Abtrust New Dawn Investment Trust plc

(Series A warrants)
Category   Investment Trusts
Activities   Investment in Far East, excluding Japan & Australia
Address   99 Charterhouse Street, London, EC1M 6AB
Telephone   0171-490 4466
Conversion terms   One ordinary share at 95.88p on 31 July 1991 to 2000 inclusive; time value protected
Number in issue   2,993,500
Number of market-makers   Six
Warrants listed in FT   Yes

Abtrust New Dawn Investment Trust plc

(Series B warrants)

Category   Investment Trusts
Activities   Investment in Far East, excluding Japan & Australia
Address   99 Charterhouse Street, London, EC1M 6AB
Telephone   0171-490 4466
Conversion terms   One ordinary share at 135p on 31 July 1991 to 2000 inclusive; time value protected
Number in issue   2,993,060
Number of market-makers   Six
Warrants listed in FT   Yes

Abtrust New Dawn Investment Trust plc

(Series C warrants)

Category   Investment Trusts
Activities   Investment in Far East, excluding Japan & Australia
Address   99 Charterhouse Street, London, EC1M 6AB
Telephone   0171-490 4466
Conversion terms   One ordinary share at 270p on 31 July 1997 to 2000 inclusive; time value protected
Number in issue   2,630,130
Number of market-makers   Seven
Warrants listed in FT   Yes

Abtrust New Thai Investment Trust plc

Category   Investment Trusts
Activities   Investment in Thailand
Address   99 Charterhouse Street, London, EC1M 6AB
Telephone   0171-490 4466
Conversion terms   One ordinary share at 100p on 31 May 1992 to 1996 inclusive; time value protected
Number in issue   3,000,000
Number of market-makers   Four
Warrants listed in FT   Yes

Abtrust Scotland Investment Company plc

Category   Investment Trusts
Activities   Investment in unlisted Scottish companies
Address   10 Queen's Terrace, Aberdeen, AB9 1QJ
Telephone   01224-631 999 Ext. 3208
Conversion terms   One ordinary share at 43p on 30 September 1995 to 2000 inclusive; time value protected.
Number in issue   13,406,184

Number of market-makers   Three
Warrants listed in FT   Yes

Advanced Media Group plc

Category   Rule 4.2
Activities   Interactive multimedia products
Address   44 Earlham Street, Covent Garden, London, WC2H 9LA
Telephone   0171-240 3868
Conversion terms   One share at 110p if exercised before 31 December 1995; at 120p if exercised between 1 January 1996 and 31 December 1996; at 150p if exercised between 1 January 1997 and 31 December 1997; time value protected
Number in issue   236,000
Number of market-makers   n/a
Warrants listed in FT   No

Aegis Group plc

Category   Media
Activities   Media and communications
Address   6 Eaton Gate, London, SW1W 9BL
Telephone   0171-730 1001
   Conversion terms   One ordinary share at 30p at any time until 9 December 1998
Number in issue   50,000,000
Number of market-makers   n/a
Warrants listed in FT   No

American Opportunity Trust plc

(formerly Leveraged Opportunity Trust plc)
Category   Investment Trusts
Activities   Investment in North America
Address   30 Queen Anne's Gate, London, SW1H 9AL
Telephone   0171-222 2020
Conversion terms   One share at 100p during the month of August in 1996
Number in issue   1,750,000
Number of market-makers   Two
Warrants listed in FT   No

Amicable Smaller Enterprises Trust plc

Category   Investment Trusts
Activities   Investment in smaller companies
Address   150 St Vincent Street, Glasgow, G2 5NQ
Telephone   0141-248 2323
Conversion terms   One share at 100p on 30 April 1993 to 2000 inclusive; time value protected

Number in issue 7,911,394
Number of market-makers Five
Warrants listed in FT Yes

Angerstein Underwriting Trust plc

Category Insurance
Activities Investment in Lloyd's insurance market
Address 43–44 Crutched Friars, London, EC3N 2NX
Telephone 0171-374 3000
Conversion terms One share at 100p on 31 August 1995 to 2000 inclusive; time value
   protected
Number in issue 15,000,000
Number of market-makers Four
Warrants listed in FT Yes

Anglian Water plc

Category Water
Activities Provision of water and waste services
Address Anglian House, Ambury Road, Huntingdon, Cambs, PE18 6NZ
Telephone 01480-443 000
Conversion terms One share at 495p at any time up to 24 August 1998; settlement
   through Euroclear/CEDEL
Number in issue 14,651,000
Number of market-makers Nine
Warrants listed in FT No

Anglo-Eastern Plantations plc

Category Food Producers
Activities Rubber, cocoa and oil palm plantations
Address 81 Carter Lane, London, EC4V 5EQ
Telephone 0171-236 7414
Conversion terms One ordinary share at 86p on 31 July 1986 to 1995 inclusive
Number in issue 1,816,309
Number of market-makers Two
Warrants listed in FT No

Anglo United plc

Category Other Services & Businesses
Activities Coal and fuel supply and distribution, operation of port facilities, property
   development and the production of chemicals and smokeless fuels
Address Newgate House, Broombank Road, Chesterfield, Derbyshire, S41 9QJ
Telephone 01246-454 583

Conversion terms   One share at 10p during the one month period following the date of issue of the company's audited accounts for each of the years ending 31 March 1993 to 1999 inclusive; estimated final expiry 21 July 1999
Number in issue   156,761,044
Number of market-makers   Three
Warrants listed in FT   No

APTA Healthcare plc

Category   Health Care
Activities   Nursing Homes
Address   39 King Street, London, EC2V 2DQ
Telephone   0171-831 5136
Conversion terms   One share at 15p at any time from 31 August 1995 to six weeks following the posting of the accounts for the first financial period ending on or before 30 April 1999; estimated final expiry 11 June 1999
Number in issue   13,600,000
Number of market-makers   Two
Warrants listed in FT   No

Asset Management Investment Company plc

Category   Investment Trusts
Activities   Investment in investment management companies
Address   Burne House, 88 High Holborn, London, WC1V 6LS
Telephone   0171-831 0066
Conversion terms   One share at 100p on 31 January 1995 to 2002 inclusive; time value protected
Number in issue   1,007,400
Number of market-makers   Three
Warrants listed in FT   Yes

Baillie Gifford Japan Trust plc

Category   Investment Trusts
Activities   Investment in Japan
Address   1 Rutland Court, Edinburgh, EH3 8EY
Telephone   0131-222 4000
Conversion terms   One share at 655p on 30 November 1992 to 1995 inclusive
Number in issue   2,198,346
Number of market-makers   Five
Warrants listed in FT   Yes

Baillie Gifford Shin Nippon plc

Category   Investment Trusts
Activities   Investment in small Japanese companies

Address   1 Rutland Court, Edinburgh, EH3 8EY
Telephone   0131-222 4000
Conversion terms   One ordinary share at 50p on 30 April 1986 to 1996 inclusive
Number in issue   3,083,834
Number of market-makers   Four
Warrants listed in FT   Yes

Baillie Gifford Shin Nippon (2005) plc

Category   Investment Trusts
Activities   Investment in small Japanese companies
Address   1 Rutland Court, Edinburgh, EH3 8EY
Telephone   0131-222 4000
Conversion terms   One ordinary share at 200p on 30 April 1997 to 2005 inclusive
Number in issue   2,518,031
Number of market-makers   Five
Warrants listed in FT   Yes

The Baring Chrysalis Fund Ltd

Category   Investment Companies
Activities   Investment in developing country equities
Address   Baring International Investment Management Ltd, Barfield House, St
   Julian's Avenue, St Peter Port, Guernsey, Channel Islands
Telephone   0171-628 6000 (Baring Investment Management)
Conversion terms   One share at US$8.78 on 30 November 1995; settlement through
   Euroclear/CEDEL
Number in issue   1,277,124
Number of market-makers   n/a
Warrants listed in FT   Yes (in sterling)

The Baring Emerging Europe Trust plc

Category   Other Investment Trusts
Activities   Investment in Greece, Portugal, Turkey, The Czech Republic, Hungary and
   Poland
Address   155 Bishopsgate, London, EC2M 3XY
Telephone   0171-628 6000
Conversion terms   One ordinary share at US$1.00 on 31 August 1997 to 2004
   inclusive; time value protected
Number in issue   24,800,000
Number of market-makers   Four
Warrants listed in FT   Yes (in sterling)

Baronsmead Investment Trust plc

Category   Investment Trusts

Activities   Investment in management buyouts/ins
Address   Clerkenwell House, 67 Clerkenwell Road, London, EC1R 5BH
Telephone   0171-242 4900
Conversion terms   One ordinary share at 100p on 31 May in any of the years 1997 to 2001 inclusive; time value protected
Number in issue   2,555,000
Number of market-makers   Two
Warrants listed in FT   Yes

Beacon Investment Trust plc

Category   Investment Trusts
Activities   Investment in Rule 4.2/AIM companies
Address   99 Charterhouse Street, London, EC1M 6HR
Telephone   0171-490 3882
Conversion terms   One share at 100p on 31 October 1995 to 2003 inclusive; time value protected
Number in issue   3,800,000
Number of market-makers   Two
Warrants listed in FT   Yes

Beta Global Emerging Markets Investment Trust plc

Category   Investment Trusts
Activities   Investment in the world's emerging stockmarkets and developing economies
Address   3 Bolt Court, Fleet Street, London, EC4A 3DQ
Telephone   0171-353 2066
Conversion terms   One share at 100p on 31 May 1992 to 1996 inclusive; time value protected
Number in issue   8,714,821
Number of market-makers   Five
Warrants listed in FT   Yes

Brazilian Smaller Companies Investment Trust plc

(formerly Brazilian Investment Trust plc)
Category   Other Investment Trusts
Activities   Investment in Brazil
Address   Exchange House, Primrose Street, London, EC2A 2NY
Telephone   0171-628 1234
Conversion terms   One share at US$1.00 at any time up to 30 September 2007
Number in issue   12,500,000
Number of market-makers   Two
Warrants listed in FT   Yes (in sterling)

Brent Walker Group plc

Category Leisure & Hotels
Activities Betting services; pubs and brewing; leisure
Address 19 Rupert Street, London, W1V 7FS
Telephone 0171-465 0111
Conversion terms One share at 60p during the 30-day periods beginning on the dates falling one day after the posting of the annual report and accounts in 1997 to 2007 inclusive; estimated final expiry 25 June 2007
Number in issue 25,869,690
Number of market-makers Three
Warrants listed in FT No

British Assets Trust plc

Category Investment Trusts
Activities Investment in an international portfolio
Address One Charlotte Square, Edinburgh, EH2 4DZ
Telephone 0131-225 1357
Conversion terms One ordinary share at 101p during the period from 1 July 2001 to 30 September 2001; time value protected
Number in issue 73,800,000
Number of market-makers Eight
Warrants listed in FT Yes

British Biotech plc

(formerly British Bio-technology Group plc)
Category Pharmaceuticals
Activities Pharmaceutical research and development
Address Watlington Road, Cowley, Oxford, OX4 5LY
Telephone 01865-748 747
Conversion terms One ordinary share at 525p at any time between 11 December 1995 and 31 January 1996
Number in issue 9,073,062
Number of market-makers Four
Warrants listed in FT Yes

British Empire Securities & General Trust plc

Category Investment Trusts
Activities Investment Trust
Address Cayzer House, 1 Thomas More Street, London, E1 9AR
Telephone 0171-702 2495
Conversion terms One share at 60p on 31 January 1991 to 1996 inclusive; time value protected
Number in issue 12,827,937

Number of market-makers   Four
Warrants listed in FT   Yes

Broadgate Investment Trust plc

Category   Investment Trusts
Activities   Investment using 'relative strength' methodology
Address   99 Charterhouse Street, London, EC1M 6AB
Telephone   0171-490 4466
Conversion terms   One share at 100p on 30 May 1995 to 2003 inclusive
Number in issue   990,000
Number of market-makers   Two
Warrants listed in FT   No

Brockhampton Holdings plc (series 'A' warrants)

Category   Saturday Dealings Page
Activities   Water supply
Address   Brockhampton Springs, West Street, Havant, Hampshire, PO9 1LG
Telephone   01705-499 888
Conversion terms   One 'A' share at 150p in the month of June 1992 to 1997 inclusive
Number in issue   156,187
Number of market-makers   n/a
Warrants listed in FT   No

BTR plc (1994/5)

Category   Diversified Industrials
Activities   Industrial conglomerate
Address   Silvertown House, Vincent Square, London, SW1P 2PL
Telephone   0171-834 3848
Conversion terms   One share at 222p in the 30-day period commencing on the date
    falling one day after the posting of the annual report and accounts and the interim
    results in 1994 and 1995; estimated final expiry 15 October 1995
Number in issue   104,749,294
Number of market-makers   Ten
Warrants listed in FT   Yes

BTR plc (1995/6)

Category   Diversified Industrials
Activities   Industrial conglomerate
Address   Silvertown House, Vincent Square, London, SW1P 2PL
Telephone   0171-834 3848
Conversion terms   One share at 258p in the 30-day period commencing on the date
    falling one day after the posting of the annual report and accounts and the interim
    results in 1995 and 1996; estimated final expiry 15 October 1996

Number in issue   130,924,446
Number of market-makers   Ten
Warrants listed in FT   Yes

BTR plc (1997)

Category   Diversified Industrials
Activities   Industrial conglomerate
Address   Silvertown House, Vincent Square, London, SW1P 2PL
Telephone   0171-834 3848
Conversion terms   One share at 258p in the 30-day period commencing on the date
    falling one day after the posting of the annual report and accounts and the interim
    results in 1997; estimated final expiry 15 October 1997
Number in issue   132,648,501
Number of market-makers   Ten
Warrants listed in FT   Yes

BTR plc (1998)

Category   Diversified Industrials
Activities   Industrial conglomerate
Address   Silvertown House, Vincent Square, London, SW1P 2PL
Telephone   0171-834 3848
Conversion terms   One share at 405p in the 30-day period commencing on the date
    falling one day after the posting of the annual report and accounts and the interim
    results in 1998; estimated final expiry 15 October 1998
Number in issue   105,416,231
Number of market-makers   Ten
Warrants listed in FT   Yes

BZW Commodities Trust plc

Category   Investment Companies
Activities   Investment in a portfolio of commodities
Address   BZW Investment Management, Seal House, 1 Swan Lane, London, EC4R 3UD
Telephone   0171-623 7777
Conversion terms   One share at 100p on 28 February in any of the years 1996 to 2004
    inclusive; time value protected
Number in issue   15,630,040
Number of market-makers   Four
Warrants listed in FT   Yes

Caledonian Media Communications plc

(formerly Worth Investment Trust plc)
Category   Media
Activities   Cable Telecommunications

Address   303 King Street, Aberdeen, AB2 3AP
Telephone   01224-646 644
Conversion terms   One ordinary share at 27p during June and December in the years 1996 and 1997 and in June 1998 and during the period of 30 days following the publication of the interim results or the preliminary announcement of the final results for any period expiring on 31 March 1996 or 31 March 1998 or any date between those dates; time value protected; estimated final expiry June/July 1998
Number in issue   29,681,059
Number of market-makers   Three
Warrants listed in FT   Yes

Canadian General Investments Limited

Category   Investment Companies
Activities   Investment in Canadian equities
Address   Suite 1601, 110 Yonge Street, Toronto, M5C 1T4, Canada
Telephone   00-1-416 366 2931
Conversion terms   One common share at C$40.00 on 30 June 2000 to 2007 inclusive; settlement through Euroclear/CEDEL
Number in issue   n/a
Number of market-makers   n/a
Warrants listed in FT   Yes

Care UK plc

Category   Health Care
Activities   Provider of healthcare facilities and services to the elderly
Address   Crown House, Stephenson Road, Severalls Park, Colchester, Essex, CO4 4QR
Telephone   01206-752 552
Conversion terms   One share at 45p in the 28-day period commencing one day after the posting of the annual report and accounts between 30 September 1994 and 30 September 1996 inclusive; estimated final expiry 10 March 1997
Number in issue   2,202,434
Number of market-makers   Three
Warrants listed in FT   No

Cementone plc

(formerly Multitrust plc)
Category   Chemicals
Activities   Property investment, paint and cement manufacturer, and securities investment
Address   Unit G, Tingewick Industrial Estate, Tingewick Road, Buckingham, MK18 1AN
Telephone   01280-823 823
Conversion terms   One share at 65p in the 31-day period following the posting of the

annual report and accounts for the years 1992 to 1996 inclusive; estimated final
   expiry 1 May 1996
Number in issue   864,070
Number of market-makers   Two
Warrants listed in FT   Yes

The Central European Growth Fund plc

Category   Other Investment Trusts
Activities   Investment in Central European companies
Address   CS First Boston Investment Management Limited, One Cabot Square,
   London, E14 4QJ
Telephone   0171-516 1616
Conversion terms   One ordinary share at US$1.00 on 30 April in any of the years
   1995 to 1999 inclusive; time value protected
Number in issue   40,000,000
Number of market-makers   Five
Warrants listed in FT   Yes
Teleshare share code: 1767
Teleshare warrant code: 1769

The China Investment Company Ltd

Category   Saturday Dealings Page
Activities   Investment in China
Address   c/o Crosby Securities (UK) Ltd, 8th Floor, 95 Aldwych, London, WC2B 4JF
Telephone   00-852 2821 3328 (Hong Kong)
Conversion terms   One share at US$10.00 on 31 March 1994 to 1998 inclusive; time
   value protected; settlement through Euroclear/CEDEL
Number in issue   800,000
Number of market-makers   n/a
Warrants listed in FT   No

The China Investment & Development Fund Ltd

Category   Investment Companies
Activities   Investment in China
Address   Westbourne, The Grange, St Peter Port, Guernsey, GY1 3BG, Channel
   Islands
Telephone   00-852 2847 0675 (Hong Kong)
Conversion terms   One share at US$10.60 on any business day up to and including 31
   December 2000
Number in issue   1,693,000
Number of market-makers   n/a
Warrants listed in FT   No

China Investment Trust plc

Category   Investment Trusts
Activities   Investment in China
Address   197 Knightsbridge, London, SW7 1RB
Telephone   0171-412 0703
Conversion terms   One share at 100p during the 30-day period commencing one day
    after the posting of the annual report and accounts in 1994 to 2002 inclusive; time
    value protected; estimated final expiry 11 August 2002
Number in issue   3,972,902
Number of market-makers   Four
Warrants listed in FT   Yes

The City of Oxford Investment Trust plc

Category   Investment Trusts Split Capital
Activities   Investment in high-yielding UK equities
Address   41 Tower Hill, London, EC3N 4HA
Telephone   0171-480 5000
Conversion terms   One ordinary income share at 36p on 30 June 1992 to 1999
    inclusive; time value protected
Number in issue   5,877,951
Number of market-makers   Two
Warrants listed in FT   Yes

Coal Investments plc

Category   Extractive Industries
Activities   Leasing and working of coal mines
Address   22 Tudor Street, London, EC4Y 0JJ
Telephone   0171-936 3513
Conversion terms   One ordinary share at 85p on 31 October 1994 and on the last
    business day of every third month thereafter up to and including 30 April 1998
Number in issue   6,227,809
Number of market-makers   Three
Warrants listed in FT   Yes

Continental Assets Trust plc

Category   Investment Trusts
Activities   Investment in smaller European companies
Address   One Charlotte Square, Edinburgh, EH2 4DZ
Telephone   0131-225 1357
Conversion terms   One share at 100p on 30 April 1987 to 1996 inclusive
Number in issue   4,036,046
Number of market-makers   Five
Warrants listed in FT   Yes

Continental Foods plc

(formerly IMC Industries plc)

Category   Food Producers

Activities   Manufacture of soft drinks, supply of in-flight information and distribution of video tapes.

Address   McAlpine House, Pytchley Lodge Road, Kettering, Northants NN15 6JN

Telephone   01536-416 900

Conversion terms   One ordinary share at 150p at any time between 1 September 1994 and 31 August 2001

Number in issue   2,082,242

Number of market-makers   Two

Warrants listed in FT   Yes

Creston Land & Estates plc

Category   Property

Activities   Building and property services

Address   25 City Road, London, EC1Y 1BQ

Telephone   0171-628 9371

Conversion terms   One share at 15p within 28-day period following the AGM in 1993 to 1997 inclusive; estimated final expiry 28 January 1998

Number in issue   n/a

Number of market-makers   Two

Warrants listed in FT   No

CU Environmental Trust plc

Category   Investment Trusts

Activities   Investment in companies which are or will become 'major beneficiaries of environmental protection expenditure.'

Address   155 Bishopsgate, London, EC2M 3YQ

Telephone   0171-283 7500

Conversion terms   One share at 100p on 30 April 1993 to 2002 inclusive; time value protected

Number in issue   3,495,000

Number of market-makers   Three

Warrants listed in FT   Yes

Czech & Slovak Investment Corporation Inc

Category   Saturday Dealings Page

Activities   Investment in the Czech and Slovak Republics

Address   PO Box 73, Queens House, Don Road, St. Helier, Jersey, JE4 8PN

Telephone   01534-73933

Conversion terms   One share at US$10.00 on any business day from 20 August 1992 to 19 August 1997

Number in issue   614,700
Number of market-makers   n/a
Warrants listed in FT   No

Czech & Slovak Investment Corporation Inc (2004)

Category   Saturday Dealings Page
Activities   Investment in the Czech and Slovak Republics
Address   PO Box 73, Queens House, Don Road, St. Helier, Jersey, JE4 8PN
Telephone   01534-73933
Conversion terms   One share at US$10.50 on any business day from 21 September
   1994 to 21 September 2004
Number in issue   964,442
Number of market-makers   n/a
Warrants listed in FT   No

Danae Investment Trust plc

Category   Investment Trusts Split Capital
Activities   Investment in 'above average yielding' securities
Address   99 Charterhouse Street, London, EC1M 6AB
Telephone   0171-490 4466
Conversion terms   One income share and one capital share at a total of 65p on 31
   March and 30 September in any year (perpetual, but company due to be wound up
   between 1 January 1998 and 31 December 2002)
Number in issue   401,774
Number of market-makers   Two
Warrants listed in FT   No

Dartmoor Investment Trust plc

Category   Investment Trusts
Activities   Investment in split-capital investment trusts
Address   23 Cathedral Yard, Exeter, Devon, EX1 1HB
Telephone   01392-412 122
Conversion terms   One share at 118p on 31 July 1993 to 2002 inclusive
Number in issue   6,820,403
Number of market-makers   Two
Warrants listed in FT   Yes

Deutschland Investment Corporation Inc

Category   Saturday Dealings Page
Activities   Investment in Eastern Germany
Address   PO Box 73, Queens House, Don Road, St. Helier, Jersey, JE4 8PN
Telephone   01534-73933
Conversion terms   One share at DM16.00 at any time from 31 December 1990 up to

and including 29 December 1995; dealt through Euroclear/CEDEL
Number in issue   1,200,000
Number of market-makers   n/a
Warrants listed in FT   No

Dragon Oil plc

Category   Oil Exploration & Production
Activities   Development of oil and gas fields
Address   502 North Circular Road, Dublin 1, Ireland
Telephone   00-353 1 874 0704
Conversion terms   One ordinary share at 2p at any time until 1 November 1999
Number in issue   56,919,853
Number of market-makers   Two
Warrants listed in FT   No

Dunedin Japan Investment Trust plc

Category   Investment Trusts
Activities   Investment in Japanese equities
Address   Dunedin House, 25 Ravelston Terrace, Edinburgh, EH4 3EX
Telephone   0131-315 2500
Conversion terms   One share at 100p during September 1995 to 1999 inclusive; time
   value protected
Number in issue   4,052,070
Number of market-makers   Six
Warrants listed in FT   Yes

Eaglet Investment Trust plc

Category   Investment Trusts
Activities   Investment in smaller UK companies
Address   119 London Wall, London, EC2Y 5ET
Telephone   0171-256 8388
Conversion terms   One share at 100p on 31 October 1994 to 2002 inclusive; time
   value protected
Number in issue   5,997,100
Number of market-makers   Three
Warrants listed in FT   Yes

The ECU Trust plc

Category   Investment Trusts
Activities   Investment in Europe
Address   5 Half Moon Street, London, W1Y 7RA
Telephone   0171-409 3185

Conversion terms   One share at 50p on 31 October 1993 to 1997 inclusive; time value protected

Number in issue   6,000,000

Number of market-makers   Three

Warrants listed in FT   Yes

Edinburgh Dragon Trust plc

(formerly EFM Dragon Trust plc)

Category   Investment Trusts

Activities   Investment in the Far East

Address   Donaldson House, 97 Haymarket Terrace, Edinburgh, EH12 5HD

Telephone   0131-313 1000

Conversion terms   One share at 40p on 31 January in any of the years 1989 to 1996 inclusive

Number in issue   5,165,286

Number of market-makers   Six

Warrants listed in FT   Yes

Edinburgh Dragon Trust plc (2005)

(formerly EFM Dragon Trust plc)

Category   Investment Trusts

Activities   Investment in the Far East

Address   Donaldson House, 97 Haymarket Terrace, Edinburgh, EH12 5HD

Telephone   0131-313 1000

Conversion terms   One ordinary share at 60p on 31 January 1991 to 2005 inclusive

Number in issue   19,672,915

Number of market-makers   Seven

Warrants listed in FT   Yes

Edinburgh Inca Trust plc

Category   Investment Trusts

Activities   Investment in Latin America

Address   Donaldson House, 97 Haymarket Terrace, Edinburgh, EH12 5HD

Telephone   0131-313 1000

Conversion terms   One ordinary share at 50p on 28 February in any of the years 1996 to 2009 inclusive; time value protected

Number in issue   16,463,200

Number of market-makers   Four

Warrants listed in FT   Yes

Edinburgh Japan Trust plc

(formerly EFM Japan Trust plc)

Category   Investment Trusts

Activities   Investment in Japan

Address   Donaldson House, 97 Haymarket Terrace, Edinburgh, EH12 5HD
Telephone   0131-313 1000
Conversion terms   One ordinary share at 100p on 31 October 1993 to 2005 inclusive; time value protected
Number in issue   4,523,324
Number of market-makers   Four
Warrants listed in FT   Yes

Edinburgh Java Trust plc

(*formerly EFM Java Trust plc*)
Category   Investment Trusts
Activities   Investment in Indonesia
Address   Donaldson House, 97 Haymarket Terrace, Edinburgh, EH12 5HD
Telephone   0131-313 1000
Conversion terms   One ordinary share at 50p on 31 May 1992 to 2000 inclusive; time value protected
Number in issue   6,000,000
Number of market-makers   Three
Warrants listed in FT   Yes

Edinburgh New Tiger Trust plc

Category   Investment Trusts
Activities   Investment in Far Eastern smaller companies
Address   Donaldson House, 97 Haymarket Terrace, Edinburgh, EH12 5HD
Telephone   0131-313 1000
Conversion terms   One ordinary share at 50p on 31 March 1996 to 2009 inclusive; time value protected
Number in issue   56,000,000
Number of market-makers   Seven
Warrants listed in FT   Yes

Edinburgh Oil & Gas plc

Category   Oil Exploration and Production
Activities   Oil and gas exploration and production
Address   10 Coates Crescent, Edinburgh, EH3 7AL
Telephone   0131-225 5454
Conversion terms   One share at 23p on 30 April 1995 to 2000 inclusive; time value protected
Number in issue   3,475,806
Number of market-makers   Two
Warrants listed in FT   Yes

Edinburgh Smaller Companies Trust plc

(*formerly EFM Small Companies Trust plc*)

Category   Investment Trusts
Activities   Investment in small UK quoted companies
Address   97 Haymarket Terrace, Edinburgh, EH12 5HD
Telephone   0131-313 1000
Conversion terms   One share at 100p on 30 September 1994 to 2008 inclusive; time value protected
Number in issue   13,798,328
Number of market-makers   Seven
Warrants listed in FT   Yes

The Emerging Markets Country Investment Trust plc

Category   Investment Trusts
Activities   Investment in emerging markets
Address   10 Eastcheap, London, EC3M 1AJ
Telephone   0171-711 0771
Conversion terms   One share at 60p on 30 June 1999 to 2006 inclusive
Number in issue   13,445,561
Number of market-makers   Two
Warrants listed in FT   Yes

Energy Capital plc

Category   Other Financial
Activities   Investment in North American gas and oil companies
Address   99 Charterhouse Street, London, EC1M 6AB
Telephone   0171-490 4466
Conversion terms   One ordinary share at 100p on May 31 in any of the years 1995 to 2001 inclusive; time value protected
Number in issue   9,000,000
Number of market-makers   Two
Warrants listed in FT   Yes

English & Scottish Investors plc

Category   Investment Trusts
Activities   Investment worldwide
Address   Gartmore House, 16-18 Monument Street, London, EC3R 8AJ
Telephone   0171-782 2000
Conversion terms   One share at 90p on 30 April 1992 to 1998 inclusive
Number in issue   32,133,000
Number of market-makers   Three
Warrants listed in FT   Yes

The Environmental Investment Company Limited

Category   Investment Companies

Activities   Investment in companies expected to benefit from increased spending on environment products and services
Address   Ecofin, 18b Charles Street, London, W1X 7HD
Telephone   0171-495 3830
Conversion terms   One share at US$10.00 any time to April 1996
Number in issue   800,000
Number of market-makers   Two
Warrants listed in FT   Yes (in sterling)

European Smaller Companies Trust plc

Category   Investment Trusts
Activities   Investment in European smaller companies
Address   Swan House, 33 Queen Street, London, EC4R 1AX
Telephone   0171-246 3075
Conversion terms   One share at 100p on 30 November 1993 to 2002 inclusive
Number in issue   7,097,140
Number of market-makers   Five
Warrants listed in FT   Yes

Eurotunnel plc (Founder warrants)

Category   Transport
Activities   Construction and operation of channel tunnel
Address   Victoria Plaza, 111 Buckingham Palace Road, London, SW1W 0ST
Telephone   0171-834 7575
Conversion terms   12.56 units for £9.72 plus FFr100 at any time to 30 June 1995
Number in issue   2,646,432
Number of market-makers   Three
Warrants listed in FT   No

Eurotunnel plc ('1991' warrants)

Category   Transport
Activities   Construction and operation of channel tunnel
Address   Victoria Plaza, 111 Buckingham Palace Road, London, SW1W 0ST
Telephone   0171-834 7575
Conversion terms   1.24 units for £1.75 plus FFr 17.50, during the period of three months commencing on whichever occurs first of: (i) the date when all indebtedness due to the banks under the financing agreements has been discharged; (ii) the date when the aggregate of all refinancing debt exceeds 10% of the eligible prepayment amount; and (iii) 31 March 2000
Number in issue   7,142,857
Number of market-makers   Two
Warrants listed in FT   No

Eurotunnel plc ('1993' warrants)

Category   Transport
Activities   Construction and operation of channel tunnel
Address   Victoria Plaza, 111 Buckingham Palace Road, London, SW1W 0ST
Telephone   0171-834 7575
Conversion terms   1.12 units for every ten warrants for £1.675 plus FFr 14.125 from 5 July 1993 to 31 October 1995
Number in issue   534,141,299
Number of market-makers   Seven
Warrants listed in FT   Yes

The Ex-Lands plc

Category   Property
Activities   Operation of golf courses in Europe; and property in London
Address   29 Charles Street, London, W1X 7PN
Telephone   0171-495 0626
Conversion terms   One share at 16.44p, 30 days after the AGM held in 1992 to 1997 inclusive; estimated final expiry 21 November 1997
Number in issue   2,206,284
Number of market-makers   Three
Warrants listed in FT   No

Fidelity European Values plc

Category   Investment Trusts
Activities   Investment in stockmarkets of Continental Europe
Address   Oakhill House, 130 Tonbridge Road, Hildenborough, Tonbridge, Kent, TN11 9DZ
Telephone   01732-361 144
Conversion terms   One share at 100p on 30 April 1993 to 2001 inclusive
Number in issue   8,229,963
Number of market-makers   Six
Warrants listed in FT   Yes

Fidelity Japan OTC & Regional Markets Fund Ltd

Category   Investment Companies
Activities   Investment in Japanese OTC & regional markets
Address   Oakhill House, 130 Tonbridge Road, Hildenborough, Tonbridge, Kent, TN11 9DZ
Telephone   01732-361 144
Conversion terms   One ordinary share at US$10.00 between 3 September 1990 and 31 August 1995; time value protected; settlement through Euroclear/CEDEL
Number in issue   1,200,000
Number of market-makers   n/a

Warrants listed in FT   Yes (in sterling)

Fidelity Japanese Values Investment Trust plc

Category   Investment Trusts
Activities   Investment in Japanese smaller companies
Address   Oakhill House, 130 Tonbridge Road, Hildenborough, Tonbridge, Kent, TN11 9DZ
Telephone   01732-361 144
Conversion terms   One ordinary share at 100p on 30 April in any of the years 1995 to 2004; time value protected
Number in issue   21,053,800
Number of market-makers   Eight
Warrants listed in FT   Yes

Fidelity Special Values Trust plc

Category   Investment Trusts
Activities   UK special situation companies
Address   Oakhill House, 130 Tonbridge Road, Hildenborough, Tonbridge, Kent, TN11 9DZ
Telephone   01732-361 144
Conversion terms   One ordinary share at 100p in any of the years 1996 to 2004 inclusive; time value protected
Number in issue   7,339,480
Number of market-makers   Five
Warrants listed in FT   Yes

The First Ireland Investment Company plc

Category   Investment Trusts
Activities   Investment in Irish equities
Address   51 Belmont Road, Uxbridge, Middlesex, UB8 1SA
Telephone   01895-259 783
Conversion terms   One share at 100p on the date 42 days after the AGM in 1991 to 1996 inclusive; time value protected; estimated final expiry 18 August 1996
Number in issue   6,000,000
Number of market-makers   Four
Warrants listed in FT   Yes

First Philippine Investment Trust plc

Category   Investment Trusts
Activities   Investment in the Philippines
Address   197 Knightsbridge, London, SW7 1RB
Telephone   0171-412 0703
Conversion terms   One ordinary share at 50p, in 30-day period commencing one day

after the posting of the annual report and accounts in 1992 to 1996 inclusive; time value protected; estimated final expiry 28 February 1996

Number in issue   9,961,600
Number of market-makers   Three
Warrants listed in FT   Yes

First Russian Frontiers Trust plc

Category   Other Investment Trusts
Activities   Investment in companies operating in the former Soviet republics and satellites
Address   Cutlers Gardens, 5 Devonshire Square, London, EC2M 4LD
Telephone   0171-283 4801
Conversion terms   One ordinary share at US$10.00 on 30 June 1995 to 2001 inclusive; time value protected
Number in issue   1,120,000
Number of market-makers   Two
Warrants listed in FT   Yes

The First Spanish Investment Trust plc

Category   Investment Trusts
Activities   Investment in Spanish equities
Address   48 Chiswell Street, London, EC1Y 4GR
Telephone   0171-600 4500
Conversion terms   One share at 100p on 31 August 1988 to 1997 inclusive
Number in issue   1,325,496
Number of market-makers   Two
Warrants listed in FT   Yes

The First Spanish Investment Trust plc

(1997 'stock' warrants)
Category   Investment Trusts
Activities   Investment in Spanish equities
Address   48 Chiswell Street, London, EC1Y 4GR
Telephone   0171-600 4500
Conversion terms   One convertible loan stock unit at 100p on 31 August 1988 to 1997 inclusive
Number in issue   5,301,340
Number of market-makers   Two
Warrants listed in FT   Yes

Five Arrows Chile Investment Trust Ltd

Category   Other Investment Trusts
Activities   Investment in Chilean securities

Address   PO Box 242, St. Peter Port House, Sausmarez Street, St Peter Port,
  Guernsey, GY1 3PH
Telephone   01481-713 713
Conversion terms   One ordinary share at US$3.26 on 31 May in any of the years 1995
  to 1999 inclusive
Number in issue   17,709,590
Number of market-makers   Four
Warrants listed in FT   Yes (in sterling)

The Fleming Chinese Investment Trust plc

Category   Investment Trusts
Activities   Investment in China
Address   25 Copthall Avenue, London, EC2R 7DR
Telephone   0171-638 5858
Conversion terms   One share at 100p on 1 February 1998 to 2004 inclusive; time
  value protected
Number in issue   12,000,000
Number of market-makers   Nine
Warrants listed in FT   Yes

The Fleming Emerging Markets Investment Trust plc

Category   Investment Trusts
Activities   Investment in emerging markets world-wide
Address   25 Copthall Avenue, London, EC2R 7DR
Telephone   0171-638 5858
Conversion terms   One share at 100p on 1 December 1995 to 1998 inclusive; time
  value protected
Number in issue   19,322,778
Number of market-makers   Seven
Warrants listed in FT   Yes

The Fleming European Fledgeling Inv Trust plc

Category   Investment Trusts
Activities   Investment in smaller European companies
Address   25 Copthall Avenue, London, EC2R 7DR
Telephone   0171-638 5858
Conversion terms   One share at 100p on 31 July 1994 to 1997 inclusive; time value
  protected
Number in issue   10,680,073
Warrants listed in FT   Yes
Number of market-makers   Three

The Fleming High Income Trust plc

Category   Investment Trusts

Activities   Investment in high yielding UK securities
Address   25 Copthall Avenue, London, EC2R 7DR
Telephone   0171-638 5858
Conversion terms   One ordinary share at 100p on 1 August 1993 to 1996 inclusive; time value protected
Number in issue   4,958,228
Number of market-makers   Six
Warrants listed in FT   Yes

The Fleming Indian Investment Trust plc

Category   Investment Trusts
Activities   Investment in Indian companies
Address   25 Copthall Avenue, London, EC2R 7DR
Telephone   0171-638 5858
Conversion terms   One share at 100p on 1 February in the years 1997 to 2004 inclusive; time value protected
Number in issue   16,800,000
Number of market-makers   Six
Warrants listed in FT   Yes

Fleming Japanese Investment Trust plc

Category   Investment Trusts
Activities   Investment in Japan
Address   25 Copthall Avenue, London, EC2R 7DR
Telephone   0171-638 5858
Conversion terms   One share at 192p at any time from 1 April 1992 to 28 February 1999; time value protected
Number in issue   34,512,494
Number of market-makers   Nine
Warrants listed in FT   Yes

The Fleming Natural Resources Investment Trust plc

Category   Investment Trusts
Activities   Investment in a portfolio of commodities
Address   25 Copthall Avenue, London, EC2R 7DR
Telephone   0171-638 5858
Conversion terms   One share at 125p at any time until 30 June 1997; time value protected
Number in issue   8,216,000
Number of market-makers   Five
Warrants listed in FT   Yes

Foreign & Colonial Emerging Markets Inv Trust plc

Category   Investment Trusts
Activities   Investment in emerging markets
Address   Exchange House, Primrose Street, London, EC2A 2NY
Telephone   0171-628 8000
Conversion terms   One share at 102p up to 31 March 2003; time value protected
Number in issue   19,999,151
Number of market-makers   Eight
Warrants listed in FT   Yes

Foreign & Colonial German Investment Trust plc

Category   Investment Trusts
Activities   Investment in the German-speaking economic region
Address   Exchange House, Primrose Street, London, EC2A 2NY
Telephone   0171-628 8000
Conversion terms   One share at 135.63p on 31 July 1991 to 2000 inclusive; time value
   protected
Number in issue   7,861,094
Number of market-makers   Six
Warrants listed in FT   Yes

Foreign & Colonial Income Growth Investment Trust plc

Category   Investment Trusts
Activities   Investment in FT-SE-A 350 companies
Address   Exchange House, Primrose Street, London, EC2A 2NY
Telephone   0171-628 8000
Conversion terms   One share at 100p on 31 July 1995 to 2003 inclusive; time value
   protected
Number in issue   8,581,980
Number of market-makers   Three
Warrants listed in FT   Yes

Foreign & Colonial Special Utilities Investment Trust plc

Category   Investment Trusts Split Capital
Activities   Income and capital growth from a portfolio of utilities
Address   Exchange House, Primrose Street, London, EC2A 2NY
Telephone   0171-628 8000
Conversion terms   One 'S' share at 100p on an annual basis until 2008
Number in issue   4,000,000
Number of market-makers   Six
Warrants listed in FT   Yes

Foreign & Colonial US Smaller Companies Investment Trust plc

Category   Investment Trusts
Activities   Investment in US smaller companies
Address   Exchange House, Primrose Street, London, EC2A 2NY
Telephone   0171-628 8000
Conversion terms   One share at 100p on 30 November 1994 to 2002 inclusive; time value protected
Number in issue   9,950,520
Number of market-makers   Six
Warrants listed in FT   Yes

French Property Trust plc

Category   Investment Trusts
Activities   Investment in French property
Address   Cayzer House, 1 Thomas More St, London, E1 9AR
Telephone   0171-702 2495
Conversion terms   One ordinary share at 100p on 30 April in any of the years 1993 to 1997 inclusive; time value protected
Number in issue   5,000,000
Number of market-makers   Two
Warrants listed in FT   Yes

Gartmore Emerging Pacific Investment Trust plc

Category   Investment Trusts
Activities   Investment in stockmarkets of the emerging economies of the Far East
Address   Gartmore House, 16-18 Monument Street, London, EC3R 8AJ
Telephone   0171-782 2000
Conversion terms   One share at 64p on 31 March 1991 to 1997 inclusive; time value protected
Number in issue   11,254,968
Number of market-makers   Six
Warrants listed in FT   Yes

Gartmore European Investment Trust plc

Category   Investment Trusts
Activities   Investment in Europe for long-term capital growth
Address   16-18 Monument Street, London, EC3R 8AJ
Telephone   0171-782 2000
Conversion terms   Four shares at 88.5p each on 2 January 1993 to 1997 inclusive
Number in issue   840,690
Number of market-makers   Two
Warrants listed in FT   Yes

Gartmore Micro Index Trust plc

Category   Investment Trusts
Activities   Investment in the smallest one per cent of UK companies
Address   16-18 Monument Street, London, EC3R 8AJ
Telephone   0171-782 2000
Conversion terms   One share at 100p on 1 December 1996 to 2001 inclusive; time value protected
Number in issue   7,101,466
Number of market-makers   Four
Warrants listed in FT   Yes

Genesis Chile Fund Ltd

Category   Investment Companies
Activities   Investment in Chile
Address   PO Box 208, Bermuda House, St Julian's Avenue, St Peter Port, Guernsey, Channel Islands
Telephone   01481-726 268
Conversion terms   One participating share at US$16.00 on the last business day of March and September from 1993 to 1995 inclusive; time value protected; settlement through Euroclear/CEDEL
Number in issue   1,554,475
Number of market-makers   n/a
Warrants listed in FT   Yes (in sterling)

The German Investment Trust plc

Category   Investment Trusts
Activities   Investment in the German stock market
Address   48 Chiswell Street, London, EC1Y 4GR
Telephone   0171-600 4500
Conversion terms   One share at 100p on the date 42 days after the AGM in 1991 to 1999; time value protected; estimated final expiry 22 July 1999
Number in issue   7,792,960
Number of market-makers   Seven
Warrants listed in FT   Yes

German Smaller Companies Investment Trust plc

Category   Investment Trusts
Activities   Investment in smaller German companies
Address   48 Chiswell Street, London, EC1Y 4GR
Telephone   0171-600 4500
Conversion terms   One share at 100p on 31 August 1986 to 1995 inclusive
Number in issue   3,344,604
Number of market-makers   Five
Warrants listed in FT   Yes

Govett Asian Smaller Companies Investment Trust Ltd

(formerly Oriental Smaller Companies Investment Trust Ltd.)
Category   Other Investment Trusts
Activities   Investment in Asian smaller companies
Address   Shackleton House, 4 Battle Bridge Lane, London, SE1 2HR
Telephone   0171-378 7979
Conversion terms   One share at US$2.77 on any business day up to and including 31
    December 1998; time value protected
Number in issue   7,500,010
Number of market-makers   Six
Warrants listed in FT   Yes

Govett Emerging Markets Investment Trust plc

Category   Investment Trusts
Activities   Investment in emerging markets
Address   Shackleton House, 4 Battle Bridge Lane, London, SE1 2HR
Telephone   0171-378 7979
Conversion terms   One ordinary share at 100p on any business day from 1 January
    1994 to 30 June 1998 inclusive; time value protected
Number in issue   7,142,565
Number of market-makers   Seven
Warrants listed in FT   Yes

Govett Global Smaller Companies Investment Trust plc

Category   Investment Trusts
Activities   Worldwide exposure to smaller companies
Address   Shackleton House, 4 Battle Bridge Lane, London, SE1 2HR
Telephone   0171-378 7979
Conversion terms   One ordinary share at 100p on any business day from 3 October
    1994 to 31 October 2003 inclusive; time value protected
Number in issue   4,350,690
Number of market-makers   Four
Warrants listed in FT   Yes

Govett High Income Investment Trust plc

Category   Investment Trusts
Activities   Investment in high-yielding securities
Address   Shackleton House, 4 Battle Bridge Lane, London, SE1 2HR
Telephone   0171-378 7979
Conversion terms   One share at 100p during the period 30 June 1994 to 31 December
    1998; time value protected
Number in issue   9,560,000
Number of market-makers   Four
Warrants listed in FT   Yes

Greycoat plc

Category   Property
Activities   Property investment and development
Address   9 Savoy Street, London, WC2E 7EG
Telephone   0171-379 1000
Conversion terms   One ordinary share at 250p at any time up to 31 December 2000
Number in issue   37,500,000
Number of market-makers   Two
Warrants listed in FT   No

Group Development Capital plc

Category   Investment Trusts
Activities   Investment in MBOs and MBIs
Address   11 Queen Victoria Street, London, EC4N 4TP
Telephone   0171-528 6200
Conversion terms   One ordinary share at 55.51p during the 28-day period following
  publication of the annual report and accounts in the years 1995 to 2006 inclusive;
  estimated final expiry 21 March 2006
Number in issue   8,310,000
Number of market-makers   Three
Warrants listed in FT   Yes

Guangdong Development Fund Limited

Category   Investment Companies
Activities   Investment in southern China
Address   39–41 Broad Street, St. Helier, Jersey, Channel Islands
Telephone   00-852 2530 5112 (Hong Kong)
Conversion terms   One ordinary share for US$1.00 at any time from 23 February 1994
  to 23 February 1999 inclusive; time value protected
Number in issue   19,380,000
Number of market-makers   Two
Warrants listed in FT   Yes (in sterling)

Hambros Smaller Asian Companies Trust plc

Category   Other Investment Trusts
Activities   Investment in small Asian companies
Address   41 Tower Hill, London, EC3N 4HA
Telephone   0171-480 5000
Conversion terms   One share at US$1.00 in any of the years 1997 to 2001 inclusive.
Number in issue   8,400,000
Number of market-makers   Four
Warrants listed in FT   Yes (in sterling)

Hanson plc

Category   Diversified Industrials
Activities   Industrial conglomerate operating principally in UK and US
Address   1 Grosvenor Place, London, SW1X 7JH
Telephone   0171-245 1245
Conversion terms   One share at 287p at any time from 28 February 1990 to 30 September 1997
Number in issue   578,512,048
Number of market-makers   Thirteen
Warrants listed in FT   Yes

Harmony Property Group plc

(formerly Harmony Leisure Group plc)
Category   Property
Activities   Investments in property
Address   24 Craven Terrace, Lancaster Gate, London, W2 3QH
Telephone   0171-512 2323
Conversion terms   One share at 15p in each of the years 1994 to 1999 inclusive
Number in issue   18,260,579
Number of market-makers   Two
Warrants listed in FT   No

Henderson Highland Trust plc

Category   Investment Trusts
Activities   Investment for a high level of income, predominantly in UK equities
Address   3 Finsbury Avenue, London, EC2M 2PA
Telephone   0171-638 5757
Conversion terms   One share at 100p on 31 July 1996 to 1999 inclusive and 31 December 1999; time value protected
Number in issue   5,199,998
Number of market-makers   Six
Warrants listed in FT   Yes

Herald Investment Trust plc

Category   Investment Trusts
Activities   Investment in small multi-media companies
Address   99 Charterhouse Street, London, EC1M 2PA
Telephone   0171-490 3882
Conversion terms   One ordinary share at 100p on 30 April in each year from 1995 to 2003; time value protected
Number in issue   13,000,000
Number of market-makers   Five
Warrants listed in FT   Yes

The Hong Kong Investment Trust plc

Category   Investment Trusts Split Capital
Activities   Investment in Hong Kong securities
Address   197 Knightsbridge, London, SW7 1RB
Telephone   0171-412 0703
Conversion terms   One ordinary share and one zero dividend preference share at 50p per share, during 30-day period commencing one day after the posting of the annual report and accounts in 1992 to 1995 inclusive; time value protected; estimated final expiry 19 October 1995
Number in issue   3,997,880
Number of market-makers   Two
Warrants listed in FT   Yes

HTR Japanese Smaller Companies Trust plc

Category   Investment Trusts
Activities   Investment in smaller Japanese companies
Address   3 Finsbury Avenue, London, EC2M 2PA
Telephone   0171-638 5757
Conversion terms   One share at 100p on 30 November 1996 to 2002 inclusive; time value protected
Number in issue   20,000,000
Number of market-makers   Seven
Warrants listed in FT   Yes

Hungarian Investment Company Limited

Category   Investment Companies
Activities   Investment in Hungarian enterprises
Address   Minden House, 6 Minden Place, St Helier, Jersey
Telephone   01534-38578
Conversion terms   One share at US$100 at any time between 30 June 1991 and 30 June 1995; time value protected; settlement through Euroclear/CEDEL
Number in issue   100,000
Number of market-makers   n/a
Warrants listed in FT   No

IAF Group plc

(formerly Greyfriars Investment Company plc)
Category   Other Financial
Activities   Investment company
Address   Knightsbridge House, 197 Knightsbridge, London, SW17 1RB
Telephone   0171-581 8015
Conversion terms   One ordinary share at 30p on 31 December 1996 to 1998 inclusive
Number in issue   1,400,000.

Number of market-makers   Three
Warrants listed in FT   No

I&S UK Smaller Companies Trust plc

Category   Investment Trusts
Activities   Investment in UK smaller companies
Address   1 Charlotte Square, Edinburgh, EH2 4DZ
Telephone   0131-225 1357
Conversion terms   One share at 93p on 31 July 1993 to 2000 inclusive
Number in issue   4,193,376
Number of market-makers   Three
Warrants listed in FT   Yes

Ibstock plc

(formerly Ibstock Johnsen plc)
Category   Building Materials and Merchants
Activities   Building materials
Address   Lutterworth House, Lutterworth, Leics, LE17 4PS
Telephone   01455-553 071
Conversion terms   One share at 162p in June 1990 to 1995
Number in issue   20,708,940
Number of market-makers   Four
Warrants listed in FT   Yes

The Indonesia Equity Fund Limited

Category   Investment Companies
Activities   Investment in Indonesia
Address   28/34 Hill Street, St Helier, Jersey, Channel Islands
Telephone   01534-606 000
Conversion terms   One ordinary share at US$10.00 at any time from 23 July 1990 to
    23 July 1995; time value protected; dealing through Euroclear/CEDEL
Number in issue   600,000
Number of market-makers   n/a
Warrants listed in FT   Yes (in sterling)

International Biotechnology Trust plc

Category   Investment Trusts
Activities   Investment in the Biotechnology sector
Address   Five Arrows House, St. Swithin's Lane, London, EC4N 8NR
Telephone   0171-280 5000
Conversion terms   One share at 100p on 31 January and 31 July 1995 to 1999
    inclusive, time value protected
Number in issue   7,540,000

Number of market-makers   Two
Warrants listed in FT   Yes

INVESCO plc

(formerly INVESCO MIM plc)
Category   Other Financial
Activities   Investment management
Address   11 Devonshire Square, London, EC2M 4YR
Telephone   0171-626 3434
Conversion terms   One and one-third ordinary shares at 140p per share at any time
   (perpetual)
Number in issue   2,068,391
Number of market-makers   One
Warrants listed in FT   No

INVESCO Asia plc

(formerly part of Drayton Far Eastern Trust plc)
Category   London Recent Issues/Investment Trusts
Activities   Investment in Asian equities
Address   11 Devonshire Square, London, EC2M 4YR
Telephone   0171-626 3434
Conversion terms   awaiting details; dealings due to begin on 11 July 1995
Number in issue   approximately 24,272,000
Number of market-makers   n/a
Warrants listed in FT   n/a

INVESCO Japan Discovery Trust plc

Category   Investment Trusts
Activities   Investment in Japanese smaller companies
Address   11 Devonshire Square, London, EC2M 4YR
Telephone   0171-626 3434
Conversion terms   One ordinary share at 100p on the date falling 28 days after the
   AGM for the accounting periods ending 31 July 1996 to 2004 inclusive; time value
   protected; estimated final expiry November 2004
Number in issue   2,068,391
Number of market-makers   Five
Warrants listed in FT   Yes

INVESCO Korea Trust plc

(formerly Drayton Korea Trust plc)
Category   Investment Trusts
Activities   Investment in Korea
Address   11 Devonshire Square, London, EC2M 4YR

Telephone   0171-626 3434

Conversion terms   One share at 100p on the date falling 28 days after the AGM for the accounting periods ending 31 March 1992 to 1997; time value protected; estimated final expiry 8 August 1997

Number in issue   6,603,482

Number of market-makers   Three

Warrants listed in FT   Yes

INVESCO Tokyo plc

(formerly part of Drayton Far Eastern Trust plc)

Category   London Recent Issues/Investment Trusts

Activities   Investment in Japanese equities

Address   11 Devonshire Square, London, EC2M 4YR

Telephone   0171-626 3434

Conversion terms   awaiting details; dealings due to begin on 11 July 1995

Number in issue   approximately 24,272,000

Number of market-makers   n/a

Warrants listed in FT   n/a

The Investment Trust of Investment Trusts plc

Category   Investment Trusts

Activities   Investment in investment trusts and other closed-end investment companies

Address   197 Knightsbridge, London, SW17 1RB

Telephone   0171-412 0703

Conversion terms   One ordinary share at 150p on the date falling 30 days after the date of posting of the annual report and accounts of the company in each of the years 1996 to 2004 inclusive; plus an annual dividend of 4.4p, payable in two equal instalments of 2.2p on 30 September and 31 March; time value protected

Number in issue   5,200,000

Number of market-makers   Six

Warrants listed in FT   Yes

Investors Capital Trust plc

Category   Investment Trusts

Activities   Investment in a UK Equity Portfolio

Address   One Charlotte Square, Edinburgh, EH2 4DZ

Telephone   0131-225 1357

Conversion terms   One growth share at 137p on any business day between 1 October 1997 and 30 September 2001; time value protected

Number in issue   49,478,400

Number of market-makers   Five

Warrants listed in FT   Yes

IS Himalayan Fund NV

Category   Saturday Dealings Page
Activities   Investment in Indian, Sri Lankan and Bangladeshi companies
Address   Indosuez Asset Management Asia Limited, Suite 2606-2608, One Exchange Square, Hong Kong
Telephone   00-852 2521 4231
Conversion terms   One ordinary share at US$19.00 on any day during the period from 21 January 1994 to 31 December 1996
Number in issue   n/a
Number of market-makers   n/a
Warrants listed in FT   No

The Israel Fund plc

Category   Other Investment Trusts
Activities   Investment in Israel
Address   Seal House, 1 Swan Lane, London, EC4R 3UD
Telephone   0171-623 7777
Conversion terms   One ordinary share at US$1.00 on 31 May in any of the years 1995 to 2004 inclusive; time value protected
Number in issue   30,600,000
Number of market-makers   Five
Warrants listed in FT   Yes (in sterling)

Ivory & Sime Enterprise Capital plc

(formerly the Independent Investment Company plc)
Category   Investment Trusts
Activities   Investment in venture capital in the UK and US
Address   One Charlotte Square, Edinburgh, EH2 4DZ
Telephone   0131-225 1357
Conversion terms   One ordinary share at 118p at any time up to 30 June 1998
Number in issue   2,966,863
Number of market-makers   Three
Warrants listed in FT   Yes

Ivory & Sime ISIS Trust plc

Category   Investment Trusts
Activities   Investment in UK growth companies
Address   One Charlotte Square, Edinburgh, EH2 4DZ
Telephone   0131-225 1357
Conversion terms   One share at 107.5p on 31 October 2000; time value protected
Number in issue   931,604
Number of market-makers   Three
Warrants listed in FT   Yes

Ivory & Sime UK Discovery Trust plc

Category   Investment Trusts
Activities   Investment in small UK quoted companies
Address   One Charlotte Square, Edinburgh, EH2 4DZ
Telephone   0131-225 1357
Conversion terms   One share at 100p on any day in the period from 1 June 1995 to 30 April 2002 inclusive; time value protected
Number in issue   5,156,800
Number of market-makers   Two
Warrants listed in FT   Yes

The Japanese Warrant Fund

Category   Investment Companies
Activities   Investment in Japanese warrants
Address   Jardine Fleming Investment Management Ltd, 46th Floor, Jardine House, 1 Connaught Place, Central, Hong Kong
Telephone   0171-382 8871 (UK investor relations)
Conversion terms   One share at US$10.00 until 31 December 1995; settlement through Euroclear; listed in Luxembourg but Salomon Brothers and Baring Securities make a market in London
Number in issue   3,000,000
Number of market-makers   See conversion terms
Warrants listed in FT   Yes (in sterling)

Jersey Phoenix Investment Trust plc

Category   Investment Companies
Activities   Investment trust
Address   Wellington House, 17 Union Street, St Helier, Jersey, Channel Islands
Telephone   01534-73377
Conversion terms   One share at 100p on 1 November 1993 to 1996 inclusive; time value protected
Number in issue   2,933,668
Number of market-makers   Two
Warrants listed in FT   Yes

JF Fledgeling Japan Limited

Category   Investment Companies
Activities   Investment in smaller to medium-sized Japanese companies
Address   Cedar House, 41 Cedar Ave, Hamilton HM12, Bermuda
Telephone   0171-382 8871 (UK investor relations)
Conversion terms   One ordinary share at 243p on any business day between 1 June 1994 and 30 June 1997
Number in issue   13,751,178

Number of market-makers   Four
Warrants listed in FT   Yes

JF Indonesia Fund Incorporated

Category   Investment Companies
Activities   Investment in Indonesian equities
Address   Jardine Fleming Investment Management Ltd, 46th Floor, Jardine House, 1
   Connaught Place, Central, Hong Kong
Telephone   0171-382 8871 (UK investor relations)
Conversion terms   One ordinary share at US$1.13 on any business day between 21
   December 1992 and 31 December 1995; settlement through Euroclear/CEDEL;
   listed in Hong Kong but Robert Fleming create a market in London
Number in issue   9,989,500
Number of market-makers   see conversion terms
Warrants listed in FT   Yes (in sterling)

JF Japan OTC Fund Inc.

Category   Investment Companies
Activities   Investment in Japanese OTC market
Address   47th Floor Jardine House, Connaught Place, Hong Kong
Telephone   00-852 2843 8888
Conversion terms   One share at US$10.00 between 1 January 1990 and 31 December
   1995; settlement through Euroclear/CEDEL; listed in Hong Kong but Salomon
   Brothers and Baring Securities make a market in London
Number in issue   1,180,100
Number of market-makers   See conversion terms
Warrants listed in FT   Yes (in sterling)

Jupiter European Investment Trust plc

Category   Investment Trusts Split Capital
Activities   Investment in Continental Europe
Address   Knightsbridge House, 197 Knightsbridge London, SW7 1RB
Telephone   0171-412 0703
Conversion terms   One ordinary share and one zero dividend share for a total of 100p
   in the 30-day period commencing one day after the posting of the annual report and
   accounts in 1992 to 2000 inclusive; time value protected; estimated final expiry 29
   December 2000
Number in issue   8,253,236
Number of market-makers   Three
Warrants listed in FT   Yes

Jupiter International Green Investment Trust plc

(formerly Merlin International Green Investment Trust plc)

Category   Investment Trusts Split Capital
Activities   Investment in UK and overseas companies which demonstrate sound environmental practice
Address   Knightsbridge House, 197 Knightsbridge, London, SW7 1RB
Telephone   0171-412 0703
Conversion terms   One unit comprising one ordinary share and one zero dividend preference share at 100p in the 30-day period commencing on the date falling one day after the date of posting of the annual report and accounts in 1995 to 2000 inclusive; time value protected; estimated final expiry 7 April 2000
Number in issue   5,027,250
Number of market-makers   Two
Warrants listed in FT   Yes

Kleinwort Emerging Markets Trust plc

Category   Investment Trusts
Activities   Investment in emerging markets
Address   10 Fenchurch Street, London, EC3M 3LB
Telephone   0171-956 6600
Conversion terms   One share at 100p on 31 July 1994 to 2004 inclusive; time value protected
Number in issue   5,640,000
Number of market-makers   Three
Warrants listed in FT   Yes

Kleinwort European Privatisation Investment Trust plc

Category   Investment Trusts
Activities   Investment in European privatization issues
Address   10 Fenchurch Street, London, EC3M 3LB
Telephone   0171-956 6000
Conversion terms   One share at 100p during the first 30 days of January in the years 1995 to 2006 inclusive; time value protected
Number in issue   100,000,000
Number of market-makers   Nine
Warrants listed in FT   Yes

Korea Liberalisation Fund Limited

Category   Other Investment Trusts
Activities   Investment in South Korea
Address   197 Knightsbridge, London, SW7 1RB
Telephone   0171-412 0703
Conversion terms   One share at US$10.50 in 30-day period commencing one day after the posting of the annual report and accounts in 1993 to 2003 inclusive; time value protected; settlement through Euroclear/CEDEL; estimated final expiry April 2003
Number in issue   1,000,000

Number of market-makers n/a
Warrants listed in FT Yes (in sterling)

Latin American Investment Trust plc

Category Other Investment Trusts
Activities Investment in South America
Address Exchange House, Primrose Street, London, EC2A 2NY
Telephone 0171-628 1234
Conversion terms One share at US$1.00 at any time from 20 August 1990 to 31 July 2005; time value protected
Number in issue 14,993,500
Number of market-makers Four
Warrants listed in FT Yes (in sterling)

Lazard Birla India Investment Trust plc

Category Other Investment Trusts
Activities Investment in listed Indian companies
Address 21 Moorfields, London EC2P 2HT
Telephone 0171-588 2721
Conversion terms One share at US$1.00 on 28 February 1996 to 2005 inclusive; time value protected
Number in issue 10,395,555
Number of market-makers Four
Warrants listed in FT Yes

Legal & General Recovery Investment Trust plc

Category Investment Trusts
Activities Investment in small and medium sized companies
Address 3 Queen Victoria Street, London, EC4N 8EL
Telephone 0171-489 1888
Conversion terms One share at 100p on 28 February 1997 to 2004 inclusive and on 31 October 2004; time value protected
Number in issue 7,365,200
Number of market-makers Six
Warrants listed in FT Yes

London American Growth Trust plc

(formerly London American Ventures Trust plc)
Category Investment Trusts
Activities Investment in US venture capital
Address 1 Charlotte Square, Edinburgh, EH2 4DZ
Telephone 0131-225 1357
Conversion terms Two shares at 75p each for every three warrants on 31 July 1995;

or one share at 105p for every three warrants on 31 March 2000; or one share for 105p for each warrant on 31 July 2000; warrants traded and transferred in multiples of three
Number in issue   18,337,715
Number of market-makers   Two
Warrants listed in FT   Yes

London Finance & Investment Group plc

Category   Other Financial
Activities   Investment and finance company
Address   25 City Road, London, EC1Y 1BQ
Telephone   071-628 9371
Conversion terms   One share at 25p in the 28-day period following the AGM in 1996 to 2005 inclusive; estimated final expiry April 2005
Number in issue   4,993,389
Number of market-makers   Two
Warrants listed in FT   No

Lucas Industries plc

Category   Engineering, Vehicles
Activities   Auto parts; civil aerospace
Address   Brueton House, New Road, Solihull, West Midlands, B91 3TX
Telephone   0121-627 6000
Conversion terms   One share at 172p during the months of June and December, starting with June 1993 and finishing with June 1995
Number in issue   69,876,768
Number of market-makers   Seven
Warrants listed in FT   Yes

Martin Currie European Investment Trust plc

Category   Investment Trusts
Activities   Investment in Continental Europe
Address   Saltire Court, 20 Castle Terrace, Edinburgh, EH1 2ES
Telephone   0131-229 5252
Conversion terms   One share at 100p on 31 August 1991 to 1998 inclusive; time value protected
Number in issue   4,575,120
Number of market-makers   Five
Warrants listed in FT   Yes

Martin Currie Pacific Trust plc

Category   Investment Trusts
Activities   Investment in the Pacific Basin

Address   Saltire Court, 20 Castle Terrace, Edinburgh, EH1 2ES
Telephone   0131-229 5252
Conversion terms   One share at 130p on 30 June 1995 to 2000 inclusive; time value
    protected
Number in issue   8,183,197
Number of market-makers   Eight
Warrants listed in FT   Yes

Matheson Lloyds Investment Trust plc

Category   Insurance
Activities   Investment in Lloyd's insurance market
Address   1 High Timber Street, London, EC4V 3SB
Telephone   0171-329 0329
Conversion terms   One share at 100p on 15 August 1997 to 1999 inclusive
Number in issue   10,000,000
Number of market-makers   Three
Warrants listed in FT   Yes

Melrose Energy plc

Category   Oil Exploration and Production
Activities   Oil and gas field development in the USA
Address   40 New King's Road, London, SW6 4ST
Telephone   0171-731 7273
Conversion terms   One ordinary share at 25p on the date which falls 21 days after the
    company announces its results for the financial year ending 30 June 1995, or at 30p
    on the later of 31 May 1996 or 21 days after the company publishes its interim
    results for the six months to 31 December 1995; time value protected
Number in issue   10,374,249
Number of market-makers   Two
Warrants listed in FT   Yes

Mercury European Privatisation Inv Trust plc

Category   Investment Trusts
Activities   Investment in European privatization issues
Address   33 King William Street, London, EC4R 9AS
Telephone   0171-280 2800
Conversion terms   One ordinary share at 100p on 31 July in each of the years 1995 to
    2004; time value protected
Number in issue   115,000,000
Number of market-makers   Nine
Warrants listed in FT   Yes

Mercury World Mining Trust plc

Category   Investment Trusts

Activities   Investment in quoted mining and metals securities.
Address   33 King William Street, London, EC4R 9AS
Telephone   0171-280 2800
Conversion terms   One ordinary share at 100p on 30 April 1995 to 1998 inclusive
Number in issue   85,158,000
Number of market-makers   Nine
Warrants listed in FT   Yes

Mid Kent Holdings plc

Category   Water
Activities   Water company
Address   High Street, Snodland, Kent, ME6 5AH
Telephone   01634-240 313
Conversion terms   One share at £6.00 on any day in January in 1990 to 1999 inclusive
Number in issue   1,859,287
Number of market-makers   One
Warrants listed in FT   No

Mithras Investment Trust plc

Category   Investment Trusts
Activities   Mezzanine finance for unquoted companies
Address   Legal & General Ventures Ltd, Temple Court, 11 Queen Victoria Street,
    London, EC4N 4TP
Telephone   0171-528 6200
Conversion terms   One ordinary share at 50p, 30 days following the AGM in each of
    the years 1994 to 2003 inclusive; time value protected; estimated final expiry July
    2005
Number in issue   8,000,000
Number of market-makers   Two
Warrants listed in FT   Yes

Montanaro UK Smaller Companies Trust plc

Category   Investment Trusts
Activities   Investment in companies with a market cap. below £100m
Address   23 Cathedral Yard, Exeter, EX1 1HB
Telephone   01392-532 25
Conversion terms   One share at 100p on 31 July 1997 to 2005 inclusive; time value
    protected
Number in issue   5,000,000
Number of market-makers   Three
Warrants listed in FT   Yes

Moorgate Investment Trust plc

Category   Investment Trusts
Activities   Investment predominantly in smaller UK companies
Address   49 Hay's Mews, London, W1X 7RT
Telephone   0171-409 3419
Conversion terms   One share at 128.5p on 31 August 1988 to 1997 inclusive
Number in issue   5,565,417
Number of market-makers   Four
Warrants listed in FT   Yes

Moorgate Smaller Companies Income Trust plc

Category   Investment Trusts
Activities   Investment in smaller UK companies
Address   49 Hay's Mews, London, W1X 7RT
Telephone   0171-409 3419
Conversion terms   One share at 100p on 31 August 1992 to 2001 inclusive; time value protected
Number in issue   9,687,165
Number of market-makers   Six
Warrants listed in FT   Yes

Morgan Grenfell Equity Income Trust plc

Category   Investment Trusts
Activities   Investment in high-yielding UK equities
Address   20 Finsbury Circus, London, EC2M 1NB
Telephone   0171-256 7500
Conversion terms   One share at 100p on 31 January 1993 to 2000 inclusive
Number in issue   4,874,254
Number of market-makers   Four
Warrants listed in FT   Yes

Morgan Grenfell Latin American Companies Trust plc

Category   Investment Trusts
Activities   Investment in Latin American companies
Address   20 Finsbury Circus, London, EC2M 1NB
Telephone   0171-256 7500
Conversion terms   One ordinary share at 100p on 30 June 1995 to 2010 inclusive; time value protected
Number in issue   12,834,190
Number of market-makers   Eight
Warrants listed in FT   Yes

The Morgan Stanley Japanese Warrant Fund NV

Category   Saturday Dealings Page
Activities   Investment in Japanese warrants
Address   John B Gorsiraweg 6, Willemstad, Curacao, Netherlands Antilles
Conversion terms   One share at US$20.00 at any time to 29 December 1995;
    settlement through Euroclear or CEDEL
Number in issue   500,000
Number of market-makers   n/a
Warrants listed in FT   No

Murray Emerging Economies Trust plc

Category   Investment Trusts
Activities   Investment in listed securities within emerging and frontier economies
Address   7 West Nile Street, Glasgow, G1 2PX
Telephone   0141-226 3131
Conversion terms   One share at 100p in any of the years from 1997 to 2004 inclusive;
    time value protected
Number in issue   10,874,800
Number of market-makers   Five
Warrants listed in FT   Yes

Murray Enterprise Investment Trust plc

Category   Investment Trusts
Activities   Investment in smaller companies
Address   7 West Nile Street, Glasgow, G1 2PX
Telephone   0141-226 3131
Conversion terms   One share at 135p on 31 January in each of the years 1996 to 2002
    inclusive; time value protected
Number in issue   4,820,407
Number of market-makers   Three
Warrants listed in FT   Yes

Murray European Investment Trust plc

(formerly The European Project Investment Trust plc)
Category   Investment Trusts
Activities   Investment in selected Western European companies
Address   7 West Nile Street, Glasgow, G1 2PX
Telephone   0141-226 3131
Conversion terms   One share at 50p in 30-day period after the posting of the annual
    report and accounts in 1992 to 1996 inclusive; time value protected; estimated final
    expiry 27 May 1996
Number in issue   5,999,600
Number of market-makers   Four
Warrants listed in FT   Yes

NatWest Irish Smaller Companies Investment Trust plc

Category   London Recent Issues/Investment Trusts
Activities   Investment in small Irish quoted companies
Address   43–44 Crutched Friars, London, EC3N 2NX
Telephone   0171-374 3000
Conversion terms   One ordinary share at 100p on 31 July 1997 to 2001 inclusive; time
    value protected
Number in issue   4,305,200
Number of market-makers   Four
Warrants listed in FT   Yes

NatWest Smaller Companies Investment Trust plc

(formerly County Smaller Companies Investment Trust plc)
Category   Investment Trusts
Activities   Investment in smaller companies
Address   43–44 Crutched Friars, London, EC3N 2NX
Telephone   0171-374 3000
Conversion terms   One share at 100p on 31 October 1993 to 1998 inclusive; time
    value protected
Number in issue   3,275,562
Number of market-makers   Five
Warrants listed in FT   Yes

Navan Resources plc

Category   Extractive Industries
Activities   Mining and mineral production
Address   9–10 Academy Street, Navan, County Meath, Ireland
Telephone   00-353 46 22363
Conversion terms   One ordinary share at 30p at any time up to 23 October 1995
Number in issue   4,567,775
Number of market-makers   Two
Warrants listed in FT   No

New City & Commercial Investment Trust plc

Category   Investment Trusts
Activities   Investment in other investment trust companies
Address   11 Devonshire Square, London, EC2M 4YR
Telephone   0171-626 3434
Conversion terms   One ordinary share at 100p, 28 days after the AGM in respect of
    the financial periods ending on 31 January 1994 to 2005 inclusive; time value
    protected; estimated final expiry June 2005
Number in issue   2,472,720
Number of market-makers   Two
Warrants listed in FT   Yes

NM Smaller Australian Companies Trust plc

Category   Investment Trusts
Activities   Investment in small Australian companies
Address   3 Finsbury Avenue, London, EC2M 2PA
Telephone   0171-638 5757
Conversion terms   One ordinary share at 100p on 31 October 1995 to 2000 inclusive; time value protected
Number in issue   10,050,455
Number of market-makers   Seven
Warrants listed in FT   Yes

North American Gas Investment Trust plc

Category   Investment Trusts
Activities   Investment in natural gas in USA and Canada
Address   21 Moorfields, London, EC2P 2HT
Telephone   0171-588 2721
Conversion terms   One share at 100p on 31 July, 31 Oct, 31 Jan and 30 April 1989 to 1995 inclusive
Number in issue   6,958,937
Number of market-makers   Two
Warrants listed in FT   Yes

Old Mutual South Africa Trust plc

Category   Investment Trusts
Activities   Investment in South African securities
Address   Fairburn House, PO Box 121, Rohais, St Peter Port, Guernsey, Channel Islands
Telephone   01481-726 726
Conversion terms   One ordinary share at 100p on 31 December in any of the years 1996 to 2001 inclusive; time value protected
Number in issue   10,451,300
Number of market-makers   Six
Warrants listed in FT   Yes

Oryx (India) Fund Limited

Category   London Recent Issues/Investment Companies
Activities   Investment in Indian equities
Address   PO Box 208, Bermuda House, St Julian's Avenue, St Peter Port, Guernsey, Channel Islands
Conversion terms   One share at US$10.00 at any time from 1 April 1995 up to and including 31 December 1999; time value protected; settlement through Euroclear/CEDEL
Number in issue   262,000

Number of market-makers   Two
Warrants listed in FT   Yes

Oryx International Growth Fund Limited

Category   Investment Companies
Activities   Investment in medium and smaller companies
Address   PO Box 208, Bermuda House, St Julian's Avenue, St Peter Port, Guernsey, Channel Islands
Conversion terms   One share at 100p at any time from 1 January 1998 up to and including 31 December 2004; time value protected; settlement through Euroclear/Cedel
Number in issue   2,755,500
Number of market-makers   Two
Warrants listed in FT   No

The Overseas Investment Trust plc

Category   Investment Trusts
Activities   Investment overseas
Address   20 Finsbury Circus, London, EC2M 1NB
Telephone   0171-256 7500
Conversion terms   One ordinary share at 202p on 31 December 1988 to 1998 inclusive
Number in issue   1,793,183
Number of market-makers   Four
Warrants listed in FT   Yes

Pacific Assets Trust plc (Series Two warrants)

Category   Investment Trusts
Activities   Investment in selected companies within the Pacific region
Address   1 Charlotte Square, Edinburgh, EH2 4DZ
Telephone   0131-225 1357
Conversion terms   awaiting details
Number in issue   n/a
Number of market-makers   n/a

Pacific Horizon Investment Trust plc

Category   Investment Trusts
Activities   Investment in emerging economies of the Far East
Address   1 Rutland Court, Edinburgh, EH3 8EY
Telephone   0131-222 4244
Conversion terms   One share at 50p, during 30-day period commencing one day after the posting of the annual report and accounts in 1992 to 1995 inclusive; time value protected; estimated final expiry 3 November 1995

Number in issue   8,154,297
Number of market-makers   Three
Warrants listed in FT   Yes

Pantheon International Participations plc

Category   Investment Trusts
Activities   Investment in venture capital funds and companies
Address   Albany Gate, London, EC2Y 5AS
Telephone   0171-710 4567
Conversion terms   One share at 250p on 31 October in any of the years 1996 to 2001 inclusive; time value protected.
Number in issue   6,786,921
Number of market-makers   Four
Warrants listed in FT   Yes

Panther Securities plc

Category   Property
Activities   Investment and dealing in property and listed securities
Address   Panther House, 38 Mount Pleasant, London, WC1X 0AP
Telephone   0171-278 8011
Conversion terms   One ordinary share at 140p during the 30 days after the despatch of the annual report and accounts in the years 1995 to 2000 inclusive
Number in issue   865,801
Number of market-makers   Two
Warrants listed in FT   No

Paribas French Investment Trust plc 'B'

Category   Investment Trusts
Activities   Investment in French companies
Address   2-3 Philpot Lane, London, EC3M 8AQ
Telephone   0171-621 1161
Conversion terms   One ordinary share at 150p in 31-day period commencing on 31 May 1996 to 1998 inclusive; time value protected
Number in issue   3,000,000
Number of market-makers   Five
Warrants listed in FT   No

Perpetual Japanese Investment Trust plc

Category   Investment Trusts
Activities   Investment in Japan
Address   48 Hart Street, Henley-on-Thames, Oxon, RG9 2AZ
Telephone   01491-417 000
Conversion terms   One share at 100p during the years 1994 to 2000 inclusive; time value protected

Number in issue   7,282,900
Number of market-makers   Seven
Warrants listed in FT   Yes

Pilkington plc

Category   Building Materials & Merchants
Activities   Glass production
Address   Prescot Road, St Helens, WA10 3TT
Telephone   01744-28882
Conversion terms   One share at 120p at any time from 14 June 1993 to 4 May 1998;
   settlement through Euroclear/CEDEL
Number in issue   78,200,000
Number of market-makers   Eleven
Warrants listed in FT   Yes

Pilot Investment Trust plc

Category   Investment Trusts
Activities   Investment in smaller companies
Address   99 Charterhouse Street, London, EC1M 6HR
Telephone   0171-490 3882
Conversion terms   One ordinary share at 100p on 31 July 1994 to 1998 inclusive; time
   value protected
Number in issue   5,112,000
Number of market-makers   Three
Warrants listed in FT   Yes

Piper European Smaller Companies Trust plc

(due to be renamed following a change in ownership of the managers)
Category   Investment Trusts
Activities   Investment in companies with a maximum market capitalization of £250m
Address   133 Rose Street Lane South, Edinburgh, EH2 4NQ
Telephone   0131-226 6985
Conversion terms   One ordinary share at 100p on 31 July 1995 to 2004 inclusive; time
   value protected
Number in issue   2,013,680
Number of market-makers   Two
Warrants listed in FT   Yes

Plantation & General Investments plc

(formerly The Chillington Corporation plc)
Category   Food Producers
Activities   Overseas plantations
Address   71 Carter Lane, London, EC4V 5EQ

Telephone   0171-236 6135
Conversion terms   One share at 138p on 1 July 1990 to 1995 inclusive
Number in issue   2,916,382
Number of market-makers   Two
Warrants listed in FT   No

Prolific Income plc

Category   Investment Trusts
Activities   Investment in high yielding UK stocks
Address   Walbrook House, 23 Walbrook, London, EC4N 8LD
Telephone   0171-280 3700
Conversion terms   One ordinary share at 100p on 30 November 1995 to 2003 inclusive
Number in issue   10,353,000
Number of market-makers   Six
Warrants listed in FT   Yes

The Prospect Japan Fund Limited

Category   Investment Companies
Activities   Investment in Japanese smaller companies
Address   Barfield House, St. Julian's Avenue, St. Peter Port, Guernsey, Channel
    Islands
Telephone   n/a
Conversion terms   One share at US$10.00 at any time between 1 January 1995 and 31
    December 1999; time value protected
Number in issue   up to 2,000,000
Number of market-makers   n/a
Warrants listed in FT   Yes

Ptarmigan International Capital Trust plc

(formerly The Castle Cairn Investment Trust Company plc)
Category   Investment Trusts
Activities   Investment in international companies
Address   45 Charlotte Square, Edinburgh, EH2 4HW
Telephone   0131-226 3271
    Conversion terms   One ordinary share at 200p on 30 September 1994 to 1999
    inclusive; time value protected
Number in issue   976,671
Number of market-makers   Three
Warrants listed in FT   Yes

Raglan Properties plc

(formerly Raglan Property Trust plc)
Category   Property

Activities   Property investment and development
Address   Orion House, Grays Place, Slough, SL2 5AF
Telephone   01753-553 388
Conversion terms   One share at 30p at any time up to 31 December 1995; time value
   protected
Number in issue   3,100,000
Number of market-makers   Three
Warrants listed in FT   Yes

R.E.A. Holdings plc

Category   Distributors
Activities   Plantation holding company
Address   7 Bedford Square, London, WC1B 3RA
Telephone   0171-631 3988
Conversion terms   One ordinary share at 400p on 31 July 1986 to 1995 inclusive
Number in issue   412,470
Number of market-makers   One
Warrants listed in FT   No

River & Mercantile Trust plc

Category   Investment Trusts Split Capital
Activities   Split-capital investment trust
Address   7 Lincoln's Inn Fields, London, WC2A 3BP
Telephone   0171-405 7722
Conversion terms   1.097 capital shares at 273.56p at any time to the winding-up date
   (proposed: 30 April 2000)
Number in issue   8,045,464
Number of market-makers   Three
Warrants listed in FT   Yes

River & Mercantile American Trust plc

Category   Investment Trusts Split Capital
Activities   Investment in North America
Address   7 Lincoln's Inn Fields, London, WC2A 3BP
Telephone   0171-405 7722
Conversion terms   One capital share at 32.5p on 30 June 1990 to 1998 inclusive, and
   28 February 1999
Number in issue   7,500,000
Number of market-makers   Two
Warrants listed in FT   Yes

River & Mercantile Extra Income Trust plc

Category   Investment Trusts Split Capital

Activities　Investment in high-yielding UK securities
Address　7 Lincoln's Inn Fields, London, WC2A 3BP
Telephone　0171-405 7722
Conversion terms　1.011 ordinary shares at 98.93p on 1 January and 1 July in each year up to 2000, and on 29 September 2000.
Number in issue　5,983,723
Number of market-makers　Two
Warrants listed in FT　Yes

River & Mercantile Smaller Companies Trust plc

Category　Investment Trusts
Activities　Investment in smaller companies
Address　7 Lincoln's Inn Fields, London, WC2A 3BP
Telephone　0171-405 7722
Conversion terms　One ordinary share at 100p on 31 October 1990 to 1995 and on the date 45 days after the 1996 AGM of the company; time value protected; estimated final expiry 15 December 1996
Number in issue　4,826,750
Number of market-makers　Four
Warrants listed in FT　Yes

River Plate & General Investment Trust plc

Category　Investment Trusts Split Capital
Activities　Investment in high-yielding securities
Address　197 Knightsbridge, London, SW7 1RB
Telephone　0171-412 0703
Conversion terms　One capital share at 250p at any time to the winding-up date (31 October 1996)
Number in issue　5,369,194
Number of market-makers　Two
Warrants listed in FT　Yes

Saracen Value Investment Trust plc

Category　Investment Trusts
Activities　Investment in UK smaller companies
Address　Stirling House, 226 St Vincent St, Glasgow, G2 5RQ
Telephone　0141-204 3442
Conversion terms　One ordinary share for 100p on 31 May in any of the years 1995 to 2001 inclusive; time value protected
Number in issue　7,397,293
Number of market-makers　Four
Warrants listed in FT　Yes

Schroder Income Growth Fund plc

Category   Investment Trusts
Activities   Investment in high yielding UK equities
Address   33 Gutter Lane, London, EC2V 8AS
Telephone   0171-382 6000
Conversion terms   One ordinary share at 100p on 31 December 1997 to 2003
   inclusive; time value protected
Number in issue   15,826,000
Number of market-makers   Four
Warrants listed in FT   Yes

Schroder Japan Growth Fund plc

Category   Investment Trusts
Activities   Investment in Japanese equities
Address   33 Gutter Lane, London, EC2V 8AS
Telephone   0171-382 6000
Conversion terms   One ordinary share at 100p on 30 November 1996 to 2004
   inclusive; time value protected
Number in issue   25,000,000
Number of market-makers   Eight
Warrants listed in FT   Yes

Schroder Japanese Warrant Fund Limited

Category   Investment Companies
Activities   Investment in Japanese warrants
Address   St Julian's Avenue, St Peter Port, Guernsey
Telephone   01481-710 651
Conversion terms   One ordinary share at US$9.55 between 30 June 1990 and 29
   March 1996; time value protected; settlement through Euroclear/CEDEL
Number in issue   1,580,000
Number of market-makers   n/a
Warrants listed in FT   Yes (in sterling)

Schroder Korea Fund plc

Category   Other Investment Trusts
Activities   Investment in Korea
Address   33 Gutter Lane, London, EC2V 8AS
Telephone   0171-382 6000
Conversion terms   One share at US$10.00 at any time to 31 December 1998; time
   value protected; settlement through Euroclear/CEDEL
Number in issue   1,000,000
Number of market-makers   n/a
Warrants listed in FT   Yes (in sterling)

Schroder Mediterranean Fund Limited

(formerly Mediterranean Fund Limited)
Category   Other Investment Trusts
Activities   Investment in Southern Europe
Address   33 Gutter Lane, London, EC2V 8AS
Telephone   0171-382 6000
Conversion terms   One share at 318.79p at any time from 31 March 1990 to 31 December 1995 inclusive; time value protected
Number in issue   20,000,000
Number of market-makers   Four
Warrants listed in FT   Yes

Schroder UK Growth Fund plc

Category   Investment Trusts
Activities   Investment in UK companies for growth
Address   33 Gutter Lane, London, EC2V 8AS
Telephone   0171-382 6000
Conversion terms   One ordinary share at 100p on 31 August in any of the years 1996 to 2002 inclusive; time value protected
Number in issue   23,400,000
Number of market-makers   Five
Warrants listed in FT   Yes

The Scottish Asian Investment Company Limited

Category   Other Investment Trusts
Activities   Investment in a diversified portfolio of securities in Asia
Address   7 West Nile Street, Glasgow, G1 2PX
Telephone   0141-226 3131
Conversion terms   Five participating share for 141.2p between 30 June 1990 and 30 June 1997; time value protected
Number in issue   700,000
Number of market-makers   Two
Warrants listed in FT   Yes

The Scottish National Trust plc

Category   Investment Trusts Split Capital
Activities   Investment for income and capital growth
Address   Charles Oakley House, 125 West Regent Street, Glasgow, G2 2SG
Telephone   0141-248 3972
Conversion terms   One capital share at 300p at any time up to 30 September 1998
Number in issue   12,771,018
Number of market-makers   Four
Warrants listed in FT   Yes

Scottish Oriental Smaller Companies plc

Category   Investment Trusts
Activities   Investment in smaller Asian companies
Address   45 Charlotte Square, Edinburgh, EH2 4HW
Telephone   0131-226 3271
Conversion terms   One ordinary share at 100p in the years 1997 to 2007 inclusive
Number in issue   4,747,800
Number of market-makers   Five
Warrants listed in FT   Yes

Scudder Latin America Investment Trust plc

Category   Investment Trusts
Activities   Investment in Latin American securities
Address   New London House, 6 London Street, London, EC3R 7BE
Telephone   0171-264 5000
Conversion terms   One ordinary share at 100p on 31 August in any of the years 1998
   to 2004 inclusive; time value protected
Number in issue   10,020,000
Number of market-makers   Six
Warrants listed in FT   Yes

Shanghai Fund (Cayman) Limited

Category   Saturday Dealing Pages
Activities   Investment in China
Address   c/o Carr Sheppards, 1 London Bridge, London, SE1
Telephone   0171-378 7000
Conversion terms   One participating share at U$10.00 at any time up to 31 December
   1995; time value protected; settlement through Euroclear/CEDEL
Number in issue   353,200
Number of market-makers   n/a
Warrants listed in FT   No

Shires High-Yielding Smaller Companies Trust plc

(also known as 'SHIRESCOT')
Category   Investment Trusts
Activities   Investment in high-yielding smaller companies in the UK
Address   29 St Vincent Place, Glasgow, G1 2DR
Telephone   0141-226 4585
Conversion terms   One share at 100p on 1 June 1994 to 2000 inclusive; time value
   protected
Number in issue   3,856,869
Number of market-makers   Three
Warrants listed in FT   No

SHK Indonesia Fund Limited

Category   Saturday Dealing Pages
Activities   Investment in Indonesia
Address   c/o Credit Lyonnais Securities, Broadwalk House, 5 Appold Street, London, EC2A 2DA
Telephone   0171-588 4000
Conversion terms   One ordinary share at US$10.40 at any time to 31 December 1995; time value protected; dealt through Euroclear/CEDEL
Number in issue   424,000
Number of market-makers   n/a
Warrants listed in FT   No

Siam Selective Growth Trust plc

Category   Investment Trusts
Activities   Investment in Thailand
Address   2 Broadgate, London, EC2M 7ED
Telephone   0171-256 4000
Conversion terms   One ordinary share at 175p on 31 August 1996.
Number in issue   5,400,000
Number of market-makers   Two
Warrants listed in FT   Yes

The Smaller Companies Investment Trust plc

Category   Investment Trusts
Activities   Investment in UK smaller companies
Address   99 Charterhouse Street, London, EC1M 6AB
Telephone   0171-490 4466
Conversion terms   One share at 100p in 30-day period after AGM in 1995 to 1998 inclusive; time value protected; estimated final expiry 25 May 1998
Number in issue   6,345,142
Number of market-makers   Five
Warrants listed in FT   Yes

The Smaller Companies Investment Trust plc (1999 warrants)

Category   Investment Trusts
Activities   Investment in UK smaller companies
Address   99 Charterhouse Street, London, EC1M 6AB
Telephone   0171-490 4466
Conversion terms   One share at 135p during the 30-day period following the AGM in each of the years 1996 to 1999 inclusive; time value protected; estimated final expiry 25 May 1999
Number in issue   3,583,520
Number of market-makers   Four
Warrants listed in FT   Yes

Smith New Court plc ('A' warrants)

Category   Other Financial
Activities   Dealings in securities
Address   20 Farringdon Road, London, EC1M 3NH
Telephone   0171-772 1000
Conversion terms   One share at 210p during four-week period ending 31 August 1989
   to 1995
Number in issue   1,500,000
Number of market-makers   One
Warrants listed in FT   No

South America Fund NV

Category   Investment Companies
Activities   Investment in South America
Address   1 Citicorp Center, 58th Floor, 153 East 53rd Street, New York, NY 10022
Telephone   00-212 832 2626
Conversion terms   One share at US$2.00 at any time up to and including the 19
   August 1996; settlement through Euroclear/CEDEL
Number in issue   6,400,000
Number of market-makers   Three
Warrants listed in FT   Yes (in sterling)

South Staffordshire Water Holdings plc

Category   Water
Activities   Water supply
Address   Green Lane, Walsall, West Midlands, WS2 7PD
Telephone   01922-38282
Conversion terms   One ordinary share at 500p during June 1992 to 1998 inclusive
Number in issue   305,737
Number of market-makers   n/a
Warrants listed in FT   No

Southend Property Holdings plc

Category   Property
Activities   Retail & office property investment
Address   1 Dancastle Court, Arcadia Avenue, London, N3 2JU
Telephone   0181-458 8833
Conversion terms   One share at 115p at any time from 19 July 1990 to 30 September
   1997
Number in issue   6,109,926
Number of market-makers   Two
Warrants listed in FT   Yes

The Spanish Smaller Companies Fund

Category   Investment Companies

Activities   Investment in Spanish smaller companies

Address   c/o State Street Bank Luxembourg SA, 47 Boulevard Royal, L-2449, Luxembourg

Conversion terms   One share at US$12.00 at any time from 1 March 1992 to 1 March 1997; time value protected; settlement through Euroclear/CEDEL

Number in issue   333,334

Number of market-makers   n/a

Warrants listed in FT   Yes (in sterling)

SR Pan European Investment Trust plc

(formerly Thornton Pan European Investment Trust plc)

Category   Investment Trusts Split Capital

Activities   Investment in European securities and derivatives

Address   20 St Dunstan's Hill, London, EC3R 8HY

Telephone   0171-929 3057

Conversion terms   One share at 39p on 31 May 1997 to 2001 inclusive; time value protected

Number in issue   4,000,250

Number of market-makers   Three

Warrants listed in FT   Yes

Superframe plc

Category   Engineering

Activities   Production of point-of-sale equipment

Address   The Old Electricity Works, Campfield Road, St Albans, Hertfordshire, AL1 5HJ

Telephone   01727-865 555

Conversion terms   One share at 50p in any of the two month periods commencing on 1 June and 1 December in 1995 and 1996

Number in issue   1,200,000

Number of market-makers   Two

Warrants listed in FT   No

Sutcliffe Speakman plc

Category   Chemicals

Activities   Carbon manufacture; environmental engineering

Address   Guest Street, Leigh, Lancs, WN7 2HE

Telephone   01942-672 101

Conversion terms   One share at 330p on 31 August 1988 to 1996 inclusive

Number in issue   215,483

Number of market-makers   One

Warrants listed in FT   No

Suter plc 1996/98 warrants

Category   Diversified Industrials
Activities   Conglomerate
Address   St Vincent's, Grantham, Lincs, NG31 9EJ
Telephone   01476-76767
Conversion terms   One ordinary share at 175p in the period 30 days after the posting of the annual report and accounts in 1996 to 1998 inclusive; estimated final expiry 12 May 1998
Number in issue   10,903,286
Number of market-makers   Four
Warrants listed in FT   Yes

Suter plc 1999/2004 warrants

Category   Diversified Industrials
Activities   Conglomerate
Address   St Vincent's, Grantham, Lincs, NG31 9EJ
Telephone   01476-76767
Conversion terms   One ordinary share at 300p in the period 30 days after the posting of the interim report in 1999, the annual report and accounts and interim report in 2000, 2001, 2001, 2002, and 2003, and the annual report and accounts in 2004; estimated final expiry 12 May 2004
Number in issue   11,674,308
Number of market-makers   Four
Warrants listed in FT   Yes

Syndicate Capital Trust plc

Category   Insurance
Activities   Investment in Lloyd's insurance market
Address   10 Throgmorton Avenue, London, EC2N 2DP
Telephone   0171-378 7979
Conversion terms   One ordinary share at 100p on 31 October 1995 to 1999 inclusive; time value protected
Number in issue   5,000,000
Number of market-makers   Three
Warrants listed in FT   Yes

Taiwan Investment Trust plc

Category   Investment Trusts
Activities   Investment in Taiwan
Address   Jupiter Tyndall (Asia) Ltd, Knightsbridge House, 197 Knightsbridge, London, SW7 1RB
Telephone   0171-412 0703
Conversion terms   One ordinary share at 100p one month after the despatch of the annual report and accounts in 1995 to 2003 inclusive; time value protected

Number in issue   9,000,000
Number of market-makers   Four
Warrants listed in FT   Yes

Templeton Emerging Markets Investment Trust plc (2004 warrants)

Category   Investment Trusts
Activities   Investment in emerging markets
Address   Saltire, 20 Castle Terrace, Edinburgh, EH1 2EH
Telephone   0131-469 4000
Conversion terms   One share at 133p annually from 1995 to 2004 inclusive; time
   value protected
Number in issue   80,234,034
Number of market-makers   Eight
Warrants listed in FT   Yes

Templeton Latin America Investment Trust plc

Category   Investment Trusts
Activities   Investment in Latin America
Address   Saltire, 20 Castle Terrace, Edinburgh, EH1 2EH
Telephone   0131-469 4000
Conversion terms   One share at 100p on 31 May in the years 1995 to 2000 inclusive;
   time value protected
Number in issue   9,240,000
Number of market-makers   Seven
Warrants listed in FT   Yes

The Thai Development Capital Fund Limited

Category   Saturday Dealings Page
Activities   Investment in unlisted Thai companies
Address   c/o Bermuda Intl. Securities Ltd, 2 Broadgate, London, EC2M
Telephone   0171-256 4000
Conversion terms   One share at US$10.00 on 31 March 1992 to 1996 inclusive; time
   value protected; settled through Euroclear/CEDEL
Number in issue   244,200
Number of market-makers   n/a
Warrants listed in FT   No

Throgmorton 1000 Smallest Companies Trust plc

Category   Investment Trusts
Activities   Investment in smaller companies
Address   155 Bishopsgate, London, EC2M 3XJ

Telephone   0171-374 4100

Conversion terms   One ordinary share at 100p on 1 July 1993 to 1995 inclusive; time value protected

Number in issue   6,710,987

Number of market-makers   Six

Warrants listed in FT   Yes

Throgmorton 1000 Smallest Companies Trust plc (1998 warrants)

Category   Investment Trusts

Activities   Investment in smaller companies

Address   155 Bishopsgate, London, EC2M 3XJ

Telephone   0171-374 4100

Conversion terms   One ordinary share at the NAV per share at 30 June 1995, on 1 July 1996 to 1998 inclusive; due to begin trading on 4 July 1995

Number in issue   approximately 8,900,000

Number of market-makers   n/a

Warrants listed in FT   n/a

TOPS Estates plc

Category   Property

Activities   Property management

Address   77 South Audley Street, London, W1Y 6EE

Telephone   0171-486 4684

Conversion terms   One ordinary share at 240p during the month of August in 1995 to 2000 inclusive

Number in issue   8,000,000

Number of market-makers   Two

Warrants listed in FT   No

TR European Growth Trust plc (participating subscription shares)

Category   Investment Trusts

Activities   Investment in smaller and medium sized companies in Continental Europe

Address   3 Finsbury Avenue, London, EC2M 2PA

Telephone   0171-638 5757

Conversion terms   One ordinary share at 100p on the date falling 30 days after the AGM in each of the years 1994 to 1997 inclusive; plus full dividend entitlement; time value protected; estimated final expiry 30 November 1997

Number in issue   5,324,602

Number of market-makers   Five

Warrants listed in FT   Yes

TR Far East Income Trust plc

Category   Investment Trusts
Activities   Investment in high-yielding Far Eastern equities
Address   3 Finsbury Avenue, London, EC2M 2PA
Telephone   0171-638 5757
Conversion terms   One ordinary share at 105p, 30 days after the AGM in 1993 to 1996 inclusive; estimated final expiry 1 January 1997
Number in issue   9,240,000
Number of market-makers   Six
Warrants listed in FT   Yes

TR High Income Trust plc (subscription shares)

Category   Investment Trusts
Activities   Investment in high-yielding UK securities
Address   3 Finsbury Avenue, London, EC2M 2PA
Telephone   0171-638 5757
Terms of subscription shares: One share at 100p, 30 days after AGM in 1991 to 1996 inclusive, plus an annual dividend of 1.5p per share; time value protected; estimated final expiry 27 May 1996
Number in issue   2,880,000
Number of market-makers   Five
Warrants listed in FT   Yes

TR Property Investment Trust plc

Category   Investment Trusts
Activities   Investment in property and property shares
Address   3 Finsbury Avenue, London, EC2M 2PA
Telephone   0171-638 5757
Conversion terms   One ordinary share at 47.5p on 31 July 1997 to 2002 inclusive; time value protected
Number in issue   93,676,316
Number of market-makers   Eight
Warrants listed in FT   Yes

Trust of Property Shares plc

Category   Investment Trusts
Activities   Investment in property
Address   77 South Audley Street, London, W1Y 6EE
Telephone   0171-486 4684
Conversion terms   One share at 110p in May 1991 to 2000 inclusive; time value protected
Number in issue   599,994
Number of market-makers   One
Warrants listed in FT   No

The Turkey Trust plc

Category   Investment Trusts
Activities   Investment in Turkey
Address   99 Charterhouse Street, London, EC1M 6AB
Telephone   0171-490 4466
Conversion terms   One share at 207.87p in the 30-day period commencing one day after the posting of the annual report and accounts in 1991 to 2000 inclusive; estimated final expiry 1 March 2000
Number in issue   1,956,400
Number of market-makers   Two
Warrants listed in FT   Yes

United Energy plc

Category   Oil Exploration & Production
Activities   Oil and gas exploration and development
Address   50 Stratton Street, London, W1X 5FL
Telephone   0171-493 9933
Conversion terms   One share at 40p during the 42 day period commencing on the date one day after the posting of the annual report and accounts and the interim results in each year up to and including 1995, and on 31 December 1995
Number in issue   1,838,748
Number of market-makers   Three
Warrants listed in FT   No

US Smaller Companies Investment Trust plc

Category   Investment Trusts
Activities   Investment in US smaller companies
Address   19 Berkeley Street, London
Telephone   0171-499 3189
Conversion terms   One share at 100p on 30 September in 1992 to 2002 inclusive; time value protected
Number in issue   9,945,744
Number of market-makers   Five
Warrants listed in FT   Yes

Utility Cable plc

(formerly Baillie Gifford Technology plc)
Category   Building and Construction
Activities   Cabling Services
Address   66 Wilson Street, London, EC2A 2BL
Telephone   0171-247 0007
Conversion terms   One ordinary share at 10.5p on 30 November 1995
Number in issue   2,193,020

Number of market-makers   Three
Warrants listed in FT   No

Vtech Holdings Limited

Category   Electronics & Electrical Equipment
Activities   Electronics, computers, telecomms and audio-video
Address   c/o Barclays Registrars, Bourne House, 34 Beckenham Road, Beckenham, Kent, BR3 4TU
Telephone   0181-650 4866 (registrars)
Conversion terms   One share at US$1.60 at any time from 1 April 1992 to 30 September 1996
Number in issue   14,898,079
Number of market-makers   n/a
Warrants listed in FT   No

Wigmore Property Investment Trust plc

Category   Investment Trusts
Activities   Investment in small and medium sized UK property companies
Address   155 Bishopsgate, London, EC2M 3XY
Telephone   071-214 1273
Conversion terms   One ordinary share at 100p on 31 January 1995 to 2003 inclusive; time value protected
Number in issue   4,049,955
Number of market-makers   Four
Warrants listed in FT   Yes

WMGO Group plc

(formerly MMI plc)
Category   Media
Activities   Financial marketing, recruitment and advertising
Address   178–202 Great Portland Street, London, W1N 6JJ
Telephone   0171-631 5135
Conversion terms   One share at 19.7p on 30 June 1992 to 2000 inclusive; time value protected
Number in issue   1,721,690
Number of market-makers   Two
Warrants listed in FT   No

The World Trust Fund

Category   Investment Companies
Activities   Worldwide investment fund
Address   1 Rockefeller Plaza, New York, USA NY10020
Telephone   00-212 346 2500

Conversion terms   One share at US$10.00 on Thursday of each week during 1993 to 2001 inclusive; estimated final expiry 31 December 2001

Number in issue   1,657,049

Number of market-makers   Four

Warrants listed in FT   Yes (in sterling)

WPP Group plc

Category   Media

Activities   Advertising agency

Address   27 Farm Street, London, W1X 6RD

Telephone   0171-408 2204

Conversion terms   One share at £10.00 on 30 June 1990 to 1996 inclusive

Number in issue   5,044,891

Number of market-makers   Two

Warrants listed in FT   Yes

The York Waterworks plc

Category   Water

Activities   Water supply

Address   Lendal Tower, York, YO1 2DL

Telephone   01904-622 171

Conversion terms   One share at 135p on any day in the first complete month after the date on which the accounts of the company for its immediately preceding accounting period are despatched to shareholders in any of the years 1992 to 1997 inclusive; estimated final expiry 31 July 1997

Number in issue   446,580

Number of market-makers   Two

Warrants listed in FT   No

Yorkshire-Tyne Tees Television Holdings plc

Category   Media

Activities   Television company

Address   The Television Centre, Leeds, LS3 1JS

Telephone   0113-243 8283

Conversion terms   One share at 200p in period of ten business days immediately following the announcement of the annual and interim results in 1992 to 1997 inclusive; estimated final expiry 7th November 1997

Number in issue   9,844,911

Number of market-makers   Three

Warrants listed in FT   Yes

Warning: Changes in this Data

The data compiled in this Appendix was correct as at 9 June 1995. Some of the issues listed may have expired by the time you read this book, and new issues will have arrived on the market. For the remaining warrants, many of which last until the late 1990s, the terms are likely to remain the same. You should be aware, however, that in a minority of cases the subscription terms may be adjusted, particularly in response to rights issues (see Chapter 1). The small number of warrants which are exercised each year (see Chapter 8) may also have reduced the number of warrants in issue. For these reasons it is imperative that you check the subscription terms before you deal (as explained in Chapter 3).

Although the author has taken all reasonable care to ensure that all statements of fact in this Appendix are fair and accurate in all material respects, such accuracy cannot be guaranteed, and accordingly he disclaims any responsibility for any inaccuracies or omissions which may make such information misleading. Investors should seek appropriate professional advice if any points are unclear.

GLOSSARY AND SOURCES OF FURTHER INFORMATION

The glossary contains a summary of some of the most important terms used in the book. Most of these definitions are to be found in the text, but they are reproduced here for ease of reference.

Asset Fulcrum Point (AFP)
Used for warrants attached to split-capital shares, the annual percentage growth of the underlying assets required for you to do equally well in terms of capital appreciation with either the capital shares or the warrant. If the AFP = 5 per cent and the assets actually rise by 6 per cent per annum to the final conversion date, then the warrants will outperform the capital shares over this period and vice versa.

Bear Market
A market in which the established trend for prices is down.

Black-Scholes Formula
Widely used model for evaluating all forms of options, formulated in 1973 by Fischer Black and Myron Scholes.

Break-Even Point
The annual percentage growth of the equity required for a warrant-holder to recover the current warrant price at final expiry.

Bull Market
A market in which the established trend for prices is up.

Capital Fulcrum Point (CFP)
The annual percentage growth of the equity required for you to do equally well in terms of capital appreciation with either the equity or the warrant. If the CFP = 7 per cent and the share price actually rises by 8 per cent per annum to the final conversion date, then the warrants will outperform the shares over this period and vice versa.

Conversion Terms
The key information defining the number of shares for subscription, the subscription price, and the subscription period.

Covered Warrants
Warrants issued by a third party, usually a major financial institution. In addition to equity issues, there is a wide range of covered warrants available for other instruments such as market indices, currencies, interest rates, and some commodities.

Delta
The rate of change in a warrant price for any given rate of change in the price of the underlying instrument. Used for the calculation of efficient holdings for **hedging** and speculation, and also as a measure of the likelihood of a warrant finishing 'in the money'.

Dilution
If the subscription price is less than the asset value per share when warrants are exercised, the net asset value per share will fall.

Euroclear / CEDEL
Five-day rolling settlement systems for a minority of UK warrants which are listed in London but which are typically denominated in an overseas currency (usually US dollars). Investors should be aware that

warrants settled through Euroclear or CEDEL may attract additional dealing and handling charges.

Exercise

A warrant is exercised when the subscription rights are taken up, the subscription price is paid, and the warrant is converted into the underlying security.

Expiry Date

The final date on which a warrant can be exercised. A warrant has no worth after its final exercise date.

Fundamental Analysis

Fundamental analysis undertakes to evaluate the underlying security to which a warrant is attached. The aim is usually to gauge the prospects for capital growth in the underlying share. Should be used in conjunction with **technical analysis**.

Gearing

The property of warrants which gives investors a greater exposure for a given investment. The gearing factor which measures this is simply the share price divided by the warrant price. If the gearing factor is 3.0, then £1 invested in the warrants will provide control over three times as many shares as £1 directly invested in the equity. This gearing benefit can be used for speculation or for **hedging**.

Giguere

Early warrant theorist who postulated a simple relationship between the share price and the warrant price based on the parity ratio.

Hedging

An investment policy which does not aim for outright capital gain, but seeks also to reduce the risks and potential losses. Typically in the warrants market, investors may take advantage of the **gearing** factor to achieve a given equity exposure for a lower outlay, investing the balance in lower-risk instruments.

Intrinsic Value

The value which a warrant would have were it to be exercised immediately. This is equal to the share price minus the exercise price. A warrant which has a positive intrinsic value is said to be 'in the money', and a warrant without intrinsic value 'out of the money'.

Investment Trust

Closed-end collective investment company.

Leverage

Linked to **gearing**, which enables larger percentage gains (or losses) on warrants because of their lower price relative to the equity, leverage measures this relationship between the share price and the warrant price. The higher the leverage, the higher the percentage change in the warrant price for any given change in the share price.

Limit Price

The maximum price at which you are willing to buy, or the minimum price at which you are prepared to sell.

Liquidity

Ease of dealing in particular issues. A good two-way market is said to be liquid, whereas a warrant which is difficult to deal may be illiquid.

Notice of Subscription

The form on the reverse of warrant certificates which must be completed when the warrants are exercised.

Parity

Parity is achieved when the share price is equal to the exercise price of the warrants attached. At this point the parity ratio is 1.

Penny Warrants

Low-priced warrants, not necessarily cheap, and only worth buying if **fundamental analysis** and **technical analysis** provide positive indications.

Premium

The extra amount you have to pay for the benefits which warrants confer. The premium equals the percentage by which the warrant price plus the exercise price exceeds the current share price. Because the premium reflects the time remaining to maturity and disappears as the warrant nears expiry, it is often referred to as 'time value'.

Put Warrants

Unlike ordinary warrants, which carry the right to buy the underlying security at a fixed price, put warrants carry the right to sell at a fixed price instead.

Spread

The dealing spread is the difference between the buying and selling prices which exists for all securities, warrants included.

Subscription Shares

Two hybrid warrants launched by the Touche Remnant management group in 1989 and 1990. The subscription shares have conversion terms like ordinary warrants, but also rank for partial or full dividend payments.

Technical Analysis

Specialised analysis of the warrant price, covering several aspects as **intrinsic value, premium, time to expiry, the capital fulcrum point, gearing, leverage, volatility,** and income forgone.

Time to Expiry

Time remaining until a warrant matures on its final expiry date.

Volatility

The extent of change in the warrant price over time, measured in various ways. Differing statistical approaches include high-low volatility, adjusted volatility, standard historical volatility, and implied volatility.

Warrant

Transferable, quoted option certificate issued by a company, conferring certain rights defined by the conversion terms.

Sources of Further Information

Warrants Alert

The Sion
Nailsea
Bristol
BS19 2EP
Telephone (01275) 855558

Association of Investment Trust Companies

Durrant House
8–13 Chiswell Street
London
EC1Y 4YY
Telephone (0171) 588 5347

'Investment Trusts' Magazine

Flaxdale Printers Ltd
120-126 Lavender Avenue
Mitcham
Surrey
CR4 3HP
Telephone (0181) 646 1031

The Stock Exchange Daily Official List

Publications Department
London Stock Exchange
London
EC2N 1HP
Telephone (0171) 588 2355

INDEX